Music and Dance
of the Tewa Pueblos

Music and Dance
of the Tewa Pueblos

by
GERTRUDE PROKOSCH KURATH

with the aid of
ANTONIO GARCIA

number 8
Museum of New Mexico
Research Records

MUSEUM OF NEW MEXICO PRESS
SANTA FE   1970

THANKS FOR HELP

Hans Kurath, Hugh M. Miller, Donald L. Roberts . . . and Carlos Garcia, Juanito Trujillo, and other Tewa of San Juan and Santa Clara.

THANKS FOR ADVICE

Edward P. Dozier, Bertha P. Dutton, Randall H. Speirs, Mischa Titiev.

THANKS FOR SUPPORT

The Wenner-Gren Foundation for Anthropological Research for eight years of indispensable financial aid for field work, tape recorders and tape recording, and photography, 1957-1965, and publication.

The American Philosophical Society Library for aid towards study of song texts in 1957.

Library of Congress Catalog Card No. 76-113265

MUSEUM OF NEW MEXICO PRESS
P. O. Box 2087 Santa Fe, New Mexico 87501

CONTENTS

LIST OF FIGURES

Music and Dance
of the Tewa Pueblos

"Corn Dance" by Pablita Velarde

Chapter 1

APPROACH TO THE STUDY OF TEWA CEREMONY

PURPOSE

To the native practitioner, the ceremonial arts have functional and religious significance. Beauty of form and execution are essential, but they are subsidiary to the communication with supernaturals and aid in social cohesion. The recording and analysis of the forms should lead to a deeper esthetic and cultural understanding of the Tewa people.

This is the purpose of this book. It is not a sociological or folkloric treatise. Neither is it a springboard for stage reconstructions by White Indiophiles. The musical and choreographic scores lead to the correlation with socio-religious factors and historical processes.

PROCEDURE

The empirical materials - the scores - derive from observation, from study of tape recordings, silent and sound films, and stills, and from descriptions by Tewa and various previous authors. The graphic presentation involves numerous problems of transcription and method. The problem of translating four-dimensional patterns into the two dimensions of paper has been undergoing solution for some years. The problems of layout, analysis, and integration are new for each dance. The solutions in this book grew out of the needs.

The system of musical notation current in the Western world serves the Tewa music fairly well, with the addition of several special diacritics and with a free handling of key and metric signatures. However, a final score displaying phrase patterns poses layout problems, because of the irregular phrase lengths. For analysis, the method devised by Erich von Hornbostel and improved by George Herzog works very well, especially the device of "weighted scales." Legend 1 translates the diacritics and abbreviations used throughout the scores. The analytic method awaits explanation in the appropriate chapter. Legend 2 shows labels for structural parts of ceremonial dances and songs.

Dance notation must compromise between the horizontal and vertical dimensions and their duration in time. The system of glyphs simplified for the needs of this book appears in the other Legends.

3. Glyphs for various kinds of participants.

4. Conventions for horizontal patterns of formation and of locomotion, that is, ground plans.

5. Scheme for reducing body movement to two-dimensional representation on a staff.

6. Scheme for indicating horizontal locomotion of body parts in various directions.

7. Glyphs for gestures, with directional indications.

8. Glyphs for basic units of steps - legs and feet and their manner of movement.

9. Quality glyphs, borrowed from the Laban system of notation.

These schemes and glyphs recur in the analyses and scores, along with other devices, such as stick figures and graphs of kinemes - spatial gesture paths. Glyphs are indispensable for integration with musical scores, for comparative displays, and for interpretation.

In complete scores the glyphs must combine effectively with the music. Generally it is convenient to place percussion beats and steps exactly above the corresponding melodic notes, and to write the texts below. Sometimes the spacing demands placement of the steps below the melody, with a connective line. With few exceptions, the corresponding ground plans appear in the right hand margin. But the arrangement depends on the melodic line and the complexity of the movements. Sometimes the ground plans appear in relation to the setting, that is, the house blocks, but without steps and music. That would be too much for a diagram.

The classifications and analyses leave no doubt about the cultural correlations, and they illuminate the questions of origin. Such interpretations require verbal explanations, in special chapters.

Legend 1 – Musical Diacritics

Ṗ	Vocal pulsation	♪	Drum
ρ↘	Down glide	℞	Rattle
ρ̄	Tone slightly flat	ᛗ	Morache
ρ⁺	Tone slightly sharp		
ρˣ	Tone indefinite	│	Bar line for phrases
ʔ	Glottal stop	▎	Tentative bar line
∿∿	Percussion tremolo	⁝	Bar line for upbeat

2

Legend 2 – Structural Labels

I II etc.	Appearance of performers		x	Introductory phrase
1 2	Station		y	Connective phrase
			z	Coda
A B	Dance section within song			
A' B'	Dance section – variant	𝄆	Repeat of song
a b	Melodic themes	𝄆	Repeat of section
		⁒	Repeat of dance step
		⁒	Reversal of step, path
		⌇	Ad lib

Legend 3 – Participants

⌐	Man – facing ahead	⌒	Buffalo
⌐	Man of other group	⌐	Buffalo with one horn
⌐	Leading man	⌒	Deer
O⁻	Woman–facing sideward	♈	Mountain Sheep
O⁼	Woman of other group	⍦	Antelope
●	Leading woman	⋀	Abuelo
		X	Singer
		⊗	Percussionist

3

Legend 4 – Locomotion

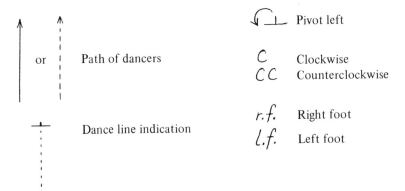

or   Path of dancers

Dance line indication

⌐⌐ Pivot left

C Clockwise
CC Counterclockwise

$r.f.$ Right foot

$l.f.$ Left foot

Legend 5 – Complete Staff for Body

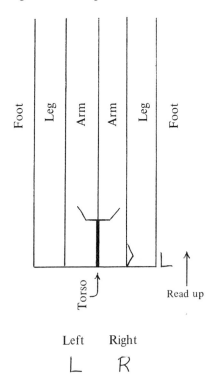

Foot Leg Arm Arm Leg Foot

Torso

Read up

Left   Right

L   R

Legend 6 – Horizontal Directions

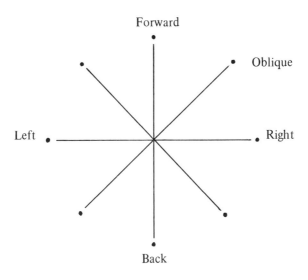

Forward

Oblique

Left

Right

Back

Legend 7 – Gesture Directions

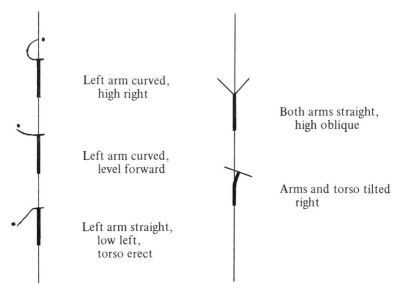

Left arm curved,
  high right

Left arm curved,
  level forward

Left arm straight,
  low left,
  torso erect

Both arms straight,
  high oblique

Arms and torso tilted
  right

Legend 8 – Steps

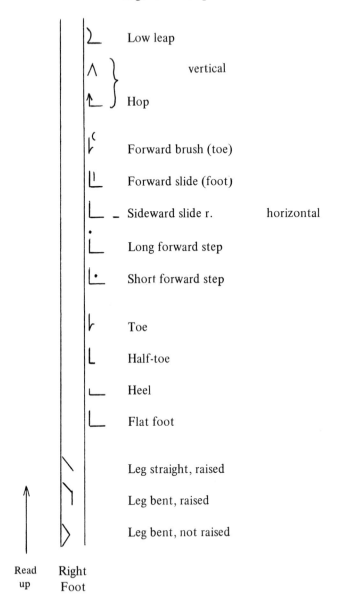

⅃	Low leap
∧ }	vertical
⅄ }	Hop
⌐	Forward brush (toe)
⌐	Forward slide (foot)
L _	Sideward slide r. horizontal
L	Long forward step
L·	Short forward step
⌐	Toe
L	Half-toe
∟	Heel
L	Flat foot
\	Leg straight, raised
⌐	Leg bent, raised
⟩	Leg bent, not raised

Legend 9 — Quality

Dynamics		Goniometry

Dynamics

𝄢 Tension

𝄢 Normal

𝄢 Relaxation

L Ordinary Foot Impact

L▬ Stamp

Goniometry

⌐⟋ Extension

⊙ Normal Position

✕ Flexion

✖ Extreme Flexion

TEXTS

Many of the songs use nonsense syllables, but the most sacred ones employ highly ceremonial texts, in current or obsolete Tewa, sometimes in Keresan or other languages. With the aid of Antonio Garcia, Hans Kurath wrote down the terminology and most of the texts in modern phonemic spelling, with indications of tones. (The tones affect the meanings of words). The glossary lists Tewa ceremonial terms in phonemic writings and also in simplified spellings employed in the course of the book. The text translations appear after the corresponding songs. In several instances it was necessary for the author to write down the texts as well as she could.

The song texts are significant as expressions of religious thought. They elucidate the meaning of specific dances, although many poetic expressions recur in songs of different purpose. The words coordinate with the song phrases in an accurate manner. But they have no effect on the dance patterns, except for gestures. It is possible that the speech melody has influenced the song melody, but this correlation needs further exploration.

The use of words from other languages also has historical significance. In the course of centuries, the Tewa borrowed many ceremonial complexes, even specific songs, from other tribes. Lately they have derived ideas and texts from the English-speaking peoples.

As the story unfolds, it will become clear that all factors enter into the ceremonial drama played in the plazas - the setting, the economy, the social patterns, the beliefs, the songs, the movements, and the song texts. The method for integration of these factors is experimental. If successful, it may prove a stepping stone for similar studies in the future.

TEWA CEREMONIAL DANCE TERMS

PHONEMIC SPELLING	SIMPLIFIED SPELLING	TRANSLATION
ʔá̜ʔá̜ge	a'age	Sweet Atole Dance
á̜kʰe	akhe	dance step
á̜ geʔi̜ŋ	ange'i	prelude and postlude
ántege	antege	footlifting step
ántege šàre	antegeshare	Footlifting Men's Dance
ʔá·šàre	ashare	Bow (and Arrow) Dance
báʔ a	ba'a	Belt Dance
búpi̜ŋge	bupinge	plaza
bùtʰáʔá	buta'a	circle, Circle Dance
cáviyò	tsaviyo	clown (in Matachina and elsewhere)
cèšarè	tseshare	Eagle Dance
céšarè	tséshare	Dog Dance
dipe̜yi	dipenyi	deer walk (they do the deer walk)
dikǫyi	dikoⁿyi	buffalo walk
ʔéheʔé	eheh	ceremonial costume
ginwéŋdiʔè	gingwendi'e	Standing Basket Dance
kɛsɛ̀ndo	kesendo	Bear Elder (priest)
koceʔi̜ŋ	kotse'ing	White Buffalo Dancer
kofɛ̜ndi	kofendi	Black Buffalo Dancer
kʔósà	kosa	ceremonial clown of winter moiety
kǫšarè	konshare	Buffalo Dance
kwá̜tèmbè šàrè	kwantembeshare	Rainbow Dance
kwá̜ šàrè	kwanshare	Rain Dance (part of xoxeye)

8

PHONEMIC SPELLING	SIMPLIFIED SPELLING	TRANSLATION
kwątuká	kwantuka	gesture calling rain from cardinal points
kwiraná	kwirana	clown of summer moiety
kwitara šare	kwitara	Comanche Dance (fance)
kwiyó	kwiyo	Priestess, old woman
Malínci	Malinche	girl in Matachina Dance
Matacína	Matachina	Hispanic Dance Drama
Monąka	Monarca	leader of Matachina (monarch)
mwὲ ʔ ὲὲ	mwe'e	scraping stick, morache
mwὲ ʔὲkwó	mwe'ekwo	second part of Basket Dance
napošun	naposhun	sacred black clay
nufaà	nufa	ash fire, Turtle Dance
o ʔὲὲ	o'e	ceremony
ohotáyo	ohotayo	gesture for luring rain
okušare	okushare	Turtle Dance
óoxuà	oxua	Raingod
òxúá	oxua	cloud
pàη šare	pangshare	Social Dance, Captive's Dance
pὲci	pentsi	deer step
pὲšare	penshare	Deer Dance
pὲsendo	pensendo	Deer Elder (spirit)
pinge cúre	pinge tsure	Parrot Dance (to take into the middle)
pįkʰέη	pingxeng	Game Priest
piηkùa	pingkua	Mountain Sheep Dancer

9

PHONEMIC SPELLING	SIMPLIFIED SPELLING	TRANSLATION
pógǫ šare (or)	pogonshare	Corn Maiden Dance
pówiŋ šare	powingshare	
pʔóhi	pohi	Scalp Dance
poʔowiye	po'pwiye	gourd rattle
pún^y abe	puñabe	shinny game (seed ball)
púutandi	putandi	clown with markings on rear
puŋkha	pungkha	first, "slow dance" in a set
sakʔo šare	sakoshare	Pipe Dance
samayo	samayo	Game Priest
šare	share	dance
save	save	Apache clown in Deer Dance
sawipinge	sawipinge	center of dance line (covetted)
sȩkʰa	sekha	song of the Rain Races
semixua	semixua	male mark, face paint
sun^yu (or)	suñu	shuffle step
šušu	shushu	
tʔa	t'a	pause in dance step
taabe	tambe	drum
taabefe	tambefe	drum stick
taʔandi šare	ta'andishare	Men's Spring Dance
tašare	tashare	Elk Dance
tembe šare	tembeshare	Hoop Dance
tembi šare	tembishare	Harvest Dance
tidi šare	tidishare	Shield and Spear Dance
tʰiʔi šare	thi'i	Butterfly Dance

10

PHONEMIC SPELLING	SIMPLIFIED SPELLING	TRANSLATION
t'o'ée	to'e	Little Antelope
t'un šarè	tunshare	Basket Dance
xá'à	xa'a	song
xá'a'egó	xa'ego	transition
xá'a kʰeegi	xakegi	loud, fast song
xáapimbè	xapimbe (hapimbe)	"chorus," repeat to come
xá'apųų	xapu	song root
xá'axánowe	xaxanowe	towards end of song
xòxéyé	xoxeye	Corn Dance
xųųcąawέin	xucawe'ing	Blue Corn Dance
xųųc'eeɲiɳ	xutseying	Yellow Corn Dance
wá'sàa	wasa	weaving formation
wènsáve	wensave	Navajo Dance
yándewá	yandewa	Sun Basket Dance
yèré	yere	Snowbird Dance
yóɳgé	yonge	slow dancing

In the phonemic version the tones are indicated, ´ for a high tone, ` for a low tone, nothing for a middle tone, and ^ for a rising-falling tone. In Tewa the tone often affects the meaning of a word, as in *oxua* and *tseshare*. In such cases, the simplified spelling contains an accent for the meanings of "cloud" and "dog," respectively. In simplifying the spelling for practical purposes various choices are possible. The choice must be consistent. In the transliteration, the vowel sounds are spelled as they would be in Spanish. Nasals are indicated by an "n" *(konshare)*. In *penshare* the "en" is similar to the German "ä". One symbol is taken from Greek, namely, the "x" for a sound like in German "ach". The "1" does not feature in daily Tewa speech, but it occurs in ceremonial speech and in song texts.

Various aspects of Tewa ceremonial and song language deserve a special study, namely, the differences between daily speech and song terminology,

11

and the relationship of speech tone to song melody. Another project would be a more detailed translation of terms from other tribes, especially Keresan and Comanche. In a book on music and choreography it is necessary to subordinate the important aspect of speech.

Part I
Ceremonial Ecology

In the fourteenth century the Tewa migrated to their present location near the Rio Grande in New Mexico. They adapted their economy and ceremonialism to the new environment and to new neighbors. They exchanged ritual features with the Keresans, who spoke another language; and even with the more distant Pueblo Dwellers, the Zuni and the Hopi of today's Arizona. (Dutton 1962:3-15).

In the sixteenth century they were forced into more drastic adaptations, when Spanish soldiers and missionaries invaded their homes from Mexico. They hid their masked rituals and outwardly accepted Catholicism. They incorporated medieval dances into their repertoire. Today even the priests of the native religion are professed Catholics, and the kiva singers often serve in the church choirs with Gregorian chants or hymns.

Since then they have opened their homes but not their kivas to other white men, "Anglos." Few Tewa have converted to Protestantism or to the hybrid Native American Church. But they have converted to modern conveniences and education in grand style. They are adept in handling machinery for agriculture or transportation. Hence they have modified their economy and the functions of some plaza dances, to which they admit tourists. But the form and the scene are affected only by incongruities like cars and TV aerials. The most progressive Tewa still revere their ceremonies. They harbor a deep love for their homeland and for their traditions.

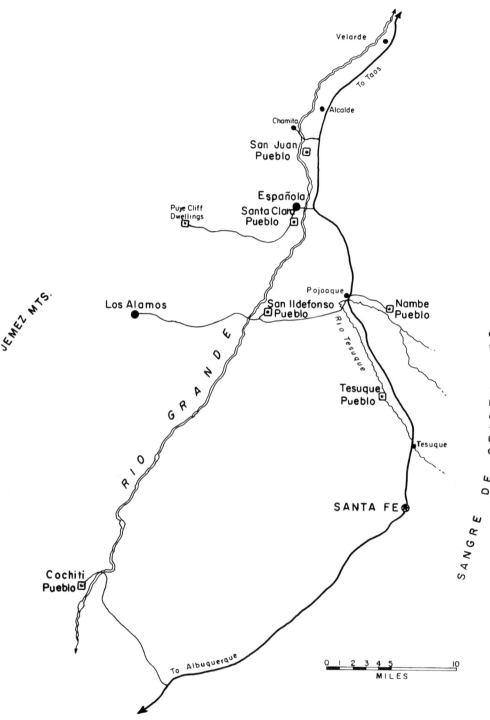

Figure 1 – Location of the Tewa Pueblos

Chapter 2

SYMBOLIC DIMENSIONS OF THE SETTING

The people in the Tewa villages live in a landscape that stretches in all directions, even towards the sky. They have developed their way of life, their beliefs, and their ceremonies in accordance with the patterns and happenings on the earth and in the sky. They have created dances, songs, poetry, and ornamental designs expressive of the natural and cultural phenomena.

SPACE: THE LANDSCAPE

The village locations refer to the cardinal directions. The five living Tewa villages are grouped in a great valley irrigated by the Rio Grande and its tributaries, north of Santa Fe. The valley's altitude is about 6000 feet, that is, midway between sea level and the summits of the Sangre de Cristo and Jemez ranges. Though the great river is the vital artery of the area, only three pueblos can irrigate their fields from its springtime surplus. They are San Juan and San Ildefonso on the east bank and Santa Clara on the west bank. Tesuque adjoins the half-dry Tesuque River. Nambe nestles in the Nambe Valley of the Sangre de Cristo mountains. On a northwest southeast axis they cluster in a diamond shape, San Juan at the northern apex, Tesuque at the south, San Ildefonso west, and Nambe east. Santa Clara lies between San Juan and San Ildefonso. All except Nambe are located near modern highways. (See Dutton 1962).

In the valleys and on the surrounding hills there are many extinct settlements. Most of them are now the haunts of tourists and archaeologists. The cliff-dwellings and mesa-top ruins of Puye have, however, remained the property of Santa Clara Pueblo, and have become the scene of an annual July festival. The mesa leans against the Jemez mountains, with views to mountains and valleys in all directions. The highway department has paved the road to the foot of the mesa. From there a gravel road winds to the top.

LANDMARKS AND SYMBOLS OF THE DIRECTIONS

The Tewa know that immense mountains extend northward, and that the lands flatten into a southern plain. They call the north *pimpiye*, "towards the north," and the south *akompiye*, "towards the plains." They designate sacred mountains of the four cardinal directions. The southerly pueblos are nearer the range of the east, *thampiyeping,* the Sangre de Cristo, which contains sacred peaks like *agatsenuping,* Lake Peak. To the south is *okuping,* Turtle Mountain, alias Sandia Mountain. The northerly pueblos are nearer the range of the west, *tsampiyeping,* the Jemez, with Santa Clara Peak, "covered obsidian mountain," *tsikumping,* and the exhilarating Valle Grande. To the north is *keping,* Bear Mountain, northwest of Taos (Harrington 1916: no. 44).

Also, each pueblo has special sacred hills in various directions. The San Ildefonso inhabitants venerate the legendary *tunyoping,* very spotted mountain, alias Black Mesa. They formerly held dances on the summit by a holy stone (ibid.:295-297). The San Juan people have a sacred northeastern mountain, *okutungwejo,* with shrines and medicine plants. A low hill to the east serves as the starting point for the dawn entrance of Animal Dancers of San Juan and San Ildefonso. Two ceremonial race tracks occupy the level lands east of San Juan.

All pueblos have sacred lakes of the four directions (ibid.:44-45). The lakes have been drying to puddles. Santa Clara and San Ildefonso no longer hold initiations at the lake of the north, *pimpiyepokwi,* which now adjoins the Espanola bridge at the mouth of Santa Cruz Creek. But they still tap it for sacred mud, *naposhun,* when they must blacken faces, bodies, and gourd rattles for a dance.

The essential water also comes from the zenith, *opamakore,* and the nadir, *nansigenuge.* From above come snow, hail, or rain; from below come spring and well water. Precipitation from the sky is associated with the cardinal directions, for snow comes from the north and the heavy rains come from the westerly Jemez range. At times the rain mixes with earth in midlevel, when a wind stirs up a duststorm simultaneously with a rainstorm. A rainstorm generates a vertical union between sky and earth in the form of serpentine lightning, especially in the summer. The rain, mist, lightning, and clouds are important themes in dance, song words, and ornaments. The clouds are equated with the raingods or *oxua,* who appear in rituals.

Ceremonies of the morning hours and some other rituals follow the course of the sun. However, many circuits follow a sinister course, especially afternoon and night ceremonies.

The male sun deity, *Thansendo,* rises in the east, *thampiye,* from a mystical lake, just as the *oxua, kosa,* and Deer spirits come to the pueblo from the east. The sun proceeds southward and upward, and sets in the westerly direction. Sometimes he sets in a splendor that illuminates sky and earth, clouds, and mountain peaks. Sometimes, close to setting time, sun and rain create a rainbow, *kwantembe,* which spans sky and earth in a

16

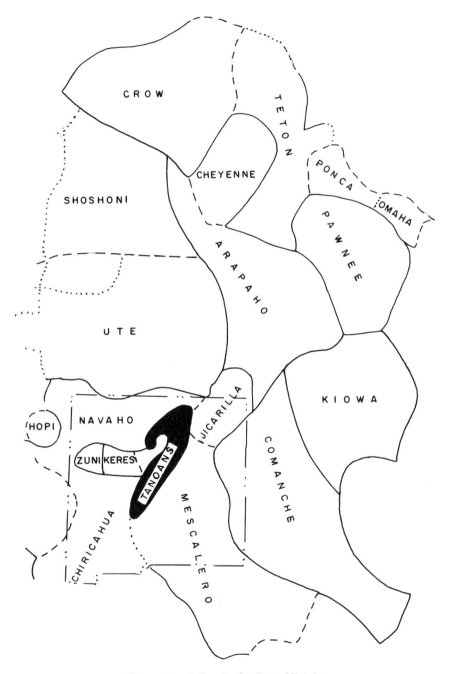

Figure 2 — Tribes in the Tewa Vicinity
(Approximate locations at time of American contact)

"Rainbow Dancers" by Pablita Velarde

"San Ildefonso Basket Dance" by Gilbert Atencio

radiant eastern arc. The rainbow has shed its form and colors across the dances and designs of the Tewa.

During the night *Thansendo* returns underground to the east, in a sinister course. Meanwhile the male moon deity, *Posendo,* travels from east to west, sets, and reappears after a journey through the realm of *Nanechukwiyo,* the earth mother. At regular intervals he crosses the sky in the daytime.

The Tewa have no moon dance, nor a star dance. However, one of the constellations, a ring-shaped cluster near the north, has the same name as the circular Harvest Dance formation, *buta'a.* This dance addresses the cosmos, but specifically it gives thanks to *Nanechukwiyo.*

The veneration of these natural features and forces has brought forth fine arts. Essentially it has a practical origin, because of the salutary effects upon living things, animals or plants, and upon human beings directly and by way of the creatures.

CREATURES OF THE LANDSCAPE

The concept of space mingles with life. In symbolism the six directions are associated with specific animals and birds (Harrington 1916:42-43). Some of the creatures appear in ritual and dance. *Pingxeng,* the mountain lion, represents the north. He is identified with the hunt chief, the master of the animals, who leads the Deer Dance, *penshare,* of San Juan. *Kesendo,* the bear elder of the east, is the tutelary of an important, esoteric curing society. The society appears in public only at the San Juan Harvest Dance, *tembishare. Katsire,* the oriole, symbol of the underworld, appears in song words but not in impersonation. The Eagle, *tse,* associated with the northern zenith, is mimed in a famous dance for two or more men. Formerly its rain-bringing power was even greater than now (Dutton 1963:135).

The water serpent, *Avanyu,* though the eagle's adversary, has great power for rain and lightning, and descends from the sky in rain. He is connected with the *oxua* or clouds and the *oxua* or raingods. Also, he dwells in pools and in the moist earth. There still is an *Avanyu* pool near Alcalde station. Snake-lightning designs decorate the kilts of male Buffalo and Eagle impersonators. And serpentine ground plans recur as dance patterns. But only one dance represents the serpent — the Snake Dance of Nambe.

Other creatures who live in the surroundings but who do not symbolize directions appear in dances. The prototypes of Deer dancers live in mountains to the east and west. Real deer are available to the hunters. But in dance it is the Deer spirits who issue from the forests and enter the pueblo at dawn. Antelope, mountain sheep, and elk are now scarce in the mountains, but they persevere as actors in Game Animal dances.

19

Their horns and hoofs decorate the headdresses and knee-rattles of impersonators.

Buffalo impersonators appear with or without Game Animals in the *konshare*. The Buffalo double as hunted and hunters, for they carry small bow-and-arrow sets. At the same time, they dance for weather. Buffalo impersonators have achieved great prestige in the repertoire, though buffalo were scarce in the land of the Tewa. When the Tewa hunted herds in eastern New Mexico, they encountered tribes from the Great Plains. Plains influences appear in the paraphernalia, the realistic buffalo headdresses and in the hide costume of the hunt chief who accompanies some groups in *konshare*. The Plains elements have mingled with Pueblo symbols: the sun splendors on women's back bustles, the snake designs on men's hide kilts, and jinglers on kilts which are now usually made of tin.

Valley creatures find less expression in dance than in song texts. A Butterfly dance fuses with vegetation and snake symbolism. The women in this dance, *thi'i,* manipulate feather clusters. Both women's and men's headdresses often contain feathers of turkey, macaw, eagle, owl, duck, or crow.

The aquatic and chthonic turtle has communicated its powers for fertility to *okushare,* the Turtle Dance of San Juan. The thunder is attracted by the tortoise shell rattles attached to the knees of men in this dance, and in esoteric *oxua,* Raingod rituals.

Plant motifs come from the mountains and from the central river valley. The mountains furnish the Douglas spruce for dance props, as symbols of everlasting life. Spruce boughs cover the shoulders of men in many dances, especially the *antege,* "Spring Dance," and the *t'unshare* Basket Dance. They dangle from the heads of animal impersonators. In Corn Dances, women jiggle spruce boughs. They sometimes combine them with other props, corn ears or scraping sticks. For certain dances, as *antege* and *penshare,* small spruce trees are holed in at the ends of dance lines. Ceremonial officials cut the trees in the mountains after midnight and bring them to the village, six for San Juan, eight for Santa Clara, four for other pueblos. After the dance they throw trees and boughs into the river.

Various trees furnish wood for esoteric prayer sticks. Cottonwood trees, which thrive along the river banks, are the favorite wood for the tall drums, and their cotton is an ornament of ceremonial racers. Willows and reeds are used for weaving baskets, essential women's props in several dances.

Instruments of wood – drums and scraping sticks – have phallic potency. So do the large and small gourd rattles wielded by men in almost every dance. The Tewa cultivate a flat gourd – *po'onwiye* – for the rattles. They treat the dried gourds in a special process, described in the Appendix, and fill them with seeds or pebbles. Seed fillers have more power than pebbles.

Corn, the traditional life staple, appears throughout Tewa dance, song, and ornament. Corn maidens symbolize the six directions as well as corn colors. Their mythological prestige is of long standing, especially the power for life sustainment of Yellow and Blue Corn Maidens (Dutton 1963:129, 132, 217). (See Robbins et al 1916:82). The Yellow Corn Dance of San Juan initiates the planting season. A Blue Corn Dance, derived from the Hopi-Tewa, helps Santa Clara crops. The Corn Dance, *xoxeye*, is an important ripening and harvest ceremony.

The corn plants also provide ritual props. In Corn Maiden dances the two women carry an ear of corn in the right hand. Priests sprinkle cornmeal in the path of dancers and in the road for visitors. They sometimes sprinkle it on dancers, as in the San Juan *penshare* Deer ritual, and in the Nambe *tashare* Elk Dance. In *okushare*, Turtle Dance, women present baskets of meal to the men dancers. A brew of cornmeal with the Nahuatl name of Atole is the focus of a kiva dance to the cardinal directions.

In this dance, the *a'age*, successive male soloists present a pipe with sacred, "Mexican" tobacco to the supernaturals. In other kiva rituals men offer tobacco, as the esoteric Bear priests and the secular Apaches for *penshare*. They do not use tobacco in plaza dances. The men do not perform the Calumet Dance, which is popular in the Great Plains.

These are examples of the relationship between dances and the natural environment. It is not a static relationship. The evershifting patterns of the dances and the changing rhythms of the songs reflect the shifting lights and shadows cast by clouds and sunlight on the landscape, the restless course of the river, the motion of animals and birds, and the growth of plants.

"San Ildefonso Corn Dance" by Gilbert Atencio

Chapter 3

TIME: THE ANNUAL CEREMONIAL CYCLE

The natural and ceremonial motions take time as well as space, from the smallest pulsations to the year's cycle. The dances express the Tewa equation of the east with sunrise and spring, the south with noon and summer, the west with evening and fall, the north with night and winter. Later chapters will describe the complex expressions in dance units and structures. This chapter outlines the effect of the seasonal and economic cycle on dance calendars and repertoires.

THE SEASONAL CYCLE

Despite the southerly location, the mountain valleys have much seasonal change, with cold winters and hot summers. The fullest dance season extends from the winter solstice to the spring equinox. As winter struggles with spring, cold days and bright days appear sporadically during the midwinter holiday period and before Lent. At this time Animal Dances predominate, because the people formerly depended on game during the winter season and they still hunt at this time. With the lengthening of the days the people turn their thoughts to the cleaning of irrigation ditches, planting corn and other vegetables. With the growth and harvesting of crops, the late spring, summer, and early fall are times for rain, corn, and harvest dances. Then comes the hunting season, with private ceremonies but not many plaza dances, and the cycle starts all over again.

Within this general cycle each pueblo adheres to certain customs, with, however, much leeway. Thus, San Juan theoretically holds the winter season *penshare,* the dance to the Deer Spirits, on February 15, but modern job compulsions have moved the date to a preceding or succeeding Sunday, any time between February 9 and 18. Traditionally, San Juan alternates *tunshare* Basket Dance with *pogonshare* Corn Maiden Dance in January, but in 1962 *tunshare* was on February 11. In that year it came after *xotsey-inshare,* Yellow Corn Dance. Yellow Corn Dance traditionally alternates with *thi'i,* Butterfly Dance in March. In 1957 Yellow Corn Dance took place on February 24; in 1963 Butterfly Dance was delayed until Easter Sunday. Nevertheless, in most years the San Juan dancers follow the traditions. They hold no dances in Lent and wait till June 13 and June 24 for summer festivals. Then their next traditional fiesta waits for the harvest season and *tembishare,* which is not held every year. The Christmas season juxtaposes two contrasting dances, the *Matachina* on Christmas Day and *okushare* for the solstice on December 26. At this time the Tewa celebrate a number of esoteric rites.

In all of the pueblos, the dances vary in sanctity according to the objective and the season. The most sacred are the rain dances of late winter and early spring. The least sacred are social dances with no specific seasonal assignment. They can be classified as follows (Edward Dozier, communication; 1957).

1. Big Dances with limited participation and supervision of sacred societies - men's *antegeshare* and other line dances; men's and women's *t'unshare* and *pogoshare*. Spring season, for rain and planting.

2. Big Dances with communal participation, arranged by social divisions, moieties, as well as societies - *xoxeye* and *tembishare*. Summer and early fall for growth and harvesting of crops.

3. Big Dances with limited participation by men and women, less sacred but still under the supervision of secret societies - *penshare* and *konshare*. Traditionally winter and spring, for hunt, but now extended to other seasons.

4. Little Dances with sacred connotations but less importance than the above - *yandewa, thi'i,* Eagle *tsehare,* for water, in the spring; *kwitara,* mostly in summer and fall, no specific function.

5. Dances of Spanish derivations, for limited participation - *Matachina* of the Christmas season, with a vaguely ceremonial significance.

6. Secular dances for social occasions - *pangshare* and Oklahoma Rounds, and show dances with no ceremonial connotation, Belt, Kiowa, Shield, Hoop, War Dances. Any time.

CALENDRIC CUSTOMS AND MODIFICATIONS

The San Juan example indicates the flexibility within calendric customs. The sample calendar at the end of the chapter illustrates general trends and deviations. In recent years there have been many changes, some for no apparent reason, as the Tesuque change from *xoxeye* or *konshare* to *kwitara* on November 12. Such gradual changes are evident in the comparison of older calendars with present events (e.g. Parsons 1939; Goggins 1937 and 1938). Some changes have historical reasons.

The Spanish missionaries influenced the calendar but not the functions during the seventeenth and eighteenth centuries. Today most of the set dates derive from the ecclesiastical calendar. One season abounds in dances, the Christmas and Epiphany period, during the solstice. The dances are native, with the addition of the *Matachina*. On the other hand, Lent is supposed to bring a recess in native dances. Most of the Tewa observe this

24

recess, except for San Ildefonso and Tesuque. In 1958 San Ildefonso held a dance every Sunday in Lent. Yet in 1957 and 1964 neither San Ildefonso nor Tesuque scheduled such dances regularly. Easter Sunday brings forth dancers at all Pueblos. In addition, each Pueblo celebrates its Saint's Day, and all celebrate San Antonio's Day, June 13, usually with *xoxeye*, a summer dance.

The fiestas for the patron saints feature native dances, but also include Catholic elements.

"Mass is held in the morning in the Catholic church of the pueblo, and the Indians in the audience and choir take their parts in the service with apparently the same reverence and fervor that they bring to their own ceremonial. After mass the image of the saint is carried into the plaza, placed under an arbor of boughs (ramada), and the Indian dance goes on in front of the improvised shrine. The Indian cosmogony includes many supernatural beings, and so they seem able to accept the Christian God even while holding to their own faith. Throughout the dancing, Indians may be observed going into the ramada and dropping on their knees before the image of the saint." (Dutton 1955:11-12).

After the day's dancing, a priest leads a procession for the return of the image to the church.

This is the schedule of the five Tewa Saint's Days, the patrons, and the customary dances:

San Ildefonso, January 23, San Ildefonso, *konshare* and *kwitara* in rotation in the two plazas.

San Juan, June 24, St. John the Baptist, formerly *konshare*, now *kwitara*.

Santa Clara, August 12, Santa Clara, *xoxeye*, *konshare*, *kwitara*, sometimes *yandewa*, two or three dances in alternation.

Nambe, October 4, San Francisco, *tashare* Elk Dance, or *konshare*, *kwitara*.

Tesuque, November 12, San Diego, formerly *xoxeye* or *konshare*, now usually *kwitara*.

Independent of the season, the dances on these ecclesiastical festivals are tending towards *konshare*, lately even more towards *kwitara*, thus towards decreasing esoteric significance.

Such modifications are also the result of Anglo-American economic influences. The increasing importance of modern jobs has decreased the indispensability of agriculture and hunting. But the native activities remain and the dances persist with a modification of function. Since *konshare* now affects weather more than buffalo hunt, it is gradually appearing at any season. Again, since irrigation now is becoming mechanized, the voluntary communal help and the ceremonies are lapsing. And the dates of persisting dances may be shifted to a weekend, as in the case of the San

Juan *penshare*, and the San Ildefonso harvest *xoxeye*, which may take place any Sunday around September 6.

The influx of tourists has promoted summer shows. Some summer public dancing is only for financial gain, but some programs, as the fiestas at Puye, and at Nambe Falls, also have artistic objectives.

REPERTOIRES

In plaza ceremonies and shows, all Tewa Pueblos favor the dances mentioned for Saint's Days, *xoxeye*, *konshare*, *kwitara*, *thi'i;* but they do not favor them equally. Tesuque presents the most spectacular *xoxeye*, and Santa Clara the most elaborate *konshare*, while San Juan shows less enthusiasm for their presentation. On the other hand, San Juan takes *penshare* and *tembishare* seriously. *Okushare* is a unique event of San Juan, but it corresponds to the *antegeshare* and *ta'andishare* of all Pueblos except Nambe. With Nambe, San Juan shares *xotseyinshare*, but not the *tashare*, Nambe's Saint's Day event. San Juan shares the Corn Maiden *pogonshare* with Santa Clara and San Ildefonso, also the *Matachina* drama. Santa Clara, San Ildefonso, and Tesuque know *ashare* Bow Dance, and *ba'a* Belt Dance. Only San Ildefonso preserves *yere*, known as the Snowbird Dance. Only Santa Clara performs *yandewa* and *kwantembeshare*.

There are fluctuations in popularity. Santa Clara's winter moiety revived *yandewa* in 1925 and *penshare* in 1965. The winter people do not give *xoxeye*, which has become a prerogative of the summer people. But the winter people have borrowed several dances from the Hopi, thanks to some Hopi-Tewa repatriates. They give a fine performance of Blue Corn Dance (Hopi Butterfly Dance). The summer people revived *tunshare* in 1951. San Juan also knows Hopi versions of several dances, of *konshare* and *thi'i*. And young men have borrowed a special Eagle Dance from Laguna.

New introductions and revivals continue. An impressive instance of renewed dance activity is the resurrection of the Nambe repertoire, for the Saint's Day and for a July 4 show. Don Roberts is interested in studying the Nambe revival.

On the other hand, some dances have become obsolete, or so it seems from English names in various publications. Santa Clara has not for some years given a Skunk or Willow-behind dance, nor a Goat Dance since Parsons' report (1929a:204). San Ildefonso has evidently not scheduled a Pinto Dance since Whitman's observation of 1937 (1947:136), nor a Bluebird Dance since Lucero-White's observation (1954). None of the Tewa villages has held a Horse Dance, Santiago, since 1920 at any rate, though Mexican villages and Keresans give this drama. *Pangshare* social dance is becoming obsolescent. And, strangely enough, San Juan has discontinued the Oklahoma Rounds which are rising in popularity elsewhere.

It is significant that the obsolescence affects less sacred dances and that perseverance and revival keep the repertoires of sacred dances intact. The fluctuations and local variations are healthy signs. They are, as a matter of fact, trivial as compared with the pervading patterns of the ceremonial cycle. While the entertaining show dances occupy a marginal position, the revered dances are still the old, ecological ceremonies, which express the interplay of seasons and human adjustment to the natural environment.

Cleto and Severa Tafoya, who assisted with explanations of Santa Clara dances, shown here with their grandchild. Cleto is a rattle maker and Severa is a potter.

Chapter 4

THE PERFORMERS: SOCIAL INTERACTION

Each pueblo is a ceremonial center. For the duration of the dance, the space between the adobe houseblocks becomes a sanctuary. The inmates do not set aside distant places for their dances, though they used to hold secret rites in mountain dells. They now have a large kiva for indoor, eso-teric ceremonies, and for ritual preludes and postludes to plaza ceremonies. They also have one or more dance kivas within the houseblocks adjacent to the plazas. They have allocated the church to a marginal location. While the performers emerge from the kivas and return to them, the spectators congregate in front of their homes or within them. Inhabitants and visitors occasionally join in phases of the activities, and they follow the performers in migrations to various plazas.

The performers are the people of the pueblo. They do not engage pro-fessionals, though they recognize competent leaders in the organization, dancing, and singing. In organization and in behavior standards they adhere to their socio-religious precepts.

THE MOIETIES AND DANCE CUSTOMS

The complex Tewa organization has had many exponents (Parsons, 1939). The moiety system formerly dominated all activities, and it still affects the ceremonies. The two basic moieties have seasonal as well as social affiliations.

"The outstanding principle of Tewa social classification is the division into moieties called the Summer people and the Winter people. Summer people are associated with the South, femininity, and squash, that is, with softness and plant life. The Winter people are referred to along with the North, masculinity, and turquoise, which is to say, a hard mineral sub-stance. The dualism of this classification impregnates the political organi-zation, ceremonial life, and social opinion of the Tewa.

"Moieties are patrilineal, and a woman who marries a man from the op-posite moiety will often join her husband's group in a ceremony called p'oku, "water pouring." Rather than being clans, moieties are divisions of the pueblo into two halves, but, according to Parsons, they may be con-sidered as 'a substitute for clans in social consciousness.' (1929:89).

"The leaders of the Summer and Winter people are the Summer Caci-que and the Winter Cacique, i.e., the ceremonial town chiefs who alternate

29

in taking charge of the whole pueblo. Each holds office for about half the year, although actually, the office of the Summer Cacique lasts somewhat longer, from March to November, 'to make the summer longer.'

"The Panyo Oke·, or Summer man of San Juan, is the lifelong head of the Panyo Oke· religious society, and ex-officio, the Summer Cacique, i.e., spiritual leader of the Summer people. His patron goddess is Panyoka·, who is considered the source of his spiritual strength. A stone figure representing her is one of his most sacred possessions.

"The O·yi·ke, or Hard Ice Man, is the head of the O·yi·ke society and simultaneously the Winter Cacique. He, too, cherishes a stone fetish of the goddess which gives him strength, the goddess O·yi·ka·" (Laski 1958:3-4).

The application of this principle to dance ceremonies is by no means uniform. In San Juan the two moieties operate in harmony. The decisions are in the hands of a unified governing body, with one Governor for public transactions and a War Chief for ceremonial transactions. The moieties unite in the dances. They use the same dance kiva and circulate through the plazas together, without any outward distinguishing marks. The men wear white, the women wear black costumes. At the fall *tembishare*, moiety representatives take turns in one large event. At midwinter, special ceremonial "clowns," called *tsaviyo*, represent the two moieties by distinctive dress and actions.

Santa Clara is split into four parties, each moiety being divided into conservatives and progressives. The government is highly organized and it even drew up a constitution on December 10, 1935 (Aberle 1948:37). The Council operates efficiently, under one Governor and a set of officers; it admits women to secular meetings. The four factions are placated by the annual rotation of officers and the election of eight representatives. The War Chief has exclusively religious duties. However, Santa Clara parties arrange separate plaza dances and give them on separate dates. They take turns on the Saint's Day and at Puye. Each party has its own dance kiva, and its dancers circulate through the plazas in a well-regulated, distinctive order, to be described in Part II. Now only three circuits are operative, because the conservative winter moiety has lost too many singers and dancers to sponsor a festival (W.W. Hill, MS.). The summer and winter people differ in their costuming. Though Deer impersonators are dressed as at San Juan, only the winter people regularly wear white kilts and mantas, while the summer men may use white or black and the women always appear in black mantas. Several more showy dances require special costumes, without moiety restrictions.

The rivalry has one good effect. It prompts each group to special exertion, in order to outdo the others. At the same time, the members of one moiety are generous with their praise of a good performance by another.

The conservative summer people admire the precision and meticulous costuming of the winter people.

San Ildefonso has another kind of split. Members of both sides live around both plazas, but a larger population inhabits the northern section. Therefore the Governor has more frequently come from the north plaza. This and other causes provoked open quarrels and secession of the southern plaza people. On February 10, 1943, an agreement on Government election in alternate years gave the two plazas equal rights and somewhat assuaged the bitterness (Aberle 1948:36, n. 62). Each side now has two representatives in the Council. But the two plazas operate their ceremonies independently. Frequently they perform dances on different days. On January 23 and Easter Sunday they schedule different dances simultaneously and in competition. In costuming they agree; they use the same types as the Santa Clara summer people. (The division may be affected by the demolition of the dividing houseblock in December 1964 – D.R.).

Each faction maintains its own kiva, a room within a houseblock on the second floor, the north plaza kiva located in a northern block and the other kiva in a western building. The dancers emerge from their respective kivas and return there. They circulate within the precincts of their own plazas, not through a series of plazas as in San Juan and Santa Clara.

The Tesuque moieties operate in harmony as in San Juan, but they use one central plaza, similar to the San Ildefonso custom. The two sides sometimes perform together as on the Saint's Day. Or they take turns during one day from home base, that is, from their respective kivas. They may alternate in the manner of Keresan moiety dancers, or they may take over half a day, the summer side in the morning, the winter side in the afternoon. They are costumed in the same manner as San Ildefonso dancers. For *xox-eye* the women dispense with the pan-Tewa silken capes. In this respect they also resemble the Keresans. Apparently the two moieties do not compete.

In Nambe the kiva ceremonies are obsolete and the moiety division is obsolescent. In a recent revival the groups have been amalgamated and have emerged from a house in the southeast section of the plaza. They circulate within this one plaza. For their costuming they have taken the cue from the two southern pueblos, though they borrow songs from Santa Clara and also remember some of their own dances.

The moieties have special ceremonial actors, generally called "clowns," *kosa* for the north and winter, *kwirana* for the south and summer. They share certain other officials who, however, differ somewhat in the various pueblos. Moieties and pueblos agree on basic customs for lay participants.

31

THE ACTORS AND THEIR FUNCTIONS

The clearest moiety representatives are the *tsaviyo* of San Juan. In their late December circuits and black vs. white costumes they symbolize the summer and winter people. These purifying agents are not comics; they are weird. The *tsaviyo* or *abuelos* in the *Matachina* drama are quite different. They do enact horseplay. The precise actions of these impersonators will appear in later chapters, as will the activities of all other actors.

The *kosa* and *kwirana,* representing the winter and summer moieties, sometimes engage in ridiculous activities and parodies, but basically they are powerfully sacred members of a brotherhood promoting fertility.

"Members of these societies accompany masked dancers in rites from which the public is excluded. They also participate in open ceremonies such as corn dances, where they dance in and out among the formal dancers." (Dutton 1955:8). They are representatives of "real" spirits who have mythological homes in the east. They serve as mediators between the people of the earth and their ancient spirits. The *kosa* are connected with the sun.

In Tewa territory their numbers and appearances are dwindling. They still sometimes appear as side dancers with symbolic gestures, or as intermission comics, in *okushare, antegeshare, tunshare,* rarely *pogonshare.* Santa Clara has no *kwirana,* but all pueblos have one or more *kosa.* Tesuque has several Tema (Keresan) *kosa,* as well as Tewa *kosa.* The Santa Clara *oke* and Nambe *kosa* visit, respectively, San Juan and Nambe. (Parsons 1929a:130; Hill MS.). The *kwirana* still wear black rags. The *kosa* sometimes wear a striped shirt instead of paint.

Several clown groups have no moiety affiliations. They are real clowns. They are the Apache in motley attire, at the San Juan *penshare,* and the obsolescent *putandi,* who collected rags from a trash pile and engaged in mischief during the *pogonshare* and *thi'i.* As all performers, these comics require ritual blessing, but they have no supernatural connotations.

Among the officials, some have moiety positions, while others represent the whole pueblo. The summer and winter caciques join the dancing in *tembishare,* but otherwise their duties are ritual and esoteric. The War Chief has six assistants, who are selected annually and installed at New Year, three from each moiety (San Juan). They serve as announcers, conductors, and guards during preliminaries and plaza performances. Each pueblo has one *pingxeng sendo* except Santa Clara and Nambe which have none. This hunt chief, who serves for life as a successor to a deceased hunt chief on the paternal side, has ritual and public duties. He is a prominent dance figure in the San Juan *penshare* and in all *konshare* of San Juan, San Ildefonso, and Tesuque. When he leads rabbit hunts, he is not in costume;

Above and Below: Dancers at Santa Clara's Feast Day (1958)

when he dances, he wears a Plains-type hide costume and carries a rattle and a bow-and-arrow set. But he does not engage in hunting mime.

The ritual officials are always older men with experience and wisdom. So are the ritual clowns. But the war chief's assistants can be younger men. In the dances, age participation is regulated by tradition. The leaders are always experienced men, usually in their thirties. They are selected because of their ability, not because of age or rank (castes do not exist). Male adults and sometimes female adults form the exclusive groups in esoteric line dances, as *okushare* and *tunshare*. But teenagers and children join in the communal and show dances, as *xoxeye* and *kwitara*. In public programs children are the preferred actors in the *tseshare* Dog Dance, Kiowa, Shield, and Hoop Dances. Boys are "shot" in *penshare*.

The great composers are always older men. But in performances they have the company of singers in middle age, and they encourage the participation of young men. Sometimes, especially in Santa Clara, they have a retinue of small boys who thus learn the songs. Sometimes the singers are members of the dance line, in the middle, *sawipinge;* sometimes they constitute a separate chorus. This is a matter for future discussion.

A dichotomy as important as the moiety dualism and more evident, is the role of men and women. Women are never ritual clowns among the Tewa, though they sometimes appear as clowns in Keresan ceremonies. They are never officials, except in their own, female kiva societies - the *kwiyo*. They are excluded from the most sacred line dances. But they feature equally and even prominently in *tunshare*, all dances with *wasa* (q.v.), all harvest dances, *konshare, kwitara,* and social dances. They never lead in mixed dances. But they monopolize some dances, especially male imitations as *ashare,* and parodies of Navaho. In these events they exhibit a sense of humor. The arrangements of the sexes in the dance formations are traditionalized and complicated.

Women do not feature as musicians. They never compose songs. They never join the separate chorus of drummers and singers. But they scrape the moraches in *tunshare* and sometimes in the San Ildefonso *antegeshare.* In the San Ildefonso *ashare* for women, a matron (Maria, the famous potter) beats the drum; and the female dancers sing their own accompaniment. Sometimes they know the songs and join in, as in Yellow Corn line dancing, but sotto voce. In Oklahoma Round Dances they join in the song an octave above the men, for female participation is customary.

Another, more informal interrelation is the performer-audience dichotomy. It is a true dichotomy, for spectators never join the ceremonial dancing, as they do among tribes to the east. They take an active part in episodes of gift throwing and in the general processions from plaza to plaza. They watch from seats by their doorways or walls, from parked cars, or from various vantage positions anywhere in the plaza. They may completely surround the performers, especially at Puye and in some San Juan and Santa Clara plazas. But usually they watch from three sides, with the chorus of musicians stationed against a background of *kiva* or house wall. The attendance may be small at very sacred line dances, especially if the weather is cold. At scheduled or advertised larger group dances there may be visitors from other pueblos. At Saint's Day fiestas and shows there is a colorful assembly of Tewa and Navaho, some in modern native attire; Santo Domingans selling their ware; and tourists in dignified clothes or in grotesque outfits and shorts. Though the attitude should always be reverent, the fiesta comings and goings are casual.

PERFORMANCE STANDARDS AND VARIATIONS

While a large audience is essential to a show dancer, a small attendance does not worry the ritual dancer. For a religious invocation a good performance achieves the purpose, audience or no. The Tewa have distinct standards of excellence, even gradations of standards for gradations of sanctity.

According to Antonio and Carlos Garcia and various other Tewa men and women, the ideal is moderation. The singing should be neither too loud nor too soft; the dancing should avoid the extremes of vigor or indifference. In general, the individual should be part of the group and conform to its style, not try to stand out. This ideal holds good for the leaders and the participating officials as well as for the line dancers. Only the ceremonial clowns are exempt, for their behavior is beyond censure. They follow special conventions which are sometimes the opposite of group standards.

Within the group repertoire there are variations in the golden mean. One kind of variation pertains to the dance type. In the *antege* sacred line dances the movements are held to a mimimum in space and effort; they are almost static. In Corn Dances the groups move about more freely and with more energy. In *konshare* the mimes may be still more energetic within the style of each particular animal. *Kwitara* and *tseshare* Eagle Dances give still more opportunity for display of skill. Oklahoma War Dance types exceed these standards. They need not conform to ritual ways.

Another kind of variation derives from the male-female dual standards in everyday life. Women always comport themselves more decorously and quietly than men, that is, ideally. They should dance with more restraint than men, never raise their knees as high as a man. In dance categories they follow a style one notch more subdued than the men. In *xoxeye* they should move as subtly as the men in *antegeshare;* in *konshare* they should be no livelier than the men in *xoxeye.* In *kwitara* they greatly contrast

35

with the men; for they bounce gently in place while their partners hop back and forth with yells. In compensation, the women and girls sometimes twist and shuffle their feet instead of merely marking time, thus in *tunshare*.

A third kind of variation is individual. Within the golden mean there is leeway for more or less skill and spirit. One person can be more buoyant or more cleancut in stepping and timing and yet fit into the group maneuvers, so long as he or she does not show off, jiggle the shoulders, hit the heels on the buttocks, or step out of line. Some men and women dance with particular absorption and with a fervent, almost masklike face. Those are often the best dancers, and they are distinguished from young people with a listless, indifferent expression and a shuffling manner.

The deviants - shufflers or show-offs - are commonly teenagers who have felt the influence of jazz dancing. Small children try to emulate the leaders and to conform to standards. Adults regard the youngsters' efforts with indulgence; the guards help them at times, and they are pleased with juvenile success.

Finally, the Tewa recognize inter-pueblo variations. They consider the performances of San Ildefonso and Tesuque as the most solemn and traditional, and the Santa Clara style as livelier, especially in the fiestas of the summer moiety. Some spectators admire the agility of the Santa Clarans, while others dub them showy. Members of the four northern pueblos approve of the resurrected Nambe style because of its adherence to the restrained ways.

The musicians also must follow a set of traditions. They show considerable variation in the use of rain-making gestures or the lack of gestures; but they must use the ritualized gestures. If a singer jiggles his arms with excessive vigor, he attracts unfavorable attention, not admiration. The manner of singing sometimes permits great range of dynamics, more than in dancing, but again within tradition. In the sacred line ceremonies the dancer-singers may let their voices soar exuberantly during high melodies and yet they begin and end in almost a growl. In these songs they propel their tones with emphatic pulsations. In contrast, the singers for Eagle and Dog Dances let their voices ring out steadily and clearly. As tempo is essential, the instrumentalists are important. They are men capable of an unfaltering beat. Generally they keep the volume of the drums below that of the singing; but in *xoxeye* they may drown out the melody, especially in the beginning and end. Not all men have equally good voices, but they all strive for the full-throated pueblo tone, and avoid a flat tone, a falsetto, or the baritone style of the Anglo. When women sing alone, they display the thin tone of Indian women, similar to that of their easterly sisters. A tremolo or bellow would be inappropriate.

The standards of restraint contrast with Euro-American ideals of acrobatic proficiency, with high kicks, leaps, and backbends. In the matter of precision the best pueblo performances satisfy Anglo professional standards. Precision is an ideal. The dancers sometimes fall short of the ideal. If someone misses a change in beat or gets onto the wrong foot, he covers up the error and remains in high regard as a traditional stylist. In certain dances it is difficult for the group to maintain a perfect line-up, as in crossovers of *xoxeye*. That too is forgiven. But a generally slovenly performance evokes criticism, even within the pueblo.

The conformity to standards and striving for precision fulfill several strivings, artistic, social, and religious. Actors and audience enjoy an artistically fine performance. The actors bask in the well-earned praise of their spectators, especially their neighbors, after a good event. Most of all, a fine performance aids the religious purpose, emotional and practical. In the words of John Collier, "the Pueblo Indian experiencer of the sacred drama knows that he is raised into vastness, made free from personal trouble, flooded with impersonal joy and ardor, and plunged into the ever-flowing tide of the tribal world soul." (1949:63). Above all, the meticulous performer has helped the pueblo by invoking supernatural aid, for a specific purpose as rain, or for the general well-being of the people.

These objectives are vital. Hence the actors spare no efforts in perfecting their presentation and in obtaining supernatural blessing on the event.

Chapter 5

RITUAL PRELUDES AND POSTLUDES
by Antonio Garcia and Carlos Garcia

The Tewa observe ritualistic customs to ensure the artistic and social success of the dance. San Juan performers follow the procedures described below. And other pueblos have similar customs.

ANNOUNCEMENT AND SUMMONS

On New Year's Day the Tewa install new sets of officers, both secular officials and ceremonial officials. For dances the most active officials are the War Chief (*ahkonutuyo*) - "Plains or Prairie governor", and his six assistants. The War Chief is elected from each moiety in alternate years. His assistants stem from both sides, three men from the winter, three from the summer moiety. When the new officers decide on the presentation of a particular dance, they choose composers, singers, and dancers.

The selection of composers presents no problem, because only three gifted men have the genius for new song creation, and they are invariably appointed for new songs, though they train young men (the talent is often hereditary). They compose new songs for *okushare, tunshare,* and *pogonshare.* For other dances they call to mind sets of traditional songs. The leading singers, who will occupy the center of the dance line - *sawipinge* are also well known, and are re-selected from year to year. However, the drummer or drummers may be newly elected for each dance, from the ranks of experienced musicians. For the dancing, especially talented and carefully selected men and women fill the roles of an exclusive nature, as the two Corn Maidens, the Buffalo Mother, the Buffalo Fathers, and leaders of large dances. All eligible males are supposed to participate in *okushare, tunshare,* and *pogonshare,* formerly all males and females in *xoxeye.* All members of Societies, officials, and representatives of both moieties attend the preparatory and final sessions of *tembishare.*

The War Chief sends his assistants to the homes of elected participants, first to the homes of the composers and the central singers, then to the other men, later on to the women. They must make formal requests to the women. "I come here aggressively, though you are a respected person." If the woman is married, the herald must speak to her in front of the husband. "We have chosen you to enlighten us and to help us gain life." It is up to the woman to accept. They address unmarried women in the same manner, but in the presence of the father, who gives his permission. The War Chief or one of his assistants can propose one of his daughters for the dance.

SONG PREPARATIONS

The song composers must obey traditional restrictions, but can also exercise ingenuity. For very sacred dances like *penshare* they try to recall the tunes exactly. If there is any disagreement about the correct version, the chorus masters, *xamayo,* Juanito Trujillo, Cipriano and Peter Garcia are the final authorities. In the case of less sacred, traditional songs, they may make a few changes, short additions or subtractions. For innovations, they can borrow melodies from other tribes, especially Keresans, and use them in toto or build a composition on the borrowed theme. They may combine traditional and new songs for the three special dances - *okushare, t'unshare, and pogonshare.*

In the process of creation they must adhere to traditional patterns, though they can develop their themes at greater or less length than the prototypes. The creation must start with a monotone, low pitched introduction. It must have a root theme, *xapu,* which is melodic and which changes tempo in *tunshare* and *pogonshare,* gradually accelerating in the latter. (This is like *antegeshare* in other pueblos.) The theme should develop into a louder section on a higher level, *xakegi,* "loud song." After statements of xapimbe comes a third theme, somewhat lower and less extensive than *xakegi.* Then the first theme comes again. Then finally a low-pitched coda ends the composition. Within each song, rhythmic changes break into the regular, duple beat of the percussion. For song texts the composers draw upon ceremonial phrases and combine them anew, occasionally contributing a new poetic image. They may use Keresan or Hopi words, though they do not understand them. English is customary only for the highly secular songs for the Oklahoma rounds, which are outside ceremonialism.

When the men of the *sawipinge* meet in the War Chief's home, the composer teaches the tune. The men must learn it exactly, so as to avoid improvisation or mistakes. Though the composer develops his themes instinctively, from long experience, without thought of terminology, the nuclear singers may refer to parts by name, especially when they realize an error. In both traditional and new songs, they may say, "We made a mistake in the *xakegi;*" or, "We made a mistake towards the end of the song, the *xaxanu.*" They try to avoid the mistake on the next try. This avoidance of errors is partly an artistic concern, for an error will not bring down supernatural wrath. It may, however, minimize the good effects of the dance.

39

SONG AND DANCE REHEARSALS

Then the War Chief's assistants summon the other men to the practice *kiva* for four or more evenings of joint rehearsal. They combine the dance steps with the singing on these occasions. The movements are set by tradition. But the dancers must memorize the songs, so they know when to expect the rhythmic changes, *t'a*, and the conclusion. They need only rehearse for a tidy rendering in the case of dances with traditional songs and choreography, like *kwitara*. But they may devise variations in step and formations for some dances like *konshare*. Gifted male leaders, usually men in early middle age, devise such variations in collaboration with the male group. Dance leaders in San Juan are David Garcia, Juanito Aguino, and Peter Aguino.

Then the officials call in the ladies for four more nights of rehearsals. Some of the mature women know the songs and they may sing them softly along with the men, if it is a self-accompanied dance. All of the women, and any children that may join the dance, must know the music well enough to avoid mistakes during rhythmic changes; and they must be sufficiently familiar with dance patterns to follow the leaders in the steps and evolutions.

Children joining in the rehearsals find the participation an honor, and they are very attentive, as a rule. In the hot season, however, young people may try to back out of participation. Anyone who consents will put forth his or her efforts. The first participation of an adult may be celebrated by tying a ribbon around the neck. Then he or she is obligated to sponsor a *pangshare* social dance in the practice kiva or at home.

Priests and dance officials introduce and end each of these rehearsals with a prayer of exhortation and thanksgiving.

PARAPHERNALIA

During the rehearsal period the officials and performers have been preparing their paraphernalia. The priests are the custodians of some communal paraphernalia, as the drums, buffalo headdresses, and the ceremonial feathers, *fe*. But each man owns his own rattle and each dancer has his or her own costume, kilt, manta, moccasins, headdress, jewelry, bells; and is responsible for their construction and repair, if necessary. If it is necessary to obtain a new drum, the officials go to the Cochiti master craftsmen for large drums, occasionally to San Ildefonso for smaller ones. San Juan men can make new gourd rattles and moraches (See Appendix II). The drums, which have supernatural power, are fed cornmeal; the gourd rattles have rain power, while tortoise-shell rattles further fertility. But most of the paraphernalia is not sacrosanct and is not connected with ritual, despite the symbolism of decorations. Only the *fe*, the down feather, has ritual power, and is attached to a man's hair by the War Chief or a priest or an old man, with gestures in the six directions.

Most of the costumes follow traditions, those of the group dancers, *kosa* and *tsaviyo*, though the women may use their judgement in the choice of jewelry and capes. For the Apaches of the *penshare* the relatives can help improvise an amusing outfit.

San Juan women are adept in the fabrication of ceremonial pottery and baskets. For other paraphernalia, men are responsible. Emissaries gather spruce boughs and cottonwood boughs for manipulation in the dances. They hold an expedition to the eastern mountains for the spruce trees which they will hole in at each plaza with an offering of cornmeal. For *penshare* the dance officials get straw, and before dawn the day of the plaza ceremony they make a smudge, a "fog."

EVE OF THE PLAZA PERFORMANCE

On the eve of the public appearance, summer dancers meet in the large kiva. In the winter the dancers meet in the practice kiva. For San Juan's Day fiesta this is June 23; for *Matachines* it is December 24; for *okushare* it is December 25. Otherwise it is a Saturday night, because the fiestas generally take place on Sundays. The performers used to fast, at least in advance of certain very sacred dances. But this is no longer compulsory. However, for the Rain Races the men must maintain sexual continence.

The performers rehearse with complete cast but not with complete paraphernalia. They execute the formations as well as possible within the confines of the kiva, knowing that their movements will be greatly expanded in the plaza. That is, they do not have "dress rehearsals" in the sense of Anglo performers.

For certain dances the men hold a very ritualistic prelude, the *ange'i*, on the eve of the public dance, before the general rehearsal. They dance *ange'i* to specially composed songs for *okushare, tunshare,* and *pogonshare,* and to traditional songs for *penshare.* The songs for *ange'i* follow the same general pattern as other songs of these ceremonies, but they are repeated three times. Between the first and second renderings the dancers, who are lined up shoulder-to-shoulder, take four steps forward, face about and repeat the song in the opposite direction from the first rendering. (If the first rendering involved a northern orientation, the second implies a southern orientation.) After the second rendering they face about similarly for the third repeat. They accompany the face-abouts with rattle, but not melodic background.

Other events may take place on the eve of the public performance. Sometimes there is a plaza dance of a less ceremonial nature. For instance on June 23, 1964, a special group performed the San Juan *konshare*. Formerly women used to dance comical transvestite versions of *thi'i*, half of them dressed as men.

On the eve of *penshare* the Apache clowns perform a special ritual, though in general they are not sacrosanct like the other "clowns." After they have been duly chosen and summoned, they go to the main kiva and smoke a pipe with ceremonial (Mexican) tobacco, or they smoke corn husks mixed with ceremonial tobacco. Such ritual smoking is usually esoteric, as in the case of the *bufona* bear doctors, and the *a'age* dance.

DAY OF THE PLAZA PERFORMANCE

A dawn prelude precedes the daytime dance of the San Juan Deer impersonators. The officials light the straw for the "fog" in the east hills. Deer dancers and their chorus enter the village from the east to special song sets, and after the ceremonial circuit they retire to their homes. In other Tewa pueblos, Buffalo dancers enter during a similar dawn prelude. The dancers return to the kiva in groups.

Just before the ultimate plaza performance, the heads of all medicine societies gather with the performers in the kiva. They are the winter cacique, *kesendo* Bear Society head, *kosa, kwirena,* and *samayo (pingxeng)* game priest. Each priest has prepared an altar, and a medicine bowl with consecrated water. They used to take water from a sacred spring, but now they can take it from a kitchen faucet. Each man has a bag of herbs and he sprinkles these into the water. They pass the bowls around to the standing performers, in counterclockwise order, first to the leaders, finally to the children. They say, "Drink, so you may have everlasting life." All drink from the bowls. The priests utter words of encouragement in Tewa. Regardless of sex, they say to everyone, "Be a man, be a woman."

Then the performers practice one song, formerly an entire set, before their emergence into the plaza. At the moment for the emergence, the *kosa* or War Chief opens the *kiva* door for the singers and dancers to file out into the sun.

POSTLUDES

At the end of the day, after the performers have made their fourth appearance, they enact a postlude *ange'i* for certain dances, for *penshare, okushare,* and *tunshare.* In *tunshare ange'i* the women join the men. During or after their *ange'i* the Deer dancers disperse into hiding places in the hills, until friends or family members find them.

42

Other dancers retire into the big *kiva.* The priests utter prayers of thanks to the performers in the *kiva.* Any male entering the *kiva* should have cornmeal and feed the fire god and other spirits by sprinkling the meal into the fireplace in the center of the *kiva* floor. Only old men do so now.

Thereafter, whenever dancers enter a home, they say, *iwowanini,* "May you have everlasting life " to the occupants of the house. This is customary even for less sacred dances like *kwitara,* but not after show dances or social dances.

After the performance, ritual cleansing is still required, though not observed in all cases. The men used to bathe in the river or an irrigation ditch after *okushare, penshare,* and *pogonshare* some thirty years ago. Primarily they bathed to wash off the paint and sacred mud, but they were also observing a symbolic cleansing. Today even the singers of the *sawipinge* do not observe this rule. Instead, they bathe at home in the wash tub after a dance in which the body has been painted.

The War Chief and his assistants observe rituals of "returning" certain paraphernalia to the supernaturals. At dawn the following morning they throw the spruce trees, spruce boughs, and sacred feathers into the river. However, the women who have participated in the plaza *tunshare* keep the scraping sticks. They place them in flower pots. Hence they call them "flower sticks."

Under certain circumstances the participants are exempt from ritual preludes and postludes. In the first place, when men or women perform for shows, they need not prepare or conclude ritualistically, even if the dances are ceremonial. Also, if anyone helps out in another Pueblo, as is often the case, rituals are voluntary.

RITUAL PRELIMINARIES OF THE TSAVIYO (Figure 3)

While group preparations have no moiety restrictions, the *tsaviyo* represent the two moieties and their seasonal-directional symbols. During the winter solstice two *tsaviyo* enact purificatory rituals. From December 21 to 25 they perform ancient rituals in the kivas and plazas. Then they join the plaza dancers.

On the eve of December 21 the white *tsaviyo* appears from the hill east of the pueblo. He belongs to the winter moiety. He wears white hide trousers, a white kilt, moccasins, and hide mask. He has a fox fur collar, mica earrings, ear flaps, eye slits, and frosted hair. On December 22 the black *tsaviyo* of the summer moiety appears in a natural colored hide costume, yellow moccasins, and a black mask similar to the white *tsaviyo's.* Both have come from Truchas Peak, *thampiyeping,* hence the frosting. They whisper in Spanish falsetto.

On December 23, in the evening before dusk, both come out to make the people sweep the plazas. Dance officials go to the head of the pueblo

Figure 3 – Circuit of San Juan Tsaviyo, December 23

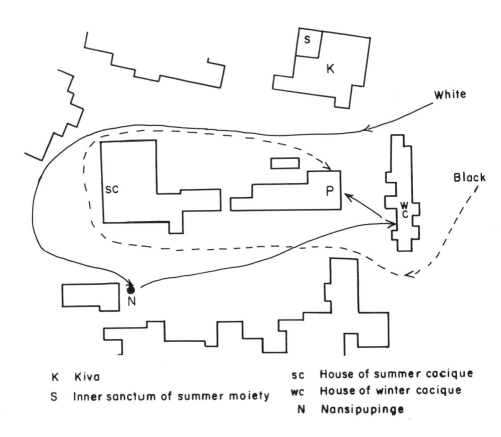

K   Kiva
S   Inner sanctum of summer moiety

sc   House of summer cacique
wc   House of winter cacique
N   Nansipupinge

below the cemetery, to meet the *tsaviyo*. The officials say "hello" and shake hands, then proceed with the *tsaviyo*. "Whitie" jumps and walks counterclockwise through the north plaza, around to the winter cacique's house south of the main house block, and strikes the ground with a whip. He strikes his whip on the *nansipupinge*, a sacred stone pile symbolic of the earth center, and the pueblo's ceremonial center. Then he enters the house. The summer "blackie" goes clockwise by way of the south plaza to the summer cacique's house west of the house block, and strikes the ground with his whip. (Since the death of the last summer cacique, in 1963, he has gone to a house in the north plaza.) They enter the house of each cacique and are welcomed to the pueblo by them. Then they retire to the big kiva with the officials. Their ritual directions are significant, counterclockwise around the north for the winter, and clockwise around the south for the summer.

On December 25 they make the circuit again after the performance of the *Matachina* drama. In the afternoon at about 4:00 P.M. they appear again from the hills. "Whitey" circuits the pueblo counterclockwise, and "blackie" enters and circuits clockwise. The *oku ange'i* has already started in the south plaza. The *tsaviyo* join the *oku* dancers when they continue the *ange'i* in the practice *kiva,* for ritual observances.

On December 26 they herald *okushare* by circulating in the morning. Then they dance around the dance line. They "catch" eligible, delinquent males and place them in the dance line, for every healthy adult male is supposed to participate. After the dance they are greeted by dance officials and caciques. Then they retire to the practice kiva, to join the *oku* dancers after their postlude *ange'i.* They go to every house to bless and say goodbye and to receive gifts of bread and money. They may cure sick persons with a touch of the whip, and they may remind naughty children to obey parents, also with light strokes of the whips. Finally they retire to the inner sanctum of the summer moiety, in the big kiva, to undress.

Though frequently called "clowns," the *tsaviyo* are not funny. They are fooling around with the kosa who make fun of them. They are uncanny in their behavior. They tread ghostlike and silently, without musical accompaniment. At times they stop and trot in place, peering about; then they trot ahead and leap soundlessly. They speak in whispers, and they lash their whips, which are curative and purificatory rather than punitive. Nevertheless, they are fearsome to children, and they may serve as threats to naughty ones any time during the year. The mother may say to a refractory child, "tsaviyo will get you." Their annual solstice circuits make an impression that lasts through the year.

Santa Clara Harvest Dance at Puye (1961)

Part II

Choreographic and Musical Patterns

In the course of a day the dancers, singers, and attendants appear several times, usually four. At each appearance they make a prescribed circuit of the plaza or plazas, in accordance with local customs. At each plaza they perform an entire dance, usually the same dance at each plaza. The traditional musical accompaniment may be one long song or a suite of two or three songs. The structure of each song or suite varies, not according to locality, but according to the function and type of ceremony.

The larger structures contain subsections and still smaller elements of gesture, steps, rhythm, and melody. The type of elements and the manner of assembly adhere to specific kinds of frames which are standardized according to function and degree of sanctity. But the compositions built on the frames vary according to the pueblo and in certain cases according to the composer.

The analysis in the following chapters will proceed from the large circuits to the smallest basic elements, and will then reassemble the pieces and demonstrate the relationships of the structures to the functions.

In Parts II and III the elements are shown by means of ground plans, glyphs, sometimes by stick figures, and, for gestures, also kinemes - abstractions of gesture paths, traced by the hands.

Except for this useful term (kinemes), the analyses avoid jargon and technical terminology, preferring Tewa and English terms to synthetic expressions.

Above and Below: San Juan Deer Dance

Chapter 6

CIRCUIT ORIENTATION

The performers relate their plaza circuits to the cardinal directions. In theory, but not always in practice, they follow a counterclockwise course. The Tewa pueblos observe two kinds of customs, depending on the architecture of the pueblo.

1. Circuit from plaza to plaza, with dancing at four stations or only two.
2. Circuit within one large plaza, with a pattern of complete or alternate use of stations.

In San Juan the 1150 residents live in the house blocks around several plazas large and small, all of them elongated. They also occupy many homes outside the central section. The 723 Santa Clarans dance in four plazas near the great kiva, in the old center, and their new homes sprawl into the valley. At the Puye performances the dancers move in a counterclockwise circuit around the four walls of the huge ruin. The 272 San Ildefonsans proceed within one huge plaza, the north people around their part of the plaza, the south people around theirs, without infringing on each other's domains. The 207 people of Nambe and 230 Tesuque residents have spread out from a central plaza, and use the center for their circuits.

The ground plans for the circuit patterns use the bird's-eye views in Stubbs 1950 for the building blocks (shaded) and plazas, and insert the paths of the dancers and singers.

LOCAL CIRCUIT CUSTOMS (Figures 4-14)

San Juan. The large plazas form a parallel design, with two smaller plazas at right angles. They run, respectively, east-west and north-south. The dancers emerge from the big kiva or the small practice kiva. They always proceed to the south, large plaza for their first station. From there on, the customs vary according to the dances, but they are always in clockwise order. The illustrations show four salient types:

1). A complete circuit of four stations, in *tembishare*. Circuits start or finish in either kiva. This aspect is optional.
2). A circuit of south, north, and east plazas, with a fourth rendering in the practice kiva. Usually the path from the south to the north plaza is by way of the east plaza, thus in *okushare, xoxeye,* and *penshare* of 1964. In 1957 the Deer Dancers proceeded through a narrow passage between the cen-

tral houseblocks. *Kwitara* dancers proceed by way of the west plaza, without stopping there. This is the path of the Dawn Deer Entrance.

3) Three stations, south, north, and big kiva, in *kwitara*.

4) Two stations, south and north, with zigzag "wasa" entrance, in *thi'i.*

Since the plazas vary in size, the performers can spread out more in the long plazas and must stand closer together in the east plaza. When there are spruce trees, they conform to the sizes and to the prospective placement of the dancers.

The numbering on the ground plans refers to the complete order, which is limited to *tembishare.* Thus, some dances use only 1 and 3.

Santa Clara. The four customary plazas, as numbered, are an open space east of the kiva, then a small space between houses just to the southwest of station 1, then a longer plaza to the north, then the large plaza south of the big kiva. Each of the three active moieties uses a different practice kiva for emergence and final entrance, as marked on the ground plan, the summer kivas south of the dance area, the winter kiva northwest. While San Juan groups generally adhere to a complete circuit at each appearance, Santa Clarans make the complete circuit only at the first and fourth appearances, and use alternate plazas, two of them, at each of the other appearances. Here the factions differ in custom, as follows -

	Progressive Summer	Conservative Summer
I.	1 2 3 4	1 2 3 4
II.	1 3	1 4
III.	2 4	2 3
IV.	1 2 3 4 5	1 2 3 4 5

	Progressive Winter	Conservative Winter
I.	1 2 3 4	1 2 3 4
II.	2 4	2 3
III.	1 3	1 4
IV.	1 2 3 4 5	1 2 3 4 5
		(obsolete)

Station 5 is the practice kiva, thus a different location for each group.

While the San Juan circuits depend on the dance type, the Santa Clara customs belong to the factions, according to tradition. "That's how it is done." No matter what the dance, the progressive summer moiety, for instance, always uses the pattern of alternation shown on the table.

Yet in the performances at Puye, each faction repeats the dance within the large plaza, in a counterclockwise direction. In 1961 all renderings of sacred dances had four complete renderings, starting in the east or the north. In 1964, only Blue Corn, Rainbow, and *kwitara* circuits were complete. *Yandewa* recurred N, W, S; other dances only N and S.

San Ildefonso. The dancers of both plazas exploit their huge open spaces, with four stations in the precincts of the plaza, around a central cairn, *nansipupinge*. They use the same alternate device for the second and third appearance, they line up in front of the kiva. This is no longer the large, circular kiva in the south plaza, but is a large room in a houseblock, as shown. In 1957 the kivas were on the second floor. In 1964, according to Don Roberts, they shifted to the first floor. The most frequent order is W S E N, but in 1957 the north plaza *antegeshare* started in the east, with the second and third appearances E W, S N; and in 1964 the south plaza *antege* started in the south, with the alternating appearances in S N, E W. In 1957 the women who danced *ashare* on March 10 added two appearances. The six appearances were W E, S N, W E, S N kiva, W E, S N. No one could explain the deviations.

In some dances everyone faces the center. When the dancers are tangent to the line, they start with a counterclockwise orientation. If the first station is at the north wall of the square, everyone starts facing west, etc. In the course of the dance they face about.

It is curious that San Ildefonsans make rare adaptation to the available space. Lines of some 30 dancers appropriately stand in close formation. But small groups also are close together, so that four Buffalo dancers occupy a mere fraction of the plaza. The ideal artistic use of space unfolds in Game Animal Dances, when Deer men can meander at large, while Buffalo impersonators adhere to their close formations.

Tesuque. Tesuque inhabitants focus on a large central plaza, and they stage all of their dances in this center. Basically, they resemble the San Ildefonso performers in the counterclockwise circuit within a given space. They differ from their neighbors in the harmonious cooperation of the moieties, similar to the people of San Juan. In practice they often deviate from the theoretical four-station complete or alternate circuit plan. On March 23, 1957, the men of *antegeshare* outlined a square in the morning, N W S E; but in the afternoon they merely lined up in front of the practice kiva, and then completed the ceremony inside the room, reportedly because of the bitter cold.

On other occasions the Tesuque dancers have tended towards a twofold pattern. For *xoxeye* on June 13, 1964, they lined up N S, then W E for successive appearances. For *kwitara* the group always occupies two stations, the first at the west end of the plaza, on a north-south axis, the second at the east plaza end, on an east-west axis. The two-fold pattern is reminiscent of customs in the Keresan pueblos, notably Cochiti (Kurath in Lange 1960).

Nambe. Nambe dancers focus on their one large plaza, leaving and re-entering a southerly practice kiva. Basically, they observe the circuit E N W S, but, according to Don Roberts, they may repeat the dance at several other stations, up to eight recurrences.

A POSSIBLE BASIC TEWA CIRCUIT

The prevalence of the fourfold station and Santa Clara's use of the four Puye walls suggest a hypothesis. The original Tewa dance circuits probably encircled one huge plaza or, in some cases, two plazas (Kidder 1951, Sinclair 1951). A complete ceremony would have involved a complete suite at four stations in a counterclockwise order, starting in the east, or perhaps variable according to the dance, emerging from and entering the kiva. The alternate pattern is, however, so common as to imply a long-standing custom. Thus, an old Tewa pattern may have been —

I.	1	2	3	4		1	2	3	4		
II.	1		3				2		4		
III.		2		4	or	1		3			
IV.	1	2	3	4		1	2	3	4	5	(kiva)

Variations have several reasons. One is political, that is, splits into factions with their separate customs. Another is the layout of the pueblo buildings, in parallel rows or around a large central plaza. A third may be proximity to the Keresan pueblos and influence from this direction on Tesuque. Variations are most evident, some local, some occasional. The variations are particularly conspicuous in San Juan, where the circuit even goes against the theory of a counterclockwise direction. The layout does not justify the deviation from theory. Could a few miles of proximity to the Great Plains account for the reversal of the circuit pattern?

Figure 4 – San Juan Tembishare Plaza Circuit (September)

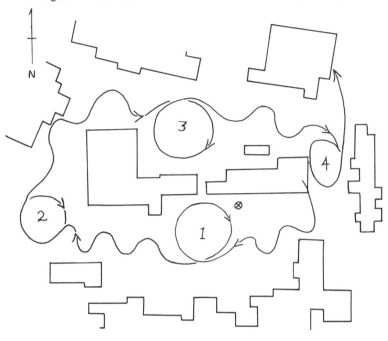

Figure 5 – Penshare at San Juan Plazas, February 10, 1957

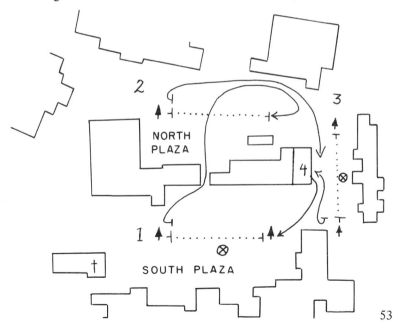

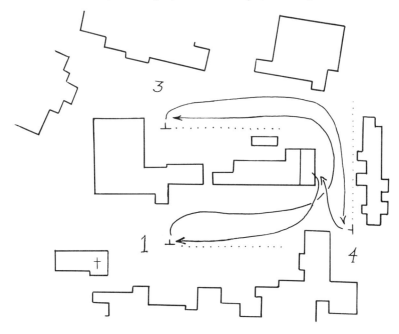

Figure 6 – San Juan Okushare, December 26, 1961
Penshare, February 9, 1964   Xoxeye, June 13, 1964

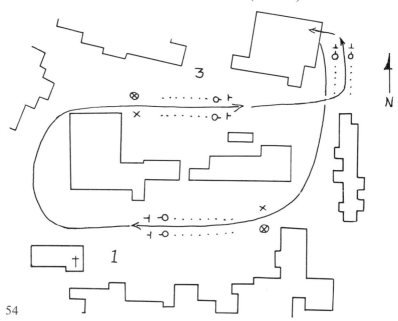

Figure 7 – San Juan Kwitara (June 24)

Figure 8 – San Juan Thi'i, Standard Circuit

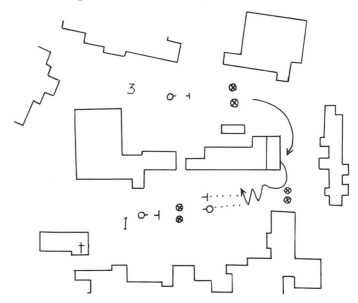

Figure 9 – Santa Clara Plazas, Circuit Pattern for All Dances

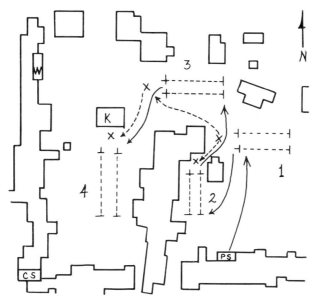

K   Kiva   CS   Conservative Summer Dance Kiva
PS Progressive Summer Dance Kiva   W   Winter Dance Kiva

Figure 10 – Puye Cliffs, Typical Plan (Kwitara, 1961)

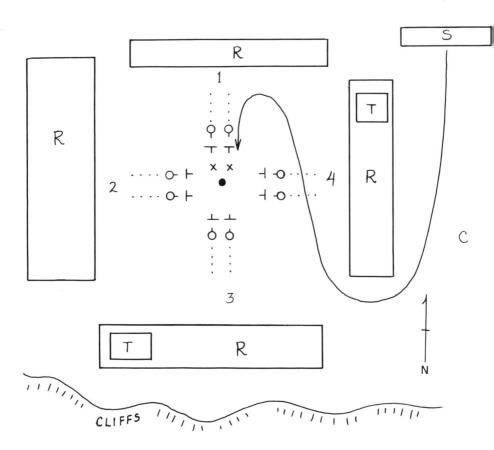

P   Central Pole   S   Shelter for dancers
R   Ruin (terraced in west)   C   Cars
T   Tower
        Concessions to west. Jemez Mts. further west.

Figure 11 — San Ildefonso Plazas, Easter Sunday, 1957

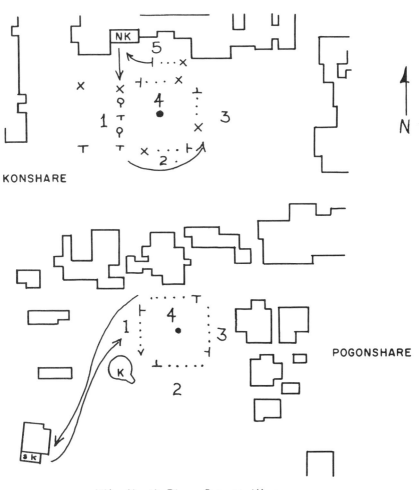

KONSHARE

POGONSHARE

NK   North Plaza Dance Kiva
SK   South Plaza Dance Kiva
 K   'Abandoned' Kiva

Figure 12 – Tesuque Antegeshare, March 23, 1957

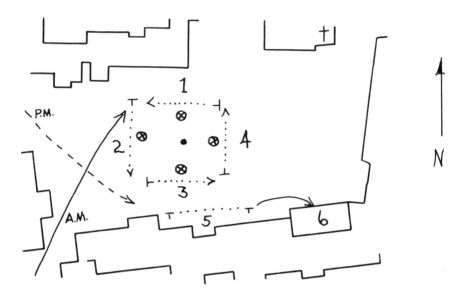

Figure 13 — Tesuque Kwitara, November 12, 1963

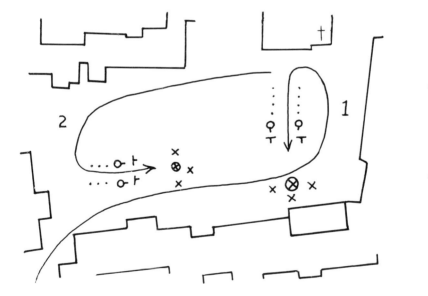

Figure 14 – Nambe Plaza Basic Circuit

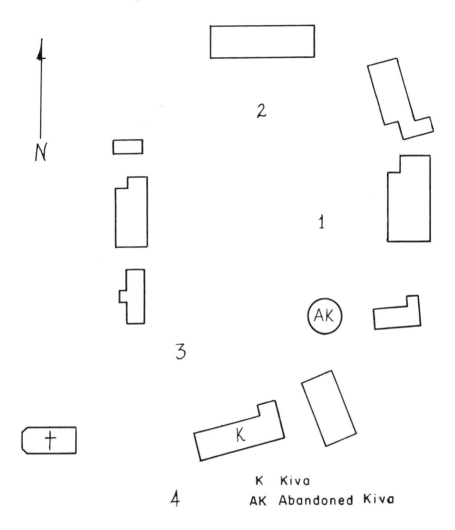

K   Kiva
AK Abandoned Kiva

Nambe Snake Dance, performed at Puye (1961)

Yandewa at Santa Clara, first part, in Kiva Plaza

Chapter 7

HORIZONTAL FORMATIONS

Within each plaza for each particular dance, the groups follow traditions as to static arrangements and mobile paths. The straight line is the basic geometric design, but the arc appears in many evolutions. Men alone, or men and women follow traditions in their orientation and in their placement in the line or lines. The comparative tables show that the simple male line is mandatory for the most sacred dances, and that combinations of the sexes mark the gradations from sacred to secular dances, by increasingly complex patterns. Paired and couple arrangements are secular, as in *tseshare* and *ba'a*.

The placement of the singing chorus shows local variations. In San Juan the chorus follows the dance group into the plaza and to ensuing stations, likewise in San Ildefonso. In Santa Clara and Tesuque they usually lead the cast into the station and take their position while the dancers circulate into a position facing the singers. Generally the singers occupy the same axis as the dancers, but sometimes they move outside the orbit of the circuit, as in the San Ildefonso *yere*. At Puye they like to stand near the central pole. The chorus is not indicated in the tables, Figures 15-17.

LEGEND FOR TYPICAL FORMATIONS AND PATHS

Line Formation (Figure 15)
1. Men in single file —
    a. Facing same direction, forwards — penshare, antegeshare, ashare.
    b. Shoulder-to-shoulder placement — okushare, ta'andishare, ange'i.
2. Men in double file —
    a. Facing ahead, static — Game, Matachina; progressive, Matachina.
    b. Shoulder-to-shoulder — side-stepping Rain Races.
3. Alternate men and women, single file —
    a. Forward progression — yandewa, yere, kwantembi, ba'a.
    b. Sideward, static — xotseyinshare; progressive, yandewa kwantembe.
4. File of men next to file of women —
    a. Ahead, static — tunshare.
    b. Face-to-face, static — tunshare, xoxeye; progress, pangshare 2.
5. Double file, men and women alternate —
    a. Ahead, static — xoxeye 2; progress konshare 1, 2, kwitara 1.

Figure 15 – Line Formations

Groupings and Paths

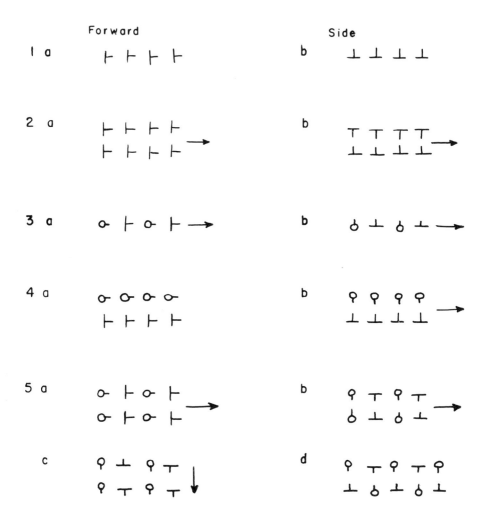

b. Face-to-face, static — xoxeye 2; progress konshare 2, 3.

c. Face same way, side-by-side, progress — konshare 3.

d. Face-to-face, alternate, static — xoxeye 2; progress xoxeye 2.

Paths (Figures 16, 17)

6. Pivots —
   a. Men in forward line-up, simultaneously face about — penshare, ashare, Matachina.
   b. Men shoulder position, simultaneous face-about — ta'andishare.
   c. Shoulder position, face about successively — antege, tembishare.
   d. Double file, men and women, face about successively — tunshare.
   e. Same in shoulder position, pivot simultaneously — xoxeye, konshare.

7. Crossing Paths —
   a. Double file men, facing — Matachina.
   b. Double file, men and women, cross in pairs — xoxeye 2.
   c. Double file, men and women, meet, pivot — panshare 3.
   d. Double file, men and women alternate, pendulum men — kwitara 3.
   e. Men circle partners — xoxeye 2, konshare 3.

8. Circles —
   a. Alternate men and women, closed circle, counterclockwise — kwanshare, yere; open circle — yandewa, ba'a.
   b. Same, facing center, closed — kwanshare, yere; open, yandewa 1.
   c. Same, backwards, closed — kwanshare.
   d. Arbitrary array, clockwise, closed — tembishare; open, 49.
   e. Castoff, two files opposite circling — men, Matachina; mixed, xoxeye, Konshare, kwitara.
   f. Castoff, two files, both C C, mixed — xoxeye, kwitara.

9. Meanders —
   a. Single file men, forward — penshare; men and women — many entrances and processionals, tembishare, xoxeye, etc.
   b. Double file, men and women, sharply sideward — wasa.
   c. Soloist meander through file — Matachina.

The choreographies in Part III will give examples of the formations, and some exceptions, and newly devised formations.

MIRROR ORIENTATION

The term, mirror orientation, signifies an exact reversal of the formation, that is, a repeat after a change to the opposite orientation. The table shows five types, reversal by face-about of individuals in a line, or a complete reversal of the line-up by means of a half circuit. All of the examples

Figure 16 – Pivots and Crossing Paths

Pivots

6. a 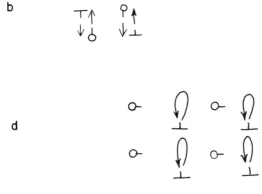   b

c

d   e

7.

Crossing Paths

a

b   c

d

e

Figure 17 — Circles and Meanders

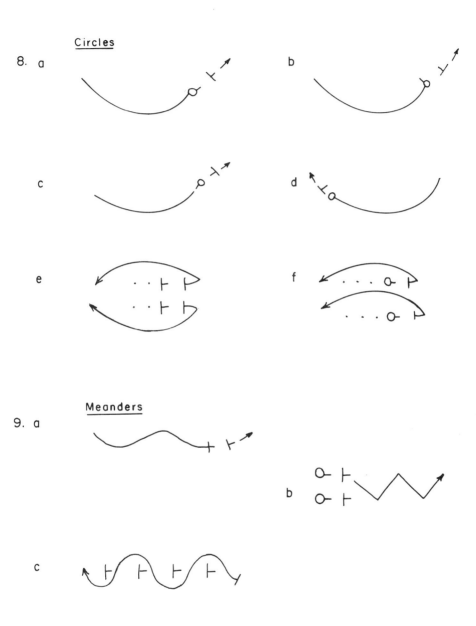

65

Figure 18 — Mirror Orientation

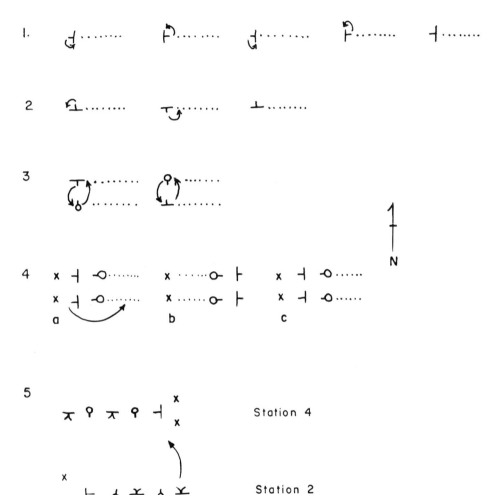

Station 4

Station 2

66

Figure 19 – Parallel and Opposite Pattern (Snake Dance)

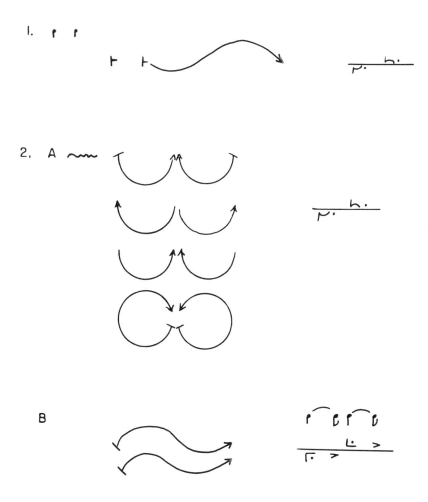

Avanyushare Snake Dance-Nambe

Figure 20 – Solar Circuit within a Plaza (Yandewa)

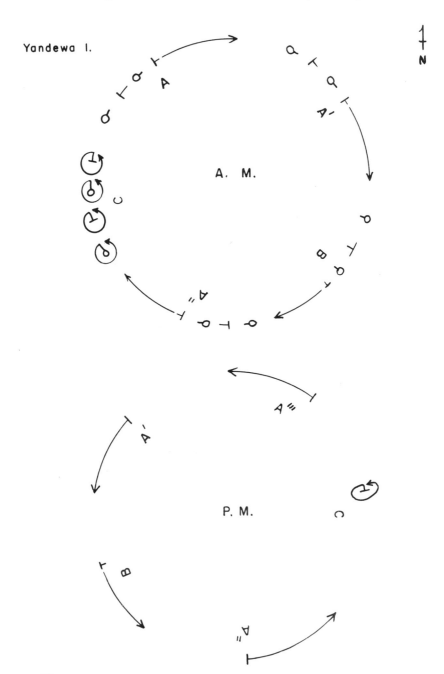

represent changes within one dance song; the last example shows a repeat of a dance in opposite orientation, but within the same plaza. (Figure 18)

1. Face-about by pivot of each man in a line, five times, so as to end in the original position - penshare, ashare.
2. Face-about by individual pivot, three times, ending in original position corresponding to melodic AB CB AB - tun ange'i.
3. Reversal of position by crossover, twice, so as to return to place - xoxeye.
4. Reversal of dancers, but not chorus, by half-circuit -
   a. Pos. a, b - kwitara.
   b. Pos. a,b,c (original) - konshare Santa Clara.
5. Reversals of dancers and chorus, for complete dance repeat -
   San Ildefonso konshare.

The orientation with regard to the cardinal points would vary with the station, say, in San Juan plazas 1 and 4.

PARALLEL AND OPPOSITE PATTERNS

Two simple means for the combination of the basic patterns in group movements are the principles of parallel and opposite designs. In parallel designs the pair of dancers or the large group moves in the same direction in the same manner. In the basic opposite designs one half of the group moves one way, while the other half progresses in the opposite direction. Both devices are common in Tewa choreography, especially the unison, parallel designs. Groups move in parallel directions in the circuits of *xoxeye* and *konshare*. They circle in opposition during *pangshare 1.*

The paired dances such as both *tseshare* use first one design, then the other. In such pairing the relationship is particularly clear. The Nambe Snake Dance, which has the same structure as *tseshare,* Dog Dance, is a good example. During the entrance the two men meander in unison. During the "fast dance" they describe opposite arcs and circles during A - apart, together, apart, together. During B they again meander in unison.

SOLAR CIRCUIT WITHIN A PLAZA

From the solar point of view it might seem fitting to begin circuits at the place of the rising sun, even if they go against the sun, and especially if they go with the sun as in San Juan. Actually, dancers usually do enter from the east, and in Santa Clara the day's events start in the east plaza. But such a custom is by no means pan-Tewa.

Santa Clara's winter moiety enacts a clearly solar dance at the time of the ceremonies for the irrigation ditch cleaning. *Yandewa* is rendered in English as Sun Basket, Rain Dance, or in Spanish, as Acequia Dance. The

69

Figure 21 – Solar Circuit within a Plaza (Yandewa)

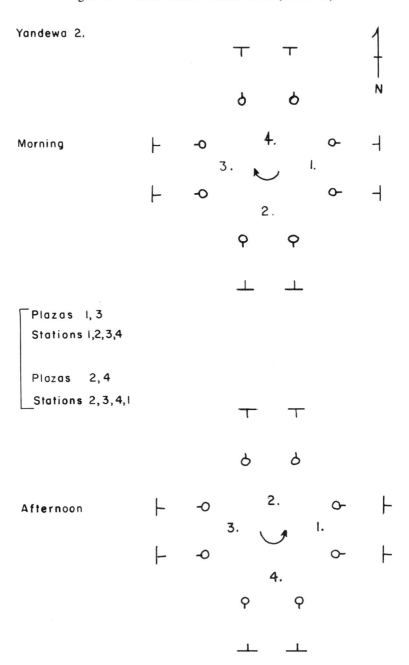

Yandewa 2.

Morning

N

Plazas 1, 3
Stations 1,2,3,4

Plazas 2, 4
Stations 2,3,4,1

Afternoon

solar symbolism takes form within each plaza. Two men and two women - thus four dancers - circulate in traditional patterns. In the morning they complete two circuits, always featuring the clockwise direction, the women wearing pink capes. In the afternoon they reverse the direction, while the women change to blue capes. The two major parts of the dance are orientated as follows -

1. The two couples, in alternate array, trot in a circle, forward, then sideward, then forward, while the women sway "sun baskets" with rays of orange angora wool.

2. In a slow tempo the men face the women in a square; bending forward, they impel their rattles, while the women sway their baskets. Then, in a fast tempo, the men hop on the left foot towards the women, then away, while lowering and raising lances in a graceful arc. They repeat the entire routine at the four points of the compass, as shown on the drawing.

This dance is one of the clearest choreographic invocations to the sun and to the cardinal directions.

Santa Clara Yandewa at Plaza 3, part 1 (1957)

Santa Clara Yandewa (part 2A)

Santa Clara Yandewa (part 2B)

72

Chapter 8

BODY MOVEMENT IN VERTICAL
AND HORIZONTAL DIMENSIONS

The ground plans, abstracted in the previous chapter, evolve because of the motions of people. The dancers move their bodies in particular postures, variations of energy, with gestures of the arms, and steps by the feet and legs. The steps are the effective agents for locomotion in a horizontal ground plan, but they will here follow the listing of gestures, because they mark the rhythms which constitute the following chapter.

The torso is essentially an erect, vertical object. It can move in all directions, but among the Tewa, the torso generally executes vertical patterns, by flexions. The arms also move primarily in vertical levels, but also from side to side, rarely in depth, forward and back (*ashare* is an exception). Sometimes they move obliquely. The feet move in vertical patterns, especially in stationary mark-times; but they can propel the entire body on a horizontal level, in any direction. Usually, in fact, the footwork uses all dimensions in space, as well as the element of time. In general the footwork synchronizes with the body flexions and gestures.

POSTURES

Flexion glyphs accompany the following stick figures, and will reappear in Part III. Generally the torso is erect, normal; sometimes it is slightly flexed forward, men more than women, in *xoxeye,* for instance. Only men use extreme flexions, as in *tseshare* and *yandewa,* and only clowns use extreme extensions and flexions. The glyphs could be applied to other body parts separately. Here they signify the whole body, as do the dynamic glyphs. (Figure 22).

GESTURES

Two devices illustrate typical and important gestures. One is the stick figure, with dotted lines for motion paths. The other is an abstraction of paths described in the air by the hands, in three levels, that is, the kineme. (Figures 23-25).

The sketches of stick figures illustrate *kwirana* gestures, specifically as witnessed in Tesuque, and *tembishare* gestures in San Juan.

Kwirana Gestures

The *kosa* and *kwirana* compel rain and gestation by traditional gestures, in kiva and plaza ceremonies. The stick figures show -
1. A gesture conjuring rainfall (*ohotayo*). It reaches into the highest level, above the head; it is lightweight and relaxed. The dancer reaches upward with open palms, then lowers the arms and hands to normal level. Frequently he gestures only with the right hand, in a vertical path. The path is the first one in the table of abstractions.
2. A gesture symbolizing cloud. It centers on the middle level of the shoulder, but swings from side to side below shoulder level. Meanwhile the body tilts from side to side in harmony with the gesture. Similar arc-shaped horizontal gestures appear in the middle section of the abstractions, all for precipitation.
3. A gesture of digging into the earth, descending from middle level to the lowest arm extension, first to one side, then the other, with natural flexions and extensions of arms and torso, and with considerable force on the downward movements. The obliquely vertical movement resembles the kwanshare gesture and its abstractions.

Gestures in Tembishare

During the San Juan Harvest celebration, the performers use two gestures -
1. The groups in the circle-dance sway their arms from left to right, in time with their clockwise side-stepping. They extend the arms in middle level, palms forward, and sway the hands from side to side. Their gesture is included in the abstraction.
2. So is the gesture of principals, who line up within the circle at their cue. Each person raises the right hand at full length, to high level, somewhat obliquely right, palm forward, with a small motion of lateral swaying.

Abstractions of Gesture Levels - Kinemes (Figure 25)

1. *Direct Paths* -
    a. *Ohotayo,* rain luring, reaching up to right with right hand.
    b. *Kwanshare,* group motion in rain dance part of *xoxeye,* from middle to low level, obliquely, one side, then the other. With closed fists, arms descend from right side of chest to left side; then from left side of chest to right low level, with emphasis on the descents.
    c. *Xoxeye* women's gesture, with alternate, oblique up-and-down movement of arms in middle level, that is, lower right arm while raising

the left to the chest; then reverse. It is a recurrent gesture, for instance, in the gesticulations of the singing chorus.

d. Men's rattle-impelling gesture in line dances, a forceful lowering of the gourd-holding hand to lower level, then recovery. (Closed hand in all gestures).

2. *Swaying in the Horizontal Dimension* -

a. *Yandewa* women's gesture with the basket in the right hand, an upward away from side to side on high level during the first dance; a downward swing on low level during the second dance.

b. *Kwantembeshare* with both hands, on middle level, by men and women.

c. *Tembishare* - abstractions of the stick figures. (Open hand).

d. *Tunshare* women's basket swing in middle level, upwards, men's downward swing in low level during *ange'i.*

3. *Swaying in the Vertical Dimension* -

a. *Tseshare* Eagle Dance, men's raising and lowering of both wings in middle level.

b. *Tseshare,* alternate raising into high level, with one wing and lowering through middle level with other wing.

c. *Ashare,* raising of bow with left hand by each man through all levels, followed by lowering.

d. *Yandewa,* men's raising and lowering of the lance through all levels, up in an arc, down in reverse arc.

The sways are controlled movements, not relaxed swings. Rarely do the dancers gesture with empty hands, only the clowns, the *kwanshare,* and *tembishare.* Even then they do not express ideas through finger codes, as do the Hindus in their *mudras.* As a rule the dancers and also the singers manipulate sacred objects.

Manipulation of Ritual Objects

While the ritual objects prevent expressive finger motions, they heighten the power for rain and fertility, because rattles, spruce boughs, rainbows, lances are invested with such power. Some props belong to men only, some to women, and some to both sexes.

The gourd rattle is the steady prop of a male dancer, sometimes in self-accompaniment with his own singing, sometimes as reinforcement of the beat by drum or morache. The downward impulse reinforces the drum's strong beat, and the retrieval synchronizes with the weak beat. At the same time the accent-and-release is welded to the vocal pulsations and to the stamp and the downward impulse of the body. In *yandewa* Part 2, the movement is especially empathic, while the men bend forward on their lances more deeply than usual. Rattle tremolo also corresponds to drum tremolo. In *xoxeye* the men shiver their rattles with a graceful movement, as they change direction at phrase ends; they swing the right arm out horizontally.

In some dances they manipulate a second prop, while pumping the rattle and singing. In *ashare* they swing the bow in the left hand through various dimensions on certain musical accents. In *konshare* each man carries a miniature bow-and-arrow set in the left hand; he propels it forward or describes a figure-8 on accented phrase beginnings. In some dances, as *tunshare ange'i,* they sway spruce boughs in the left hand. In *kwitara* and *tseshare* Dog Dance they hoist a small banner at changes of direction. In Nambe Snake Dance they simultaneously propel and twirl a rattle and a feather cluster.

In four dances the men manipulate props independent of rattle rhythm. In *yandewa* they swoop the lances with both hands. In *thi'i* the man holds up a tomahawk with one hand, while he rests the other hand on his hip; he changes the tomahawk to the other hand at phrase end. After the entrance in *ba'a,* the boys dance back and forth, swaying the belts side to side in front of their waists. The bearer of the huge standard in the Saint's Day *xoxeye* uses both hands and all of his strength to carry and sway his object.

The singers (not drummers) in the separate chorus sometimes keep hands free for luring rain. Sometimes they carry spruce boughs, and they sway or jiggle them with a pumping motion, in rhythm with the drum. They do not impel rattles.

Women always hold spruce boughs in every type of Corn Dance, and they jiggle them with the alternating gesture which is the same as that of the chorus, and which has already been described. In two dances they hide an ear of corn in a bough and manipulate it along with the spruce, namely in *xotseyinshare* and *pogonshare.* Thereby they add the symbol of food and fertility to the symbol of everlasting life. In the San Juan *xoxeye* they manipulate cottonwood boughs, which signify moisture.

In two dances the women sway baskets horizontally in various levels. In *yandewa* the baskets symbolize the sun, with their orange rays of angora wool. In *tunshare* they sway their disc-like baskets, then they invest them with the double function of resonator for the morache which they set on the inverted baskets, as symbolic recipient for ground corn.

In two dances the men and women manipulate the same objects. In *yere* of San Ildefonso they hold feathers in the left hand and sprigs in the right, as they execute the typical *kwanshare* motion into the earth and up to the chest. In *kwantembeshare,* each dancer holds a rainbow symbol with both hands and sways it in keeping with the music, everyone in unison.

76

Either men or women can end a dance with a special ritual gesture, while holding whatever prop is customary in the dance. They may conclude *xoxeye* by holding the hands in front of the face, close together and separating them quickly. The gesture signifies the dispersal of goodness and health, and it resembles a gesture of the *kosa* in kiva ceremonies. At the end of the Nambe *thi'i* the woman makes the consecrating gesture at the finish - an indication of the respect for this half-secular dance. When the dancers disperse the power, the knowing spectators catch it in the air and collect it to their bodies.

Ritual Status of Gestures

Gestures have a covert rather than an overt significance. They are not as conspicuous as other elements — formations and steps — but they constitute integral aspects of the movements. Generally they are stylized and and are either decorative or symbolic because of the power of the manipulated objects. In many cases the original symbolism has been forgotten. Two types of performers still use gestures with known symbolism, the clowns and members of the singing chorus. Their gestures impel rain and hence help crops. In some less esoteric dances, as *kwantembeshare,* abstract gestures are compulsive. In semi-secular dances, like *kwitara* and *Matachines,* they are decorative.

Figure 22 – Extension and Flexion

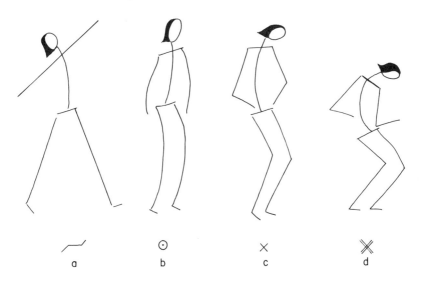

a   b   c   d

Figure 23 – Kwirana Gestures

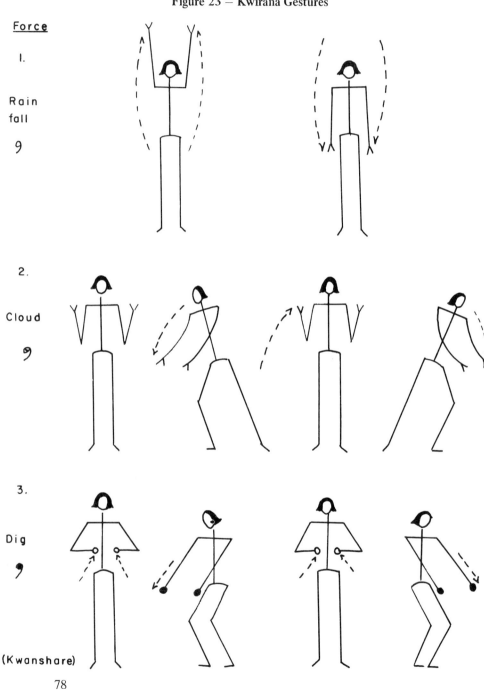

Force

1.

Rain
fall

9

2.

Cloud

9

3.

Dig

9

(Kwanshare)

Figure 24 – Tembishare Gestures

Circle   Group   Principals

Upright posture of San Juan Deer Dancers, "Apache" clown in foreground

Figure 25 — Kinemes of Gesture Levels

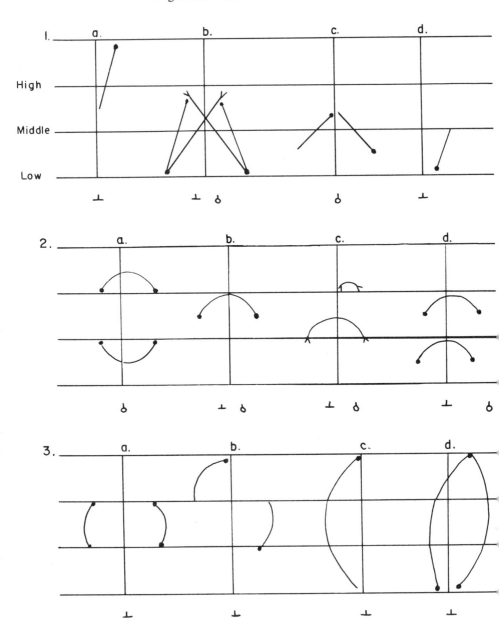

The footwork and inevitable action of the knees are essential to loco-motion and hence to dances with complex, mobile formations. The Tewa call a step *ankhe* and they may speak of *ankhe* for *xoxeye.* They have spe-cific terms for some steps, but not for all. Their basic step is the "footlift-ing" *antege,* which they can perform in place, in various directions, and in various minetic versions. They also trot, walk, hop, and jump. For the stride of the Deer they use the term *dipenyi;* for the tramping of the Buff-alo they say *dikonyi.* They have terms for special foot-brush, *sunu* or *shu-shu,* and for hops forwards, on one foot, *yandewa* step.

Figure 26 – Steps: Antege, Walk

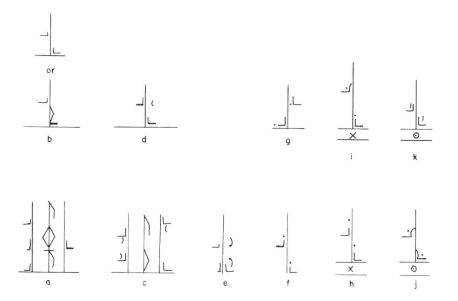

The three tables of typical steps use the glyphs presented in Chapter I. The classification here depends on weight transfer. The first group depends on ground contact with alternate feet; the second group on contact with alternate feet and repeated knee bounce; the third group includes steps with simultaneous ground contact, at times alternating with contact by one foot. Each group proceeds from steps that remain close to the ground, to steps with elevation, except the third group. In the case of several impor-tant steps the graph shows the step in detailed notation, then in simplified notation, which will recur in the choreographies of Part III.

As already indicated, the steps emphasize rhythm even more than space. In temporal patterns, they always synchronize with the arm movements and usually they underscore the gestures and instrumental self-accompaniments.

LEGEND FOR GLYPHS

1. *Antege and Walk* (Figure 26)
   a. *Antege,* footlifting, with emphasis on right foot: upbeat of raising right knee, while supporting weight on left foot; accented lowering of right foot, while raising left heel and slightly flexing knees; unaccented raising of right knee while lowering left heel.
   b. *Antege,* in two versions of simplified writing.
   c. Mimetic *antege* variant for fast Buffalo dance, with a pawing motion: with weight on right foot, brush left foot forward on secondary beat; brush back on strong beat, and immediately brush back right foot with raised knee, weight on left foot.
   d. Abbreviation of the same.
   e. *Antege* with *shushu* by women in *tunshare:* execute strong beat on right foot with forward shuffle, weak beat with back shuffle.
   f. Simple, forward walk with moderate sized steps, in many entrances and changes of formations.
   g. Side stepping to left, as in *tembishare.* Can also be to right.
   h. *Dipenyi,* Deer walk, distinguished from ordinary walk by longer stride with straight knees, and simultaneous forward torso bend, arms leaning on foresticks; even duple beat.
   i. *Dipenyi* in uneven, iambic rhythm, resembling a low gallop: step onto right foot on beat 1, land with low leap onto left foot on beat 3.
   j. *Dikonyi,* Buffalo gait: step from foot to foot heavily, and yet with a slight lift from the ground at each step, in erect posture (but often with a bowed head). This is male step in *xoxeye* 1.
   k. Women's step in *xoxeye* 1 and *konshare* progressions, like men but with continuous ground contact.
2. *Bounce and Hop* (Figure 27)
   a. Double bounce in *xoxeye* 2: with erect posture: step onto right foot with flexed knee, bounce again on right knee; same on left foot. Steps are short.
   b. Same step for Deer mimes, except that step is in place and posture is flexed, while leaning on foresticks.
   c. Pat-step: Pat right half-toe, step on right; same on left; in San Ildefonso *ba'a,* for instance; variant in *tseshare* Eagle.

82

Figure 27 – Steps: Bounce, Hop

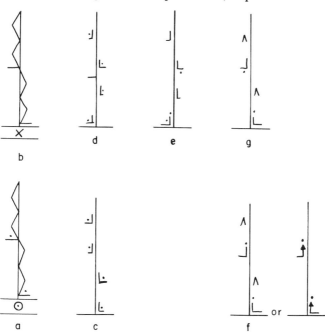

Figure 28 – Steps: Jump, Suñu

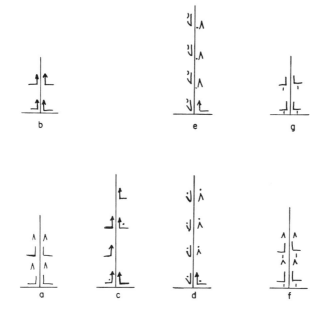

83

d. Same step, but with step on accent, pat on offbeat.

e. *Kwanshare* and *yere* step of San Ildefonso: step forward left foot, bring up right; very short step back right, bring left half-toe to right foot.

f. Same with hopping, right forward, left back, in men's version of Santa Clara *kwanshare.*

g. Forward hop from foot to foot for instance, in *ba'a.*

3. *Jump and Jump-hop* (Figure 28)

a. Take off from both feet and land on both with evenly distributed weight - not common, *kosa* and Nambe *kwitara.*

b. Abbreviation of same.

c. Jump-hop: jump off both feet, left foot ahead, hop on left; reverse - *kwitara* men's fast step.

d. *Yandewa* step: hop repeatedly on left, touching left toe.

e. Variant in *tseshare* Eagle dance: hop on right foot to left, brushing left toe forward on each hop.

f. *Sunu* of *thi'i*: pull back with both feet, slightly leaving ground at each pull.

g. Abbreviation of same, especially for women, who do not jump.

CHOREOGRAPHIC PATTERNS AND FUNCTIONS

Circuit customs owe their variability to local and moiety factors. But other patterns generally relate to the functions, to the gradation from sacred to profane.

The ground plans of the most sacred dances are simple static lines, for male participants. Double, mobile files, with women partners, gradually become more complex, in horticultural and then in Game Animal Dances. Double or quadruple files, or huge circles unite great numbers from the entire community, for the sake of crops. While certain paths, as serpentines, reappear in dances of many categories (especially in San Juan), interweavings and counterpoint of several groups characterize *xoxeye* and *konshare.* Some secular dances and all show dances exhibit special and often elaborate designs.

Conversely, the most elaborate gestures are the prerogative of the most esoteric dancers, the *kosa* and *kwirena.* Their gesture code for rain is also at the disposal of singers in the separate chorus. The gestures of line dancers are limited but functional. They serve the manipulation of self-accompanying gourd rattles or symbolic props. The female arm jiggling gesture is especially pervading. Mimetic and special gestures are distributed through the miscellaneous, less sacred repertoire.

The *antege* step threads through much of the ceremonial dancing of all categories, sometimes in mimetic variants, but it is the most basic step in the sacred line dances. The double bounce also has a ritual connotation for crops or for hunt. Walks and trots reappear as entrance steps. Hops, jumps, and other specialties are strewn through the repertoire, but they are most conspicuous in show dances.

Above and Below: Game Animal Dance at San Ildefonso

Chapter 9

DANCE AND MUSIC INTEGRATION

In all Tewa rituals, the dancing and the music interlock. The fusion is most complete in the self-accompanied dances, when the dancers shake their own rattles while they sing their own melodic accompaniment. But the connection is also very close in the events with a special chorus of singers and drummers. In both dance types the instruments form the link between the songs and the dance movements, in terms of tempo and rhythm. The dances unfold visual designs on this basis, and the melodies weave special tonal designs around the instrumental beats.

PERCUSSION AND MOVEMENT

The large, flat gourd is the sole instrument in the self-accompanied male line dances. The men vertically shake their rattles with a forceful gesture which emphasizes the vocal accents and the *antege* step. In several line dances a single drum or a scraping stick reinforces the fundamental beat, namely in *penshare, xotseyinshare, pogonshare,* and *antegeshare.* The Buffalo Dancer's small gourd rattle is an incidental noise maker in Game Animal Dances, and tinklers on the kilts automatically underscore the step rhythms. Dog Dance and War Dances also have small gourds and ornamental bells. Drums, with special singers, accompany these dances and also the great communal harvest dances. They have less ritualistic connotations than gourds with or without turtle rattles.

Several types of ideophones require no conscious manipulation, namely the turtle shell and bell knee rattles, and the various jinglers.

INSTRUMENTAL AND KINETIC TIMING

The instruments mark the basic tempo, and the dancers synchronize their movements with the speed and with the accents of the beats. To a slow drum beat the dancers tread slowly; during a fast beat they move quickly. During a tremolo they break up the tempo and amble leisurely. They synchronize their rattles with the drums, except in the second phrase of *xotseyinshare wasa.*

The tempo of most songs ranges from 92 mm. to 116 mm. to the quarternote as written, though there are a few very slow songs, as *tembishare,* and some very lively ones, as parts of Eagle Dance. A common pattern is a

Chorus of singers and drummers at Santa Clara Matachina Dance (1956)

San Juan Yellow Corn Dance (1957)

set of slow and fast dance, as in *tunshare, xoxeye, konshare,* and *kwitara.* The choice of writing in quarter notes or eighth notes is at the discretion of the transcriber. In writing *tunshare,* the choice was as follows. In the paired slow and fast songs the basic rattle beats are written in eighth notes, and the tempi are distinguished by metronomic 76 and 108 readings; but the *ange'i* is in quarter notes, at 104 mm. The quarter note beat shows that the *ange'i* movements are half as fast as in the fast dance.

Usually the songs maintain a strict tempo. But there are some traditional departures from a relentless tempo. In several dances for springtime fertility - *antegeshare, xotseyinshare, pogonshare* - the songs start slowly and accelerate to the predominant tempo. The fast dance songs of *tunshare* shift from slow to fast tempo, back and forth, before they establish the regular beat. They state hapimbe fast, then slow.

The percussion beat guides the melodic tempo. Sometimes the drum and song agree, note for note, as in monotone pulsations, and in passages of *tembishare* 8 and *tunshare* 1. Usually, however, the melodic configuration is more rapid and complex, or more sustained than the percussion beat. It may syncopate the drum. In a few dances with special chorus the drum beat lags behind the melodic accents, though the timing is the same, for example, in *xoxeye* slow dance and in *thi'i.* The dance steps fit the drum and hence pulse against the melody. This never happens in self-accompanied dances, with their identification of rattle and dance movement and the absence of a drum.

In the customs of tempo and its manipulation the Tewa Pueblos agree. But they may vary in the speed, nevertheless, because some Pueblos prefer a solemn style and others tend to liveliness. Santa Clara tempi are often faster than those of the other Pueblos. The Santa Clara *konshare* is 124 mm., *thi'i* is 108 mm., as against San Juan 116 mm. and 96 mm. Santa Clara's fast Eagle Dance is 132 mm., San Ildefonso's is 108 mm. Tesuque has a reputation for more sedate tempi, even in the fast *kwitara,* in keeping with a dignified dance performance.

CHANGES IN KINETIC RHYTHMS

The basic temporal unit is a duple rhythm, in a majority of the dance songs. That is, the kinetic, percussion, and melodic patterns lean on the pulsation - accent, release, accent, release. The *antege* and other steps usually time the two impulses equally. A few dances use triple time, as the Eagle Dance of Santa Clara and the *pangshare* waltz. But even here the step has two movements, with a pause on the third beat. In rare cases there is a two-to-three ratio between the components. In parts of *thi'i* and in some social rounds the melody and step superimpose a duple beat on the triple drum beat.

T'a

T'a, literally, "a pause," is one characteristic Tewa device for shifting from duple to triple rhythm. The term also covers another kind of rhythmic change, a pause by means of a temporary retard. The rhythmic changes have puzzled spectators, but they are in fact quite simple. The two basic kinds of *t'a* are -

1). After a series of duple beats, a change to a triple beat (not a triplet). Each of the three beats has the same value as the basic eighth note. The most characteristic form has a pause on beat 3. The dancers vary their *antege* step by holding the right foot in suspense for the third count, while the percussion and the melody pause. In another form the music marks the third beat, while the dancers pause.

2). A slower tempo for an even number of beats, from two to ten. The music - percussion and melody - marks evenly accented beats in a slower tempo from the bulk of the song, while the dancers tread right and left, with equal emphasis on each foot. They need an even number of slow beats, so they start the typical *antege* with the right foot, when the music returns to normal. The temporary changes could be indicated by a new metronomic signature, but they find a simpler and clearer visual expression in dotted eighth notes. This is feasible, because the new time value is very close to one-and-one-half times the regular basic beat of an eighth note.

Another characteristic shift is not *t'a,* but a simple change from duple to triple time, for an undesignated number of measures. This is especially common in *xoxeye* and other dances using the double bounce step. The kinetic correlary is very simple and obvious. Instead of bouncing twice in their knees, the dancers bounce three times, with a forward step on the accented first beat.

T'a changes are unpredictable in that they need not occur at any specific time, at a given part of a song. In each song the change is different in length and placement. Yet the placement appears to be natural, and, for this particular song, inevitable, somewhat like the complexities in a fugue by Bach. The dancers and the singers usually follow the changes unerringly, even if the dancers have not memorized the songs. Usually, let us say, because sometimes they miss.

The changes are most common in the sacred line dances that are self-accompanied. They also ornament more complex dances like *xoxeye,* especially in the static B sections. They are rare in *konshare* and non-existent in show dances.

After phrases of steady duple pulsation, the momentary changes correspond to the effect of dissonance in harmonized music.

CONFIGURATIONS IN TIME AND SPACE

Within the apparent restrictions, the Pueblo dances display an almost unlimited variety of patterns in time and space. That is, they follow the rules, yet differently in each case, be it a dance to traditional or newly composed songs. The only efficient manner of illustration is by excerpts, by careful selections of typical applications. The five pages of excerpts demonstrate the most typical manipulations of the duple rhythm in terms of *t'a* changes and in changes of orientation by pivots. Three of the pages exploit the *antege* step; one exemplifies variants of the double bounce; one shows combinations. On each page, and also throughout the series, the examples proceed from small and simple units to longer and more complex patterns. The examples show how closely musical and temporal patterns and changes intertwine with kinetic patterns and changes.

The examples show only the steps. In performance, any gestures would synchronize with the steps. If the dancer changes direction, the gesture is of course directed to another cardinal point, without altering the relationship to the torso. The rhythmic changes are timed exactly with the footwork.

A final page in this series includes the spatial gesture design. That is the score for *kwantembeshare* or Rainbow Dance. The illustration shows the basic foot-gesture-percussion-melody identities in the duple beat and *t'a*. Also, it shows the varying combinations in a two-part structure.

1. *Antege and Triple Time T'a.* (Figure 29)
   a. Basic *antege* with duple time music - common, especially introductions and conclusions, in place.
   b. *Antege,* repeated with forward progression - *pangshare.*
   c. Basic, stationary *antege* with pivot - *antegeshare.*
   d. *Antege* with *t'a* and return to duple - San Juan *penshare.*
   e. *Antege* with gradual change of orientation and return - Santa Clara *konshare.* (See Figure 108)
   f. Buffalo *antege* with *t'a* and change of orientation - same.
2. *Antege and Slow T'a.* (Figure 30)
   a. Basic, duple step, followed by two slow steps and return - *xotseyinshare.*
   b. Combination of triple time and slow *t'a,* return to basic duple timing - Tesuque *antegeshare.*
   c. *Kwanshare* step in duple time, followed by *antege* in slow *t'a,* pivot during *t'a* - San Ildefonso *kwanshare.*
3. Combinations of basic *antege* with both kinds of *t'a,* half-pivots, and retard; varying phrase lengths, dwindling at end - Santa Clara *xutsaweingshare* (Blue Corn Dance). North-south orientation at first station varied according to station orientation. (Figure 31)

4. *Double Bounce in Metrical Change and Step Combinations.* (Figure 32)
   a. Stationary bounce in duple time - Deer in Santa Clara *konshare.*
   b. Forward progression in duple time - Santa Clara *xoxeye.*
   c. Forward progress in triple time, followed by slow *t'a,* with same melodic cadence as 4 b – Santa Clara *xoxeye.*
   d. Trot and duple time bounce, forward - San Ildefonso Eagle Dance. (See Figure 118)
5. *Combinations of Steps and Rhythms.* (Figure 33)
   a. *Dikonyi* forward in duple time; double bounce in triple time *t'a; dikonyi* in duple time - Santa Clara Winter *konshare.* (Figure 101)
   b. Bounce and straight, in triple time with pause - Santa Clara *tseshare* Eagle Dance. (Figure 113)
   c. Forward trot, in duple time, then two measures of triple time *t'a* – Santa Clara *kwitara.*
   d. Pat-step forward, in duple time; one measure in triple time, with pause on beat 1 (not 3 as in regular *t'a*); continuation by double bounce in duple time - San Ildefonso *ba'a.* (Figure 129)

Configurations in Relation to Ritual Status

The most sacred line dances adhere to the *antege* step, but they make much use of *t'a,* especially in the middle of a song. The pivots usually take place during regular, duple time passages. The social *pangshare* makes traditional use of the *antege* and rhythms. Corn and Animal Dances complicate their special steps with rhythmic changes and changes of orientation. *Konshare* shifts are particularly ingenious in terms of direction and steps, less in terms of *t'a.* Combinations of steps are common in *kwitara, tseshare, ba'a,* and various show dances, but *t'a* is rare. Examples of *t'a* could be multiplied for the line dances; step combinations could be multiplied for more secular dances. Corn Dances change rhythms and orientation more than steps, which remain consistent throughout a dance.

Combination of Elements in a Larger Structure: kwantembeshare

Figure 34 shows the combination of regular rhythm and *t'a* in movement, with these same features in the music. The two parts are melodically similar but they are unlike in rhythmic patterns.

Figure 29 – T'a: Antege Step Duple and Triple Time

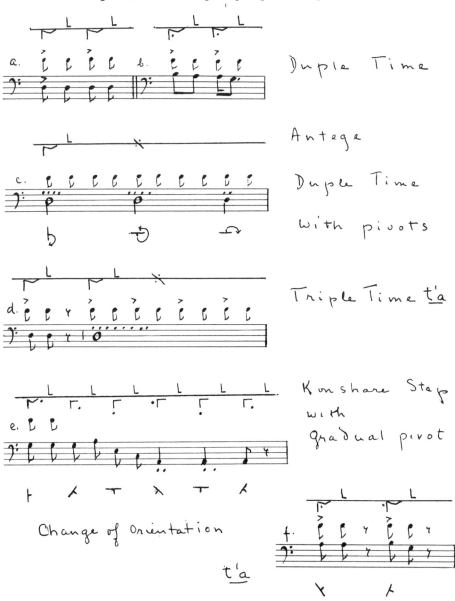

Duple Time

Antege

Duple Time

with pivots

Triple Time t'a

Konshare Step
with
gradual pivot

Change of Orientation

t'a

Figure 30 – Slow T'a

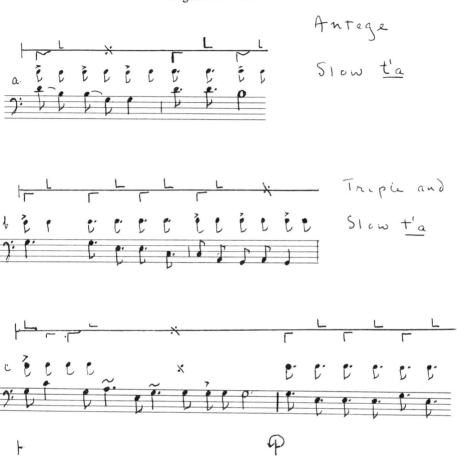

Antege
Slow t'a

Triple and
Slow t'a

Kwan share   and   Slow ta

Figure 31 – T'a: Complex Pattern

Figure 32 – Timing of Double Bounce

Figure 33 – Steps in Rhythmic Combinations

Dikonyi and Bounce

Bend - Step
Triple Time

Trot - t'a

Toe - heel
and
Double Bounce

Figure 34 – Combinations in Large Structure: Rainbow Dance

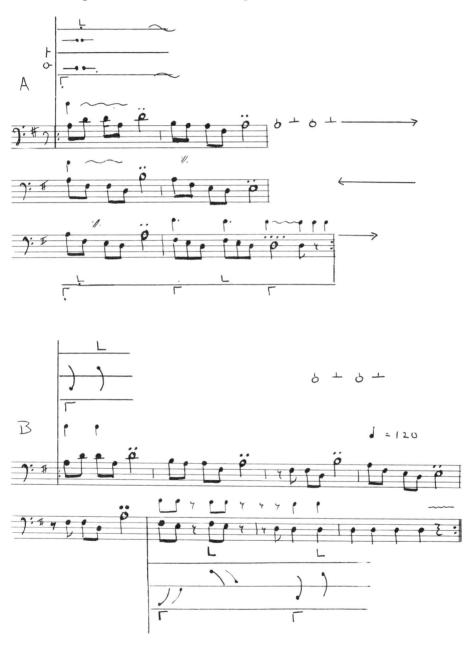

Figure 35 – Rhythmic Units

98

Chapter 10

TONAL PATTERNS

MELODIC RHYTHMS

The previous examples show that the melody synchronizes with the kinetic rhythms in terms of accent and *t'a,* but that it usually has independent patterns. The Tewa melodies are diversified in the rhythmic units and in the combinations of units. The most common rhythmic units, on Figure 35, are combinations of even quarter notes and eighth notes. Half notes and whole notes are rare, except as prolonged pulsations.

Slower, even units have a stately quality. Triplets are more animated, as in *thi'i.* "Dotted" figures (4 and 5) are still livelier. They are scattered throughout the repertory, but they are rare in *penshare* and *tembishare.* The "scotch snap", 5, is the reversal of dotted unit 4; it appears in *ashare, pangshare* 3, and other songs. Grace notes, which resemble scotch snaps except for the placement of the accent, are rare.

Syncopations (7 and 8) are slow in *tembishare* and fast in *thi'i* and *penshare* 13. They are not as common as rapid figures, combinations of eighth and sixteenth notes (9-11), which prevail in *okushare* and *tunshare.*

Pulsations are very characteristic of Tewa music. They appear at many positions within melodies, and they are almost inevitable in the openings, connectives, and codas. They set the tempo and rhythm, alongside the percussion. Pulsations are most propulsive in the line dance songs and also most frequent. They are less persistent in *konshare,* and are absent in social dances.

Rhythmic figures serve as a sort of artistic compensation, for they embroider melodies in dances with simple choreography.

PHRASES AND SECTIONS

The devices for combining rhythmic units into phrases are almost limitless, and in the line dances they are ingenious. Any of the units can appear in combination with any others in any amount. The resulting phrase lengths are very irregular in the line dances, as is obvious in the scores of Part III; but the phrases are of more even length in the secular dances. The phrases are always clearly defined. They end on a longer note, often a pulsation, though the percussion accompaniment may continue without pause. The phrases have a clear effect on the dance movement.

They mark changes of direction or pivots. Sometimes a new phrase has a different step, but only in more secular dances like *ba'a*.

The phrases contain a variable number of measures. In the scores the measures are set off by half bar lines, the phrases by complete bar lines. As much as possible, a phrase occupies a line, for easy recognition.

Phrases combine into sections by several devices. Simple repetition is rare, and is limited to *pangshare*. Sequences - recurrences at a lower, occasionally a higher level - characterize *konshare, kwitara,* and related songs. They are less frequent and exact in line dances. Line dance songs are skillfully composed, with inversions, curtailments, expansions, and every other device known to Western art music.

The sections, which are labelled A, B, etc., may or may not have a kinetic corollary. In *xotseyinshare* line dance and *tembishare* the step continues unchanged through the melodic sections. The same is true of *pangshare* waltz, with its completely different function. Usually, however, a new section has choreographic significance. As will appear in later analyses, sections may be clustered previous to a change. In *okushare*, A and B have the identical choreography, but C brings a change of orientation, which continues through a recurrence of B. In many line dances, including *xoxeye,* the second section, with its special melodic material, is a solidifying factor. It reinforces the position of the dancers. If there has been a re-orientation in A or C, B confirms the orientation, and compensates for a static alignment by *t'a.*

In the line dances, each section contains new material. Usually the distinct melodic sections are three, sometimes four, thus, A B C, sometimes A B C D, never more. In line dances the various sections maintain the same tempo and percussion beat, though they may start with a slow tempo and acceleration. In *konshare* and *kwitara* fast dances and others of their types, the two major sections, marked A and B, have identical melodic material and distinct percussion. Part A has a percussion tremolo, while part B has a duple beat. Each section prompts a traditionalized type of movement, ambling during A, and a complex step figuration during B. The details will appear in the concordance of structural patterns.

We must not overlook connectives. Besides the monotone or near-monotone introductory and terminal pulsations, many songs have connectives between sections. *Tembishare* has special formulae. But many songs use a connective, marked "y," with the vocables, "hapimbe."

Hapimbe and Song's Middle

The word *hapimbe,* sometimes *hapimbe hayambo,* is always in the middle of a song or a series of songs, exclusively in the sacred line or

100

circle dances. It marks a change of orientation. During *penshare* line dancing it is monotone, on the tonic. It concludes a song; the men face about, and go on to the next song. In *penshare ange'i* there is a melisma on "ha" and a montone on "pimbe." *Hapimbe* is two-tone, on 1 and 2, in the San Juan Harvest entrance song. In *okushare* it has three tones, 1, 3, 4, and it introduces part C. In *tunshare,* also before C, it plays on 1 and 3, but for the *ange'i* it is monotone. In *xotseyinshare wasa, hapimbe,* on 1 and 3, marks the face-about for a backward progression. In *pogonshare,* also on 1 and 3, it signifies the meeting of the two women in the center of the dance line. Then the song is repeated.

In *pogonshare* the *hapimbe* is really in the song's and dance's middle. But in the sacred line dances, *okushare* and *tunshare,* it is placed one third through the song. Another face-about has the same monotone "x" as the beginning, with the syllables, "heye hoye." The entire form is: x A B hapimbe C B x A B.

The scores in Part III will show the choreographic application of the melodic sections. They will display the variety of structures in the repertoire, but they will also demonstrate the prevalence of two salient types with different functions, the agrarian line dances with three parts and *hapimbe;* and the animal and war types with binary form and tremolo. Also, they will display examples of entire suites.

TONAL MATERIALS

The tonal materials define functional types and also subsections of songs. The scales and intervals are fullest in the sacred dances and most limited in social dances. These melodic aspects have no effect on the dance movements. That is, large scales and intervals do not imply larger movements.

Scale and Range: selected examples.

Monotone - in pulsations, in parts x, y, z, frequent.

Two tones - same limitations as monotone.

Range of 2	tembishare 1					2	1
	xotseyinshare, pogonshare				3		1

Three tones - connectives and pangshare 5 (Round) 8   5 4   1

Four tones - fairly common above tonic, sometimes dip below.

Range of 5	penshare Dawn 1, San Juan kwitara 1			5 4 3	1
8	San Juan kwitara 4	8	6	4 3	1
	kwitara 7	8 7	5 4		1
	pangshare 2, 3, 4		4	2 1 6 4	
9	Santa Clara konshare 1 (Type 4)		6 5 4	2 1 6	
11	Santa Clara ba'a 2	11 10 8	6	4 3	1

101

Five tones - very common.

Range of 8   tembishare 4   8   6 5 4 3   1
             penshare Dawn 3   8   6 5 4   2 1
             penshare Line 3-6   8   6 5   3 2 1
             kwantembishare   8   6 5   3 2 1
        10   tunshare 1   10 8 7 6   4 3   1
             Santa Clara konshare 3   10 9 8   6 5 4   2 1
        12   okushare 2   12 11 10 8 7   5 4 3   1
        13   xotseyinshare   10 8 7   5 4 3   1 7 5

Six tones - less common, also above tonic.

Range of 13   okushare 1, xoxeye   13 12 11 10 8 7 6 5 4 3   1

Seven tones (diatonic) - uncommon, above tonic.

Range of 8   Santa Clara tunshare ange'i   8 7 6 5 4 3 2 1
         9   xutsawe'ingshare (Blue Corn)   9 8 7 6 5 4 3 2 1

Intervals

Semitones - Rare: penshare Dawn 1, xutsawe'ingshare, Eagle Dance.
            okushare C and C sharp not adjacent.
Major seconds - all song types, rising and falling, especially line dances.
Thirds, minor, major, often "blue" - more common than seconds,
            especially in songs with tertial scales (3 1):
            penshare Dawn, xotseyinshare, xoxeye; in songs
            with quartal scales (4 21), connecting 4-2, 6-4: konshare.
Fourths - most common in songs with sparse scales of wide range:
            kwitara, 49 round; in San Juan kwitara 6, two
            adjacent, descending fourths. Sometimes in line dances
            with large scales.
Tritone (augmented fourth) - rare: okushare 1, tembishare 4, 5.
Fifths - rare as direct interval: San Juan kwitara 4.
Larger intervals not customary, except octave beginning xotseyinshare.

Medium-sized tonal materials prevail. In sacred line dances the scale and range are generally larger, while in konshare and kwitara types the intervals are larger. In line dances the intervals could be wide, but they are not. In small scales they must be small, as in *pangshare*.

TONAL MATERIALS WITHIN STRUCTURE (Figures 36-43)

The weighted scales show that the melodic material behaves variously in subdivisions, depending on the ritual type. A weighted scale shows the relative frequency of tones, the most frequent one by a whole note, the next one by a half note, and so on. A hold marks the final tone, an inverted hold marks the opening tone. Common intervals are connected by

102

Figure 36 – Scale: Okushare

Figure 37 – Scale: Xotseyinshare

104

Figure 38 – Scale: Xoxeye (Santa Clara)

Figure 39 – Scale: Tembishare

Figure 40 – Scale: Penshare

Figure 41 – Scale: Konshare (Santa Clara)

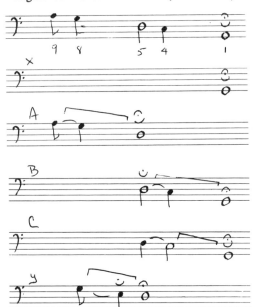

Figure 42 – Scale: Kwitara (San Juan)

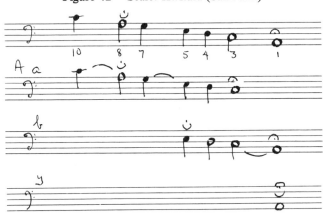

Figure 43 – Scale: Pangshare

brackets (fourths) or arcs (thirds). The character of the note, which has nothing to do with rhythms in this device, shows whether the song has low weighting, that is, with most melodic material near the bottom of the scale, or whether it has high weighting, or whether the material is evenly distributed. It also shows whether the melody is entirely above the tonic, or whether it dips below the maintone. The method, which is the invention of Erich von Hornbostel, and a favorite device of George Herzog, maintains its usefulness.

By the graphic display, the few samples show that Tewa songs manipulate the tonal material in many ways, but that the agrarian line dances differ from the rest of the repertoire. The breakdown displays the increasing expanse and higher pitch in the middle of the song, with shrinkage towards the end. All of the other songs, including *tembishare,* start at the highest point, and shrink or lower or both, towards the end. Their structure is less complex than that of the line dance songs.

Correspondingly, the line dances have a pyramidal contour, with the apex in the middle, while the other songs have descending trend, often in a "terrace" contour. However, within this large contour, all melodies waver up and down.

Turtle Dance (okushare) (Figure 55)

Six-tone scale, range 13 tones, begin 8, end 1.

x – 2-tone pulsation, begin on 3, end on 1.

A – 4-tone scale, range 10 tones (10-1), begin 8, end 1, emphasize thirds, often consecutive, descending.

B – 6-tone, range 13 (13-1), begin 10, end 1, melismatic semitone, emphasize fourths, also thirds, direct or by steps.

y – 3-tone, range fourth, begin 3, end 1.

C – 4-tone, range 9, begin 12, end 8, fourths in upper range, thirds in lower range.

z – like x.

B – as above.

x – as above.

A – as above.

B – as above.

z – as above.

Yellow Corn Dance (xotseyinshare) – *Wasa*

Five-tone scale, range 13 tones, begin 1, end 1.

x – 3-tone, range 6 (3-5), begin 1, end 1, fourths and thirds.

A – 5-tone, range 9 (8-7), begin 5, end 1, fourths.

BC – 5-tone, range 10 (10-1), begin 5, end 4, fourths.
y – 2-tone, range 3 (3-1), begin and end 1.
D – 5-tone, range 8 (8-1), begin 8, end 1, thirds.
z – monotone.

Line Dance

Six-tone, range 13, begin and end 1.
x – monotone.
A – 4-tone, range 8 (8-1), begin and end 1, fourths in upper range, thirds in lower range.
y – 2-tone, range 3 (3-1), begin and end 1.
B – 5-tone, range 13, begin 8, end 1, fourths and thirds.
z – 3-tone, range 4 (4-1), begin and end 1.

Corn Dance (xoxeye) (Figure 78)

Five-tone, range 11, begin 5, end 1.
x – monotone.
A – 4-tone, range 6 (8-3), begin and end 5, thirds.
B – 5-tone, range 8 (10-3), begin 10, end 5, fourths and thirds.
C – 5-tone, range 9 (11-3), begin 10, end 5, fourths.
D – 4-tone, range 8 (8-1), begin 5, end 1, fourths above, thirds below.

Harvest Dance (tembishare) (Figures 89, 91)

<u>1.</u> Five-tone, range 10, begin and end 1 (E and F not adjacent).
x – unitone, range 8 (8-1), begin 8, end 1.
A – 4-tone, range 10 (10-1), begin 8, end 1, thirds.
y – monotone.
B – 4-tone, range 8, begin 8, end 1, thirds.
z – 3-tone, range 5 (5-1), begin 3, end 1, thirds.
<u>3.</u> Same plan, but range 8 and B only 3-tone, range 4.
<u>1.</u>for Clowns *(kosa)* is repeated four times in full; that is the form.
<u>3.</u> for the Winter Cacique is A A B B A- B B A- A A, plus connectives.

Deer Dance (penshare) (Fig. 46, 47, 49)

Dawn Entrance 2
Four-tone, range 5, begin on 5, end on 1.
a. 3-tone, range 3, begin 5, end 3, seconds, semitone.
b. c. 3-tone, range 5, begin and end 1, thirds.

Dawn Entrance 3
Five-tone, range 8, begin 6, end 1.
A.a. Same as whole song, thirds.
b. 4-tone, range 6, begin 4, end 1, thirds.
c. 3-tone, range 4, begin 4, end 1, thirds.
B. 4-tone, range 6, begin 4, end 1, thirds.
Line Dance 1
x – monotone.
Whole song and a. Five-tone, range 8 (7-7), begin 5, end 1, thirds, some fourths.
b. 5-tone, range 6, begin 4, end 7, thirds.
cz. (coda) 5-tone, range 6, begin 5, end 1, thirds.

Buffalo Dance (konshare) (Fig. 107)

Santa Clara Summer Moiety 2 (slow dance)
Four-tone, range 9, begin 5, end 1.
x – monotone, on 1.
A – 3-tone, range 5 (9-5), begin and end 5, fourths.
B – 3-tone, range 5 (5-1), begin 4, end 1, fourths.
C – 3-tone, range 5 (5-1), begin and end 1, fourths.
y – 3-tone, range 4 (7-4), begin 5, end 4, thirds.
z – monotone, on 1.

Comanche Dance (kwitara) (Figure 122)

San Juan 3 (fast)
Five-tone, range 10, begin 8, end 1.
A a – 5-tone, range 8 (10-3), begin 8, end 3, thirds, indirect fourth.
b – 4-tone, range 5 (5-1), begin 5, end 1, thirds, seconds.
y – monotone on 1.
B. Same as A, with different percussion.

Social Dance (pangshare) (Figure 133)

Santa Clara 3
Whole song and A – 4-tone, range 5, begin 5, end 1, thirds, seconds.
B – 2-tone, range 2, begin 2, end 1, seconds.

All songs use seconds, but they are prominent where mentioned and marked. When not otherwise indicated, the song repeats without change. In cases of structural complexity, the sections are listed.

INTEGRATION

The tonal analysis could fill a volume. The samples show the relations and independence of the artistic constituents, and they suggest certain relationships between form and function.

1. *Formal Integration*

The tempo ties together all aspects. The percussion beat guides the steps and gestures, and underlies the melodies. The melodic form guides the dance patterns and changes in ground plans, though the tonal patterns and materials do not directly affect the movement. The sum total of the entire repertoire proves consistent artistic compensation, with complex melodies for simple dances, and simpler melodies for complex dances.

2. *Form and Function*

The ceremonies with complex melodies and simple choreography are the most sacred line dances for rain and crops; the reverse combination characterizes social dances, while semi-sacred dances for animals, war, and peace have fairly simple music and simple to complex choreographies. The analyses reveal several significant groupings of ceremonies according to form and function, but also transitional examples, and unique ceremonies, with their special patterns and somewhat ambiguous functions.

3. *Integrated Classification*

a. The clearest type is the sacred line dance, with antege step; stationary choreography except for pivots, re-orientation after specific song sections, in three-part total structure, and elaborate, full melodies in pyramidal contour. The traditional form is the same as for kiva dances by "kachina" (*óxua*), as described by Hill (MS.). The parts are those mentioned in Chapter 5 by Antonio and Carlos Garcia. The form is A (xapu), B (xakegi), C (hapimbe), B, A, B, with certain repeats. *Okushare* is the clearest example, but *tunshare* uses the same pattern. The Corn Dances share the basic choreographic and melodic characteristics, with variations. They have two parts, a *wasa* and line dance, or a slow and a fast dance. *Xoxeye* shares certain characteristics with the next category, namely, the slow-fast form, and the double-file elaborations of ground plans, with special step.

b. Semi-sacred ceremonies using variations of *antege* or special steps, mobile choreography in double files with both sexes or special male dancers, new formations for each song section and distinctive choreography for each part. They have simple melodies with medium-sized scales and some large, quartal intervals, often in sequential pattern and always in a

112

general descent of contour. This type, avowedly inspired by Plains cere-monies, has a series of song-dances, entrance, slow, and fast, with a binary structure, most clearly defined by percussion in the fast songs. *Konshare* is the most important representative. *Kwitara* shares the general structure, as do Eagle and Dog Dances, also Nambe Snake Dance. One dance, which has a connection with rain symbolism, not with animals or war, is the Rainbow Dance. This shares the structure of this type.

c.   A less homogeneous assortment of semi-sacred or social dances for couples using *antege* step *(pangshare)* or special steps *(yandewa, thi'i, ba'a),* mobile choreography, different for each part of a suite and for each section of a song within the suite. They repeat a single melody, either with change of tempo or change of level, limited scales and intervals, and generally descending contour. They tie in with the most sacred type in various ways, by the *antege* step *(pangshare)*, *wasa* (*thi'i*), and rain-crop symbolism (*yandewa*); with type two in the slow-fast combination (*yan-dewa, ba'a*).

d.   Distinctive, important rituals limited to San Juan using *antege* step or a mobile variant, simple choreography, without change for the duration of a song, distinctive patterns of song repeats, average-sized scales and intervals, generally descending. *Penshare* resembles the line dance pat-tern 1a (Fig.15), with stationary arrangement and face-abouts by pivots, but it contains short songs, rendered twice, and melodic characteristics different from any other Tewa music. The Dawn songs differ even more from the Tewa style. As a whole, *penshare* is a day-long drama of many parts and several styles. *Tembishare,* which is homogeneous within itself, differs from other Tewa ceremonies in ground plan, participation, and song structure. It resembles other ritual songs in the ideology and phrasing of the texts. As to origin, *penshare* line dance and *tembishare* lay a claim to Tewa origin, while the Dawn Entrance shows distinct Apache influence. The *penshare ange'i* resembles Type two choreographically.

In a ceremonial tradition so rich and ancient, any pigeon-holing would be disastrous, and indeed impossible. There are always exceptions, and cross-connections. It is remarkable that at least two types stand out in their integrated characteristics, the one very sacred and no doubt Pueblo, the other semi-sacred and half-Pueblo, half-imported.

Santa Clara Buffalo Dance, type 2 (Easter 1957)

Part III
Symbolic Pageantry

The Tewa dances are among the most startling spectacles of North America. Consequently, they have lured photographers and have inspired eloquent authors – Erna Fergusson, Elsie Parsons, John Collier, and a host of others. Their media can now supplement the novel feature of this book, the choreo-musical displays.

Each display illustrates a dance or suite at one station; the same patterns would recur at other stations with reorientation and minor variants. A complete dance drama may fit into one page, or it may spread over many pages, depending on the musical length. The ingenious reader can decipher the choreographic aspects with the help of the introductory legends and the explanations in Part II.

The reader can also divine the meanings in the mystical song texts. They repeatedly tell about the *oxua* who come from sacred lakes with song, rain, and corn growing power. They speak of game, birds, flowers, and of men and women in ceremonial array. They have ultra-natural symbolism beyond the words, as in the very ceremonial recurrent phrase – indíví tʰ ǎmù xɛ·n wínulíŋ – the verbal Leitmotif of *penshare:* "at dawn they stand prepared."

Penshare will lead the series of pageants. For it fuses the patterns of agrarian line dances and of game animal mime. It bridges the seasons, from winter to spring. Thus it introduces the series of ceremonies from the awakening season through the joyous summer back to the dormant season, and the series from sacred line dances to great communal pageants to pleasure dances.

115

Game Priest with Deer Dancers at San Juan (1957)

Chapter 11

DEER SPIRITS HERALD THE DAWN

Penshare, the Deer Dance of San Juan, also of Santa Clara, is a drama in four acts - a prelude, a dawn entrance, a plaza dance-song series, and a postlude.

1). The Prelude, *ange'i*, takes place in the plaza the eve of the main dance. *Pingxeng*, the game priest, renders a prayer, but the performers do not engage in ritual purification. They practice the songs and the beat of the step. Several decades ago the singer-dancers were exclusively men and teenaged boys. Now they include small boys. About 40-50 dancers assemble for the festival.

2). The *Dawn Entrance* takes place on the Sunday nearest the middle of February. In the cold dawn, just before sunrise - before 7 A.M. - a chorus of seven singers gathers at the northeast edge of the pueblo and faces east. The Deer assemble around the fog-making fire about 200 yards east of the big kiva. After 20 minutes *pingxeng* leads the Deer in single file and they serpentine past the chorus to the first entrance songs. Then they form a large circle so that the spectators can touch them. They pass through the chorus and enter the east plaza from north to south, ambling with *dipenyi* to drum tremolo. In the east plaza they begin dancing to song 3, first in a straight line, rhythmically to duple or iambic beats. During the second, tremolo Part B they meander. With repetitions of this song and dance, the performers make a complete circuit, through the south, west and north plazas, back to the east plaza, and into the practice kiva. The Apache clowns engage in horseplay. (Adapted from description by Don Roberts.)

3). The *Plaza Dance* lasts from late morning, after mass, to late afternoon, about 5 o'clock. Silently the Deer and one drummer follow *ping-xeng* into the south plaza from the practice kiva. They line up west to east between two small spruce trees, holed in for the occasion. They are dazzling white with ordinary shirts, Tewa kilts and crocheted leggings; but their faces are blackened or reddened. Deer antlers surmount tiaras of yucca stalks. The game priest, with a hide costume and long, flowing hair, stands at the west end of the line, north of the first Deer. The drummer, in ordinary clothes and headband, stands south of the line, in the center, facing the *sawipinge*, the main singers.

The Deer stand shoulder-to-shoulder, facing north. With a yelp and a sideward swing of their blackened rattles, they pivot left a quarter turn. For the remainder of the performance at this station, they all face in the same direction. (In 1964 they started in the latter alignment, facing west. D.R.). They intone the first set of songs and mark time with the *antege* step, in position 1. They stand erect, leaning on a tall, feathered staff held in the left hand. Then, during a brief pause, they face about. In position 2 they sing the same set of songs, while the game priest stands by the line's center, facing east. They again pivot and face west in position 3, singing the next song set 3-7. The game priest has moved to line's east end. He returns to the center for position 4 and a repeat of songs 3-7. For position 5 he and the Deer have their original placements. They sing only song 1. Then silently the Deer follow *pingxeng* to the north plaza. They perform as in the south plaza, then proceed to the east plaza, lined up south to north. They hold the fourth performance in the practice kiva.

For the second, third, and fourth appearances, the dancers use the same choreographic plan; but they sing other sets of songs. In positions 3 and 4 they replace the first song of the set by a new tune - song 8b instead of 8a. Between the second and third appearances they have a lunch recess. During their appearances the two Apache clowns wander around in a motley array of trousers, smocks, and fur caps. They speak Spanish, the lingua franca of the Jicarilla. With tiny bow-and-arrow they stealthily approach small Deer, hold the arrow to the dancer's ear, and pretend to shoot. Some of the Deer fall down, and are carried on an Apache's shoulder to the home of a purchaser. For the last appearance of 1957, one Apache, dressed in long skirts, tottered around like a decrepit old woman, falling down amidst audience uproar.

4). The Postlude *ange'i* takes place between 3:30 and 4:00 P.M. Before the emergence of the Deer, the War Chief addresses the people in Tewa and Spanish, begging the women to let the dancers complete the *ange'i.* The Deer file into the south plaza, with *dipenyi,* on foresticks. They line up shoulder-to-shoulder, facing north. The head singer moves from the *sawipinge* to the west end of the line. Several non-costumed dancers may help the drummer and the remaining singers in the middle. Usually they barely start the song, when the women and girls dash from the crowd; the Deer run away; the women chase them into the hills. In 1964 the War Chief and assistants kept the stampeding women in check till the song's end. Formerly the Apaches would "kill" a Deer for each Society, and the others would vanish during the singing. Now, as before, the Deer hide in the hills or in homes and the people hunt them until dark, on foot or in cars. When a Deer is caught, the family must redeem him with gifts of meat or bread, carried in baskets. A thanksgiving prayer by the Game Priest concludes the drama.

The songs are traditional and should be the same from year to year. Two recordings of the plaza songs (the second tape in entirety) display small differences within six years, particularly in 1963 a rendering in a lower pitch, a fourth lower. The general activity seems to have persevered, judging by descriptions of Spinden (1915: 11), Buttree (1930:52-54), and others. But their descriptions are not detailed and they include no music. A few items have changed, as the present inclusion of small boys and the deer-killing during the *ange'i.*

But the Deer Spirits are as awe-inspiring as ever. At dawn they stand at attention and then they cautiously enter through the dim light and the snow, as white, wintry animal supernaturals. In broad daylight they take root in the ground and rear their forest of antlers towards the sky, like a prophecy of a new season and new growth.

SONG TEXTS FOR PENSHARE

As the dancers do not mime the song words, they have led many writers to consider them meaningless vocables (Stevenson 1963:33). However, the texts mingle Tewa and Keresan phrases with vocables, during the plaza dance, while the dawn songs are Apache. The words speak of animals but also of the raingods and cloudblossoms.

Dawn Songs

Each verse contains one meaningful word, which the leader utters softly as a cue. The song recurs 11 or 12 times, with a different word on each repeat. The third song mixes Tewa with the same Apache words. The order for song 1 is -

mase	yellow buffalo
shitepe	mountain goat, male
kutipe	mountain goat, female
pian	deer, male
piande	deer, female
tsebahe	antelope
paschuye	red deer
pischuye	red deer
kutipe	mountain goat, female
shitepe	mountain goat, male
kahe	rabbit
sukahe	jack rabbit

Song 2 uses a different order of these words. So does song 3, along with initial and terminal vocables, and interpolations of the Tewa word for "little one" - navitsini'e.

Plaza Day Songs

As the complete texts are written under the music, the Tewa versions need not accompany the translations. When the same text recurs for each line of music, the translation is given once. When a new text belongs to each line of music, the translations appear line by line.

1. ho'o'owe (Keresan) It will be the shiwana singing. he . . . .
2. he. . . ha'aya'a (Keresan) Once upon a time.
    (Meaning unknown).
3. hapimbe (Tewa) At Kaya village in the middle of plains of San Juan
    Deer Elders (old women, old men) reside in a cloud blossom.
    At Kaya village in the valley of San Juan
    Deer Elders at dawn stand prepared (to enter San Juan).
4. On the oriole tail path, at dawn they stand prepared (1)
    At the ? path they are approaching at dawn (2)
5. On the river path they are approaching at dawn.
    Deer Elders are approaching at dawn.
6. On the parrot tail path at San Juan village
    They have arrived at dawn.
7. Same as 2.
8a. he. . . (Keresan) At the Keresan place. . .
8b. hapimbe (Keresan) From the north, from the east.   ?
9. (Vocables)
10a. ho'o . . . (Keresan) Early in the morning
    Early in the morning, from the north, from the east katsina, shiwana (are coming?)
11. weya . . . . . (Vocables)
    (Vocables) Once upon a time.
    (Vocables)
10b. hapimbe (Vocables)
12a. ho ha (Vocables)
    (Same vocables) (Tewa) A cloud blossom.
13. weyaye Once upon a time, from the east.
    (Obsolete)
14. heye . . . . From the east
    (Obsolete)
12b. hapimbe At Kaya village, in San Juan
    Deer Elders stand prepared at dawn hohe

120

Some obsolete terms have lost their meaning. Some expressions are highly ceremonial but are understood; terms with obsolete "1."

Ange'i

1. ha . . . Now the shiwana
    Are singing, the shiwana oho . . . (Vocables)
    hapimbe
2. At Kaya village, at Kaya village
    Deer Elders stand prepared at dawn.
3. At Kaya village, there to San Juan pueblo
    Deer Elders are prepared to enter at dawn (bringing fertility, goodness).
4. cf. 2.

Figure 44 – Penshare Dawn Circuit

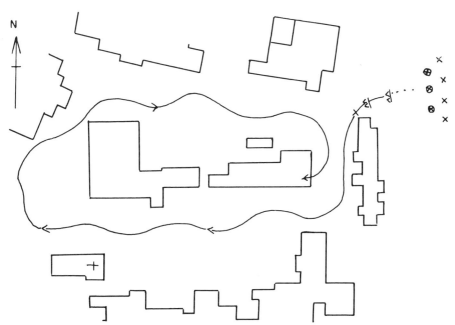

Figure 45 — Dawn Song

Figure 46 — Dawn Song

Figure 47 – Dawn Song

Figure 48 – Orientation of Plaza Deer Dance

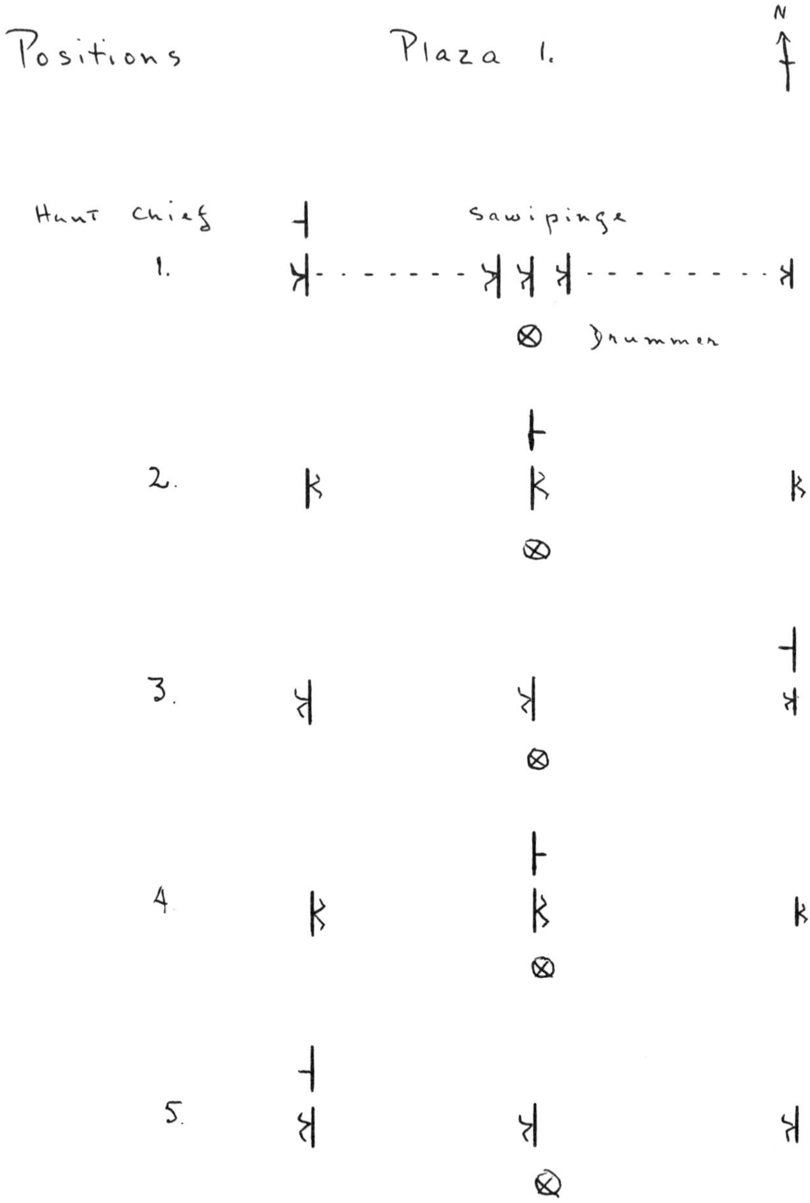

Positions   Plaza 1.   N ↑

Hunt Chief

Sawipinga

1.

⊗ Drummer

2.

3.

4

5.

Figure 49 – Penshare Plaza Dance Songs

Figure 50 – Penshare Plaza Dance Songs

Figure 51 – Penshare Plaza Dance Songs

Figure 52 – Penshare Plaza Dance Songs

Figure 53 – Penshare Plaza Dance Songs

Figure 54 – Penshare Ange'i Song

Chapter 12

THE AWAKENING SEASON:
FROM DAWN LAKE COME THE RAINGODS

Penshare does not usher in the New Year. It falls between an important solstice ceremony and a series of dances for fructification. *Okushare* belongs to the old year according to the Christian calendar, but by the solar calendar it welcomes the lengthening days. Just before and after *penshare*, in January or February, San Juan women join in the celebrations for corn planting - *tunshare, pogonshare* in alternate years; then a bit later, usually in March, they feature in *xotseyinshare* and *thi'i*. At this time Tewa men perform line dances resembling *okushare* in form, but not entirely in objective. They help the rain, as do *ashare* and *sekha* Rain Races.

The presentation could follow the calendar exactly. But it seems preferable to group the male line dances together, then the male-female fertility dances.

OKUSHARE, Turtle Dance or *Nufa* of San Juan

Antonio Garcia tells about the significance of this dance:
"The Turtle Dance is an annual ceremony in San Juan on December 26 and of course has nothing to do with the Christmas celebration. It is also called Nu-Fah, which literally translated means Ash-Fire. No one seems to know the exact function of the dance but I think it must be a winter solstice ceremony, perhaps for ushering in the winter solstice. It is not the prerogative nor the property of any particular clan, society or moiety and every able bodied male in the pueblo is expected to participate. This was particularly true before we started becoming acculturated. Today, only the "obedient" males take part.

"The dance is performed outside in the plazas and then, like other important ceremonies, there is a very short performance of the same in the Kiva before and after the outside performance. You might call this a prelude and postlude." (Letter December 3, 1957 to Willard Rhodes, quoted in Rhodes 1963).

The men line up shoulder to shoulder. They *antege* and sing their own accompaniment, with newly composed songs or at times traditional, successful songs. The songs are of the very sacred, complex type, pyramidal in contour, and structurally a cross between "rondo" and ternary form, ABCBAB with repeats. The orientation is of the three-fold mirror type. The dancers start, say, facing north. After the first B they face about to look south. After the second B they face about again to the original position. This resembles the five-fold mirror orientation of *penshare.* Also, as in Deer Dance, they file silently from one plaza to the next.

The first song was composed in 1954 and it recurs from time to time. The second song was newly composed by Cipriano Garcia in 1961. While the latter uses time-honored Tewa words, the former inserts English words between Keresan words and vocables. Of this innovation, Garcia says:

"When the composer came out with the English text for this song, I think most of the Pueblo members were pleased and delighted, and although I was horrified at first, I now feel that the words fit into the music very well and that they serve the purpose well. I am sure that this has been the first time that English words have been used in a religious song in San Juan and perhaps the main reason was because most Pueblo members now speak and understand English and some of us can express ourselves better in English." (ibid.) Since 1957 the rumor has been confirmed that this tune is of Keresan origin.

The line-by-line translation of the 1961 song is -

A.   ho he   When dawn was breaking,
                 From dawn lake the oxua came,
                 Beautifully singing   ha . . . heya we
B.   The kosa produced clouds to make rain.
       (tham faya chamu - esoteric term for kosa)
       They saw oxua, that's what they said.
       1)   With their wheat-growing power now they come (tota - wheat).
       2)   With their corn-growing power now they come (xu - corn).
C.   hapimbe The kachina in San Juan beautifully stand in ceremonial formation.

The dancers do have the company of sacred clowns, the *tsaviyo,* formerly also *kosa.* Parsons describes a satire on a priest and his acolytes (1929a:183). Pablita Velarde includes striped kosa in her painting of Turtle Dance (La Farge 1960:120); she shows the white kilts, feather pinwheels on the hair, painted torsos, and the tortoise-shell knee-rattles. The rattles gave the name, *okushare.*

SPRING RAIN DANCES FOR MEN

The other Tewa Pueblos hold very sacred plaza dances that resemble *okushare,* but they invoke rain at the time of the spring equinox. For their Spring Dance - *ta'andishare* - the men line up as for *okushare.* For the

132

Footlifting Dance - *antegeshare* - they line up as for *penshare,* but they sing entirely different songs.

TA'ANDISHARE or Spring Dance (Rain Dance, Cloud Dance)

The men, dressed very much as for *okushare,* but without the tortoise knee rattles, file in silently and line up shoulder-to-shoulder. They start marking time in silence, vibrating their gourd rattles. With the *antege* step they sing their own melodies which have the same style and structure as *okushare* songs, namely, a monotone opening, a rising and expanding contour, and a final return to a low level and monotone pulsation. However, the form is ABC, repeated. The example from Santa Clara, recorded by Donald Brown, has meaningful words, but is untranslated.

The choreography has local variants. In the San Ildefonso north plaza on March 3, 1957, the nineteen men and boys started facing the central *nansipupinge.* In the course of the song, at section ends, they turned in unison to face the opposite direction. They did this five times, ending as they started. That is, they used the five-fold pattern of mirror orientation. They filed in silence to the next station, with a circuit ENWS for the first and last appearances, and EW, SN, for the second and third appearances. They had the support of a male drummer, who stood by the *sawipinge.*

On March 23, 1957, Tesuque men danced with a similar alignment and mirror orientation, but without a drummer. They appeared only once, in the afternoon, after a morning's performance of *antegeshare.*

Despite the esoteric nature of the dance, the Santa Clara summer men performed a variant of *ta'andishare* at Puye Cliffs on July 23, 1961. They wore black kilts and small coronets. Without a drummer they shook rattles and spruce branches, and they sang their own accompaniment. In a complete circuit of the plaza, WSEN, they always started facing center. During the monotone pulsations they turned slightly to the right or left and reverted to the original shoulder-to-shoulder position. They used irregular combinations of *antege,* for instance, 4 antege R, 6 antege L 180°, 4 antege to center. They varied the regular, throbbing duple beat with both kinds of *t'a,* the triple and the slow types.

ANTEGESHARE or Footlifting Dance (Rain Dance)

This male line dance differs from the previously discussed dances in several ways, in the initial line-up with shoulders to the center, all facing the same direction, in morache accompaniment, initial acceleration, and successive pivots (Figure 16, 6c). Also, *kosa* and *kwirana* appear as side dancers and as intermission clowns.

133

During the morning of March 23, 1957, thirty-two men gave a most solemn performance in Tesuque. In their two appearances they lined up NWSE, then NS (Figure 11). One man, by the *sawipinge*, scraped a morache. The singers started low and slow; they accelerated and they raised their voices to an exultant melody, in songs resembling those of *okushare* in character. For each of the nine song parts they turned successively. A song fragment written down on location is in Figure 30.

Two *kwirana* and a *kosa* served as prop men and as side dancers. They used the *antege* step or gesticulated for rain and crops (Fig. 24). Sometimes the three conversed in jibberish, fluttering their hands. During the lunch period, after 2 o'clock, the *kwirana*, in black rags, entered homes and emerged into the freezing temperature, to carry the offerings into the kiva. They started at the north and went from house to house counterclockwise. During their emergence they chanted the simple song written down by ear and here reproduced. Women also carried food.

For a San Ildefonso south plaza performance on March 29, 1964, Don Roberts has provided a good description of the salient features:

"Twenty four men danced in a single line. The last two on each end were quite young, probably about 8-10 years old. The dance leader was in the center of the line. The dancers sang and no chorus was used. Two women scraped notched sticks. They knelt on a blanket exactly in the center of the line and faced the line, with the blanket carefully placed exactly in front of the dance leader. The women also sang and at times their voices were audible. Once, when their voices were carrying above the men's, one of the dance officials made a motion to the women which looked as though he wanted them to sing softer. They had laid one stick across the top of a large gourd which served as a resonator, and they scraped the other stick on the horizontal stick. (Notched sticks are often used in the kiva.)

"The women wore black mantas and their hands were painted orange – a shade very close to that of the gourd (pumpkin?). The men wore white kilts. The upper half of their torsos were painted black, as were their legs below the knees. The area above the knees was white. [Same painting as for the other line dances.] They wore moccasins with skunk fur anklets, a large necklace of evergreen which covered most of the upper half of the torso, and bands holding evergreen on each arm. Most dancers shook black rattles, but the three dancers adjacent to the main dancers on one side used plain gourds. For headdress they had stuck three turkey feathers on each side of the head, in most cases in a horizontal V between the two feathers and stuck in behind.

"Four evergreen trees marked off the dance area, just northeast of the round kiva which remained unused. The trees represented the SE, NE, NW, and SW of the area. The dance line just fitted between the trees. In the first of four appearances, the circuit progressed to stations SENW. The last appearance was the same. In the second and third appearances the men used only two sides, SN and EW.

"The dance leader began each station by shaking his rattle. The dancers, who had been facing the center of the area, did a 3/4 turn to the left and began to mark time. This occurred at each station. After a song section the dancers at the front of the line slowly made a 180° turn. This movement travelled down the line, from man to man. After 6-8 beats they repeated this procedure starting from the opposite end. It was a most beautiful sight to watch the ripple go down the line, first in one direction and then the other. At certain intervals, the dancers all faced the center of the area for a short time before returning to the regular movement. This pattern continued for all of the stations and circuits.

"The men used no entrance or exit song; they simply filed into the plaza from the practice kiva, progressed silently to the next station, and returned to the kiva. Each song started out VERY slowly (ca.♩=35). Then came a gradual accelerando which was nothing short of breath-taking. It was perfectly paced. Each beat was slightly faster than the previous one until the fast tempo was reached. Then a ritardando was perfectly paced until a return to the slow tempo. The performers repeated the same songs for each station in a circuit, but a different set for each circuit. The songs were rather simple, with little ornamentation. The fast part was quite long and recurred four times. [Not recorded.]

"In the last appearances two kosa were out. Between the second and third stations of the fourth circuit they enacted a burlesque on the Catholic Church, while the dancers halted. One kosa was dressed as an Archbishop complete with staff and mitre; the other was dressed as an acolyte. During the first two stations, the Archibishop had sat inside the dance area watching the dancing. At his cue he arose and delivered a sermon, part English and part Tewa. With florid gestures he reminded the congregation to tithe and pray for their sins. During the next station, his assistant gathered up a congregation of both Anglos and Indians. The Archbishop dipped a long handled car washing brush into a can of water and proceeded to sprinkle the congregation with "holy water." Most of the Indian ladies even crossed themselves. Church was then dismissed. The kosa removed their religious attire and continued as side dancers with hand motions for the rest of the day."

Other, earlier writers do not describe the musical features. In fact, Whitman (1947:138) and Parsons (1929a:186) do not mention clowning in San Ildefonso. In 1937 (Whitman) the fifteen men were led by an old *kosa* from Santa Clara. Parsons, speaking of San Ildefonso and Santa Clara, refers to the "maskless kachina" in the "antere" dance, because they dance like kachina but wear no masks.

135

Figure 55 – Okushare (Turtle Dance) Song and Choreography (San Juan, 1954)

Figure 56 – Okushare (Turtle Dance) Song and Choreography (1961)

Figure 57 – Okushare (Turtle Dance) Song and Choreography (San Juan, 1964)

Figure 58 – Ta'andishare (Santa Clara)

Figure 59 – Food Collecting Song of Kwirana (Tesuque)

howe howe ho

139

ASHARE or Bow Dance (Bow-and-Arrow Dance)

Ashare shares features with all of the preceding line dances and stands alone in its **bow** manipulation. It has the line-up of *penshare* and the five-fold mirror orientation. It would in this respect resemble *ta'andishare,* but the Spring Dance has shoulder-to-shoulder alignment. For *ashare* the numerical pattern is not as rigid as for *penshare.* Sometimes the repeats of song sections prompt seven pivots; at San Ildefonso I even counted eleven. The men use the *antege* step, with occasional *t'a.* They accompany themselves in songs of pyramidal contour, but not as steeply rising and falling as in *okushare.* The form is simply ABC with repeats and the usual monotone pulsations, which prompt pivoting.

The costuming differs in that the dancers wear hide capes across one shoulder. The action differs in that each man carries a bow in the left hand and manipulates it in a stylized fashion. (Despite the English name, "Bow-and-Arrow Dance," they carry no arrows.) Usually the men hold the bow horizontally, with the left arm in natural, vertical position. During each of the major song sections, they raise the bow in a special way, during A with an arm swing forward and back to position; during B with a swing overhead, then right, left, and down; during C with a swing to the left and return. This is the only dance that conforms gesture levels to melodic levels.

Santa Clara men - ten from the summer moiety - performed this dance in most solemn fashion at Puye on July 22, 1961. They used the same complete orientation as the men for the Cloud Dance. Tesuque men danced it at the Santa Fe Indian Market on August 22, 1964.

The women of San Ildefonso have for some years taken a liking to Bow Dance, and they perform it very well, albeit in the thin, traditional female timbre. They have a drummer, no less a person than the famous potter, Maria Martinez. On March 10, 1957, a long line of women with hide capes performed *ashare* in the north plaza. They performed always in alternate double stations - WE SN - and they appeared six times because it was a fine day and they felt like dancing. They also appear at semi-commercial events, "Benefit Dances" in the pueblo, the Indian Market in Santa Fe. They call themselves the Tunyo Woman's Club.

Ashare has deep ceremonial associations, in other pueblos too. The bow priesthood of Zuñi has lightning power (Dutton 1963:82), and the Tewa dance has the same potentiality. However, it seems to be gradually moving towards secularization.

SEKHA or Rain Race Singing

In the early spring, men of San Juan - formerly also of other Tewa pueblos - conjure rain by ceremonial relay races. After ritual preludes the best runners of the two moieties compete on the race track east of the pueblo, early in the morning. After recess they dance in the plazas, singing their own accompaniment. They face each other in two lines and side-step, changing direction after each song section.

The song example (recorded by Manuel Archuleta) illustrates the long, three-part structure, the melodic complexity, and the thematic recurrences like the persistent coda. In *t'a* the melody and rattle rhythms sometimes agree, sometimes complement, as in the fourth line. The musical type fits into the sacred pyramidal category, though the double file face-to-face, moving sidewards, is unusual.

Figure 60 – Ashare (Santa Clara)

Figure 61 – Sekha (Rain Races)

143

San Juan Butterfly Dance

Santa Clara Basket Dance at Puye Cliff (1961)

144

Chapter 13

SAN JUAN GIRLS ARE SINGING BEAUTIFULLY, SWAYING DEW BASKETS

Men and women prepare the planting season with *tunshare, pogonshare, xotseyinshare,* and *thi'i.* Dancers of all Tewa pueblos know the four early spring dances, except for San Juan's monopoly of *xotseyinshare.* San Juan has the most regulated alternation of the four dances.

Formally *tunshare* is distinctive in the springtime repertoire. The songs resemble *okushare* songs in their structure and contour, while the songs of *pogon* and *xotseyinshare* state three or four themes in a manner resembling *ta'andishare* and *xoxeye,* and *thi'i* songs vary one theme. Then, *tunshare* lacks a feature of the other three, a weaving entrance, termed *wasa.*

TUNSHARE or Basket Dance

The famous Basket Dance promotes fertility in vegetation and in human beings, by the symbolic power of baskets and of the women who carry them:

"The baskets symbolize that which they contain - the food which pre-serves the life of the people. They contain the seed which is planted in the ground, and which must be fructified in due time; the fruit or grain which the earth yields in response to the efforts of the people; the meal which is produced when the harvest of corn is ground; and, finally, the loaves of of bread ready for the sustenance of the Pueblo group. The invocations for fertility which occur in the Basket Dance embrace not only the food plant life, but the human race, which must multiply and transmit the gift of life from generation to generation. A complete series of the scenes presented in this ceremonial would constitute the epitome of woman's life, her conse-cration to childbearing and the sustaining of the life of the pueblo." (Dutton 1955: 15-16).

The two symbolic scenes are:

1). *Gwingwendi'e,* the standing dance. After a silent entrance, a line of women parallels a line of men who sing the accompaniment. The women embroider the basic *antege* step with *shushu* foot shuffles in place. They move disc baskets up and down in front of their faces. Towards the end of each song section the two lines reverse their orientation, with successive pivots, as in the men's *antegeshare.* Three song sections add up to the same structure as in *okushare* songs, and they represent similarly new creative efforts. The men are dressed as for *okushare,* in Santa Clara, with the addi-tion of squash blossoms in their headdresses. The women wear black mantas and black or white capes.

Above and Below: San Ildefonso Butterfly Dance (ca.1930)

2). *Mwe'ekwo,* the dance with the *mwe'e* or scraping stick. The men stand shoulder-to-shoulder and sing with the *antege* step. Meanwhile, the women kneel on a blanket, place their basket face down to serve as resonator for the scraping sticks. They had carried these in disguising spruce clusters and they now use them as musical instruments, with phallic symbolism. This is the "Fast" dance.

1). Slow, standing dance again.

Choreographically simple and musically complex, this solemn dance has long been one of the most famous Pueblo performances. It has evidently not changed, judging by the comments of Parsons (1929a:187-189), Buttree (1930:8 for Cochiti), Lea (1957:18) and others. It has entered the repertoire of public programs, as at Puye, without losing dignity.

Tunshare has an esoteric corollary - a very ceremonial prelude in the kiva. Formerly it also featured *kosa.* In the kiva it is a male line dance. The *ange'i* prelude is for men. But the postlude *ange'i* is held in the plaza and includes women line dancers. However, the songs are the same for both types of *ange'i.* The choreography of the men's *ange'i* resembles that of *okushare,* but the tempo is slower, with a more swinging movement; the reversal of direction is more complicated. The men sway their whole bodies to right and left, along with the rattles and evergreen boughs. In San Juan they step as notated, R right, L in place, R left, L in place. In Santa Clara they double-bounce R and L.

For the reversal after each song section B, they tremolo their rattles; meanwhile they walk ahead a few steps, pivot 180°, and return to place facing the opposite direction. Thus they pivot say from N to S, the next time from S to N. In San Juan they take four steps forward, in Santa Clara three, as shown.

Though the male *ange'i* is a kiva dance, the Santa Clara summer people honored their spectators by concluding their 1964 Puye events with the "Morning and Evening Dance." The men and boys entered silently, in long black capes, portending solemnity. They danced twice, in the north, then the south area, with the triple orientation at each area. As they sang (fortunately without amplifiers), their voices rang out exultantly in a haunting melody. As they filed out and as visitors' cars snorted into action, the melody continued to pulsate towards the blue mountains and soar towards the cloud blossoms.

SONG TEXTS FOR TUNSHARE (San Juan, 1964)

1. Slow Dance
A. Over there where the rivers join at confluence lake
Beautifully game is emerging;

147

coming to San Juan right now.

B. 1) The oxua came with lightning
With rainfall they came
2) The oxua came with thunder
With dewfall they came.

C. hapimbe 1) San Juan boys are singing beautifully, decorated with parrot feathers.
2) San Juan girls are singing beautifully, swaying sacred dew baskets.

2. Fast Dance
A. (Vocables)
B. (obsolete)
C. 1) They are wearing spirit flowers
2) They are swaying spirit baskets.

3. Slow Dance
A. When dawn is breaking, at dawn lake
1) Dawn boys are singing (thamuyoge enung olinxatung)
2) Dawn girls are singing (thamuyoge anung olindingtung)
B. From the inner sanctum black, rain-promising clouds they bring.
1) With their wheat-producing power they are singing.
2) With their corn producing power they are singing.
(Vocables)
C. (Keresan?)

4. Fast Dance
A. 1) Now that the dawn is breaking, oxua boys have come, Beautifully singing. He . . .
2) Now that the dawn is breaking, oxua girls have come Beautifully singing. He . . .
B. Oxua boys are arriving, Oxua
girls are arriving
With their wheat growing power.
C. They come to see our fields
B. Oxua boys (girls) are arriving
With their corn conjuring power.

Ange'i
A. Here in San Juan pueblo the winter cacique (our great winter mother)
With his children he came.
B. 1) San Juan boys swayed fir boughs.
2) San Juan girls swayed sacred dew baskets.
From turtle lake the oxua came.

148

C. Katsina shiwana (Keresan)
    1) San Juan boys are wearing sacred clay.
    2) San Juan girls are swaying dew baskets.

XOTSEYINSHARE or Yellow Corn Dance

The Yellow Corn Dance of San Juan is in two parts, *wasa* and line dance. The cast includes men and women, the women symbolizing the sacred Yellow Corn Maiden of Tewa mythology (Parsons 1926:104).
1). *Wasa,* the Weaving Dance. The men and women - up to 56 from both moieties - zigzag into the plaza, at San Juan from east to west. Of the four leading couples, the first two couples step obliquely forward-sideward R for a phrase, then L for a phrase. The next two couples conversely step L, then R. Then follow other couples in groups of fours (8 dancers), alternating their directions. They progress with the *antege* step, always accenting the right foot, no matter which direction they proceed. At "hapimbe" everyone faces about and continues the weaving, backward-sideward. At song's end all face about again, and proceed forward-sideward during the song repeat. The men sing their own accompaniment, with the aid of one drummer by their side.
2). *Single Line Dance.* In silence the men and women line up in alternate array, shoulder-to-shoulder, facing north in the first plaza, the drummer by the *sawipinge* south of the line. During a slow section the singer-dancers flex and straighten both knees and simultaneously lower and raise their rattles and spruce clusters, as shown by the kineme in the choreography. During the fast part they *antege* in place with the typical male and female arm movements, and with t'a. They do not pivot.
    They *wasa* only in the first and fourth appearances. For the second and third appearances they line up single file right away.

SONG TEXTS: SAN JUAN YELLOW CORN DANCE
    (The same each year)

Wasa
A. 1). Here in San Juan pueblo San Juan boys (enung)
        Beautifully are singing (dinxadung)
    2). Here in San Juan pueblo San Juan girls (anung)
        Beautifully are making their special sound (holingdengdung)
B. (Vocables) In the inner sanctum of the kiva
    1) oxua boys make their sacred path; they have their flower path.
    2) oxua girls make their sacred path; have their flower path.

149

C. (Vocables)
    (Vocables)
    hapimbe
D. (Keresan?)

Line Dance
A. Slow: (Vocables)
    (Vocables)
    (Keresan) North, West, South, East
B. Fast: o'e
    Here in San Juan pueblo
    In San Juan, in the Keresan place wiya. . .
C. (Vocables)

POGONSHARE or Corn Maiden, Squash Blossom Dance, Rainbow Dance

Pogonshare has an alternate name, *powingshare,* "Three Time Dance."
The cast includes a large group of men and eight young women, who appear
successively in pairs, two at each of the four appearances. The men do not
wear shirts as for Yellow Corn Dance, but have orange discs painted on
their nude torsos, and wear squash blossoms in their hair. The Corn
Maidens, in black mantas and capes, wear gaudy feather crowns, and carry
an ear of corn. This all-Tewa dance includes *wasa* and line dance, as
follows:
1). *Wasa.* The men shuttle onto the plaza in a thick group, four abreast,
ten deep, with the women in the center, one front, one back. The drummer
progresses with them, at the right, aiding their self-accompaniment. *Wasa*
starts each entrance.
2). *Line Dance.* The men form a long line, at San Juan the length of the
plaza, at San Ildefonso along one side of the circuit square. Three men
from the end stand the two women, that is, at opposite ends of the line.
While the men *antege* in place, the maidens *antege* in a zig-zag progression
in front of the line:
A. During an accelerando both *antege* forward, say north, away from
the line, then quarter-pivot to face each other.
B. C. y. At San Juan they zigzag towards each other with light, low leaps,
pass each other, face-about, and return to the middle. The diagram shows
the path of the first woman; the second woman's path is the reverse. In San
Ildefonso they cover one-third as much space, so they get to the middle by
the "hapimbe."
Hapimbe. They stand still, right arm across the chest, face-to-face.
A.B.C. During the song repeat they pass each other, face about, and re-

150

turn to their original location in front of the line.

z. During a song ritartando they *antege* towards the men, and take their places in the line as at the beginning of this song.

In the kiva each Corn Maiden passes her fan-shaped headdress to her successor. This very sacred dance for crops requires kiva rituals of purification. Formerly the dancers had the company of *putandi,* ragged clowns who teased the women (Parsons 1929a:189-190). They also used to appear at the other *wasa* dances - Yellow Corn and Butterfly.

SONG TEXT: POGONSHARE

San Juan, recording by Manuel Archuleta.
A.   In San Juan pueblo San Juan boys
     Are beautifully making their flower path.
     (Same for San Juan girls).
B.   (Vocables).

THI'I or Butterfly Dance

Dancers of *thi'i* employ *wasa* in still a different way. And then they perform in couples, not in a great line. In San Juan they *wasa* into the plaza only once, all participating couples together. In Santa Clara they do not *wasa* at all, but *antege* in a circle as in *yandewa,* forward, sideward, forward. The San Juan choreography is:

1).   *Wasa.* From the practice kiva the participating couples zigzag into the first, south plaza, with the separate chorus of singers and drummers in their wake. There may be any number of couples, never more than 16.

2).   *Couple Dance.* While the chorus stands, the first couple performs the following dance:

A.   While the woman steps sidewards in a straight line, the man meanders in front of her with a rooster prance, raising a knee at each step, thrusting the head forward rhythmically. She steps left for a phrase, then right for a phrase.

B.   Both partners move backwards with the *suñu* step, passing each other, turning at phrase ends, and returning. As they zigzag, they bend from side to side, especially the man. During *suñu* to the right, they lean L. The man holds a tomahawk in the right hand and the left hand on the hip. During each reversal he switches the tomahawk to the other hand. The woman holds the left hand overhead, grasping a cluster of feathers; she has the other hand on the hip.

After the first dance, everyone goes to the north plaza. The chorus sits down on chairs. Each successive couple dances to another song, while the

151

non-active couples watch. At the end of the contest (for such it is) the performers return to the practice kiva.

While the songs for *wasa* resemble those for other spring dances, the song for the *suñu* dance is quite different. The scores include a recording from 1957 of the *wasa* and the dance song in honor of the winter cacique, then, from a 1963 recording, a song for the summer cacique. The recording also included *wasa,* song for *suñu* 2, and other songs for other couples. The songs repeat one long theme, of which song 3 is the clearest example. During the first recurrence the dancers perform choreography A, pausing for knee-flexions during the episode of quarter note drum beats. During faster recurrences (first with vocables, then with words) they *suñu* and *t'a.* Finally, in the original slower tempo, they revert to choreography A - the rooster prance.

Though the dance is now becoming a social dance and has shed various ceremonial features, it used to be quite ceremonial. At Nambe, strangely enough, its revival inspires reverence. The dancers think of it as an oxua kiva dance, even when they perform it at Puye. In the end the woman opens her feather cluster with the ceremonial good-dispensing gesture. It is also questionable whether the women always wore the present antennae and butterfly wings (or vast set of feather wings). However, it is possible that the springtime symbolism is associated with the metamorphosis of the butterfly out of the chrysalis. (The *suñu* ground plan has a remarkably caterpillar-like aspect).

The ambiguity of *thi'i* - which does not mean butterfly - increases in a comparison with the Hopi version of the dance. San Juan, as well as Santa Clara dancers, know the Hopi version and perform it at times. This is a line dance for alternate men and women like *xoxeye,* according to Antonio Garcia. Parsons equates the Hopi version with the Tewa "Saint's Day Dance " (1939:975). Lange illustrates the resemblance with photographs (1957:60-61).

SONG TEXTS: SAN JUAN THI'I

1. *Wasa*
A.   (Vocables)
B.   (Keresan) Once upon a time. (Vocables)
C.   (Vocables)
2. *Line Dance* for Winter Cacique
A.   (Vocables)
B.   In San Juan pueblo right in the middle of the plaza outside the
              kiva here, white corn goddess stands.
      With her living plants she stands prepared at dawn.

C.   (Vocables)
3. *Line Dance* for Summer Cacique
A.   (Vocables)
B.   (Vocables)
C.   At Kaya village, over there where the rivers join at confluence lake.
They come right here, carrying flowers; the oxua have flowers there.
They come to see our fields. (Vocables)

Note the overlap of texts with *tunshare* and *tembishare.*

COMPARISON WITH THE HOPI BUTTERFLY DANCE

A description by Mischa Titiev shows resemblances of the Hopi Butterfly Dance to both *thi'i* and *xoxeye* (communication). Each woman picks
her partner, who must be the son of one of her mother's brothers. The
woman or ikya'a (of the father's clan) stands in a warm joking relationship, involving sex, to the young man or imuyi (grandson). Sometimes
another ikya'a partners with the boy during the dance. In San Juan the
woman also picks her partner for *thi'i;* as in Hopi land, the boy recipro-
cates with a gift for the honor of dancing with her. As in San Juan there is
a separate chorus, a Hopi drummer with a cluster of singers. Sometimes
successive couples dance as in a contest, but in Hopi land this is uncommon,
although customary in the Hopi Buffalo Dance.
Usually the Hopi line up in single or double file with men and women
in alternation; or they can dance face to face, as in *xoxeye.* They can invent formations. At times they even dance in ballroom clinch, counting
"one-two". The women wear tablitas with a variety of decorations. They
do not wear wings.
Nevertheless, the Hopi term "politikive" literally means Butterfly
Dance. It is a social dance, and is set apart from the masked kachina dances
in function as well as in form. It is more secular than the Tewa *thi'i.*
The Tewa sometimes perform a Hopi Butterfly Dance in the spring or
summer. At San Juan a resident Hopi, Preston Keevama, directs the performance. At Santa Clara a former Hopi-Tewa, Philip Dasheno, has trained
the winter moiety in a meticulous rendering with splendid tablitas. At
Puye Cliffs the Santa Clarans call it "Blue Corn Dance."

Figure 62 – San Juan Tunshare (1964) (Slow)

Figure 63 – San Juan Tunshare (Fast)

Figure 64 – San Juan Tunshare (Slow)

Figure 65 – San Juan Tunshare (Fast)

157

Figure 66 – San Juan Tunshare

Figure 67 – Santa Clara Tunshare Ange'i

Figure 68 — Santa Clara Tunshare Ange'i

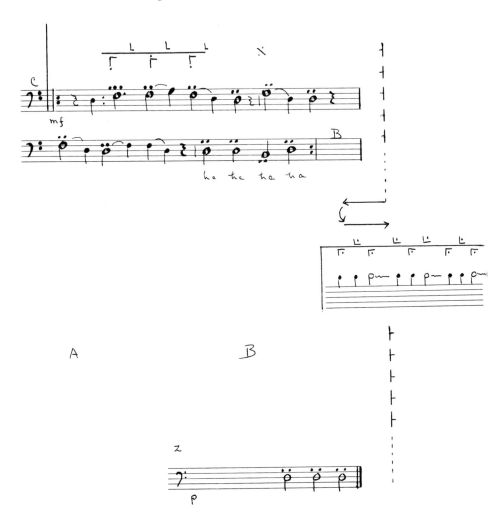

Figure 69 – Choreography of San Juan Yellow Corn Wasa

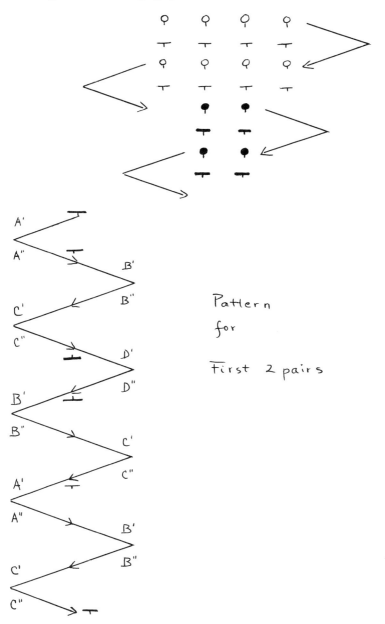

Pattern
for

First 2 pairs

Figure 70 – Yellow Corn Songs and Choreography

162

Figure 71 – Yellow Corn Songs and Choreography (continued)

Figure 72 – San Juan Pogonshare (Corn Maiden Dance)

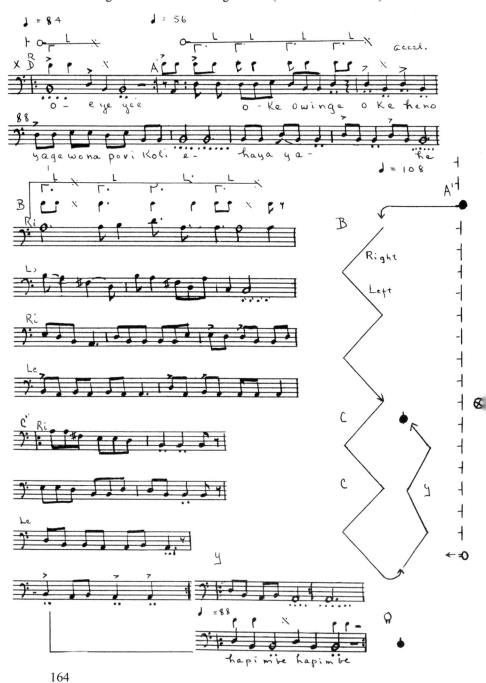

Figure 73 – San Juan Pogonshare (continued)

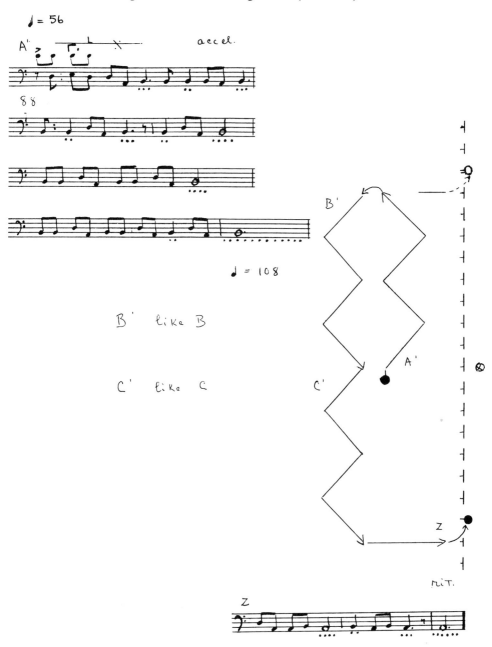

Figure 74 – San Juan Thi'i

166

Figure 75 – San Juan Thi'i (continued)

Figure 76 – San Juan Thi'i (continued)

Chapter 14

THE RIPENING SEASON:
WITH THEIR CORN GROWING POWER THEY COME

Throughout the summer the Tewa pueblo residents unite in large, communal dances for the ripening of the corn and for the successful harvest. Sometimes they give the summer dances during the cold season. The Corn Dance, *xoxeye,* is an important, widespread dance. It also has some "satellites," minor dances with similar forms and objectives. *Tembishare,* less spectacular and less well known, reaches into the whole Tewa social structure.

XUTSAWE'ING or Blue Corn Dance, alias Hopi-Tewa Butterfly Dance

This is the dance introduced by Philip Dasheno. It is the only Corn Dance of the Santa Clara winter people, who do not perform *xoxeye.* The winter men and women like to dance it on Puye Cliffs. They have two variants. In 1961 they danced in double file, two men, then two women - the typical *xoxeye* alignment. In 1964 they alternated in a single file. (Hopi Butterfly dancers can use both patterns).
In any event the dance has two parts:
1. An entrance dance, so-called slow, but actually quite lively. The dancers circle the plaza C C; they face forward, sideward, forward, as shown in the diagram with the music. The song is of the pyramidal structural type; it has semitones, which are not a Tewa characteristic.
2. A stationary dance, with *t'a* and many face-abouts (Figure 31) after ambling back and forth to a drum tremolo.
1. Exit to entrance song.

XOXEYE or Corn Dance, Tablita Dance, Harvest Dance

The "Corn Dance" has for years been one of the most publicized Pueblo dances because of the large cast and beautiful formations. As the usual "Saint's Day Dance," it has achieved more prestige and also more geometric complexity in Keresan Pueblos and Jemez. It is not the typical Tewa Saint's Day Dance, except for Santa Clara's summer moiety. In Tesuque it has been supplanted by *kwitara.* In San Juan it was becoming obsolescent, but it was revived in fine form for San Antonio Day, June 13, 1964. San Ildefonso and Tesuque also like to celebrate San Antonio Day with

Santa Clara Blue Corn Dance at Puye (1961)

xoxeye. Santa Clara's summer people like to bring a day on Puye Cliffs to a rousing conclusion with the so-called "Harvest Dance." Under that name it is an annual early September celebration in San Ildefonso.

Except for Tesuque, the Tewa pueblos adhere to traditional ground plans, which are basically simple but look complex in the multiple line-up. Tesuque approaches the Keresan complexities and variety. And it emulates the double appearances by the moieties in two performances at each appearance. All Tewa pueblos adhere to the traditional two-part structure - slow dance and fast dance - and to the pyramidal song type of the spring dances for men and women. At the second or third appearance the Tewa change to a different kind of formation and step in a circle dance for rain - *kwanshare* - which is equivalent to the Keresan *yorañi,* and which also resembles the Tewa *yere.* (For Cochiti see Kurath in Lange 1959: 545-556).

The two typical *xoxeye* dances are as follows:

1. *Slow Dance* (pungkha):

The dancers enter the plaza dancing, in double file - two men, two women, etc. They trot in time with the drums which lag slightly behind the melodic accents. At the end of each songphrase the men swing the right arm out, shivering their rattle, and swoop it back to the body in a graceful motion. Their gesture is the signal for a slight change of direction, in the course of a flat meandering ground plan. When they arrive at the first station, the two male leaders guide all of the dancers in a parallel, oval circuit (Figure 17, 8f) and return to the front of the double line. Meanwhile, the women jiggle their arms as in Yellow Corn and other vegetation dances.

2. *Fast Dance:*

The chorus of singers and drummers, who brought in the dancers and then dropped behind, group themselves to one side. In silence, the dancers stretch out into two parallel files, face-to-face, men and women alternating. With the double-bounce (or triple-bounce) they maneuver through certain formations for each of the song sections:

A. Partners circle around each other, after the mark-time of part x.

B. Both lines are stationary, while the dancers follow the rhythmic complexities of both kinds of *t'a,* triple and slow, with double bounce.

C. The two lines cross over or describe some other formation, with forward progressing double bounces.

B. Both lines are stationary.

C. The lines describe some other formation, to the climactic tune.

Coda. The dancers return to their original positions.

Two Figures of ground plans show the traditional formations for the different song parts.

LEGEND FOR XOXEYE FORMATIONS, FAST DANCE

Letters refer to musical sections.

Typical Formations (Figure 79).
x - Opposite rows face-to-face, in place.
A - Partners a. Circle each other (all couples moving as shown).
     Opposites b. Circle each other.
B - In place - a. Like x.
              b. Line of women facing line of men (especially *Santa Clara*).
              c. Two lines face ahead, alternate array (*Santa Clara*).
C - In motion - a. Circle by fours.
               b. Two groups of fours meet obliquely, circle by fours, and return to place.
               c. Couples change places with each other.
               d. Quadruple file, couples back-to-back with opposite couples, after c.

Quadruple Formations (Figure 80).
Variants on C d, above, specialties of *Tesuque*.
C - Two lines meet and return, cross by pairs.
B - In place as shown, opposite side from before.
C - Reverse positions by C C path, each man followed by partner.
B - In place as shown.
C - Each couple small C C arc.
B - Face ahead, men in center.
C - Partners change position.
B - In two files, alternating men and women, face ahead.
C - Women to center, men to outside.
B - In place as shown. To original position (x), by C C passing of partner.

KWANSHARE

On the day of a *xoxeye* celebration, when the Tewa replace the usual Fast Dance by *kwanshare*, they proceed as follows:
A.   After the line-up and stationary x, the male leader guides a single file into a large circle, with the *kwanshare* step and gesture to an accented quadruple drum beat, R and L by phrases.
B.   All face center and step-bend sidewards R., turn on *t'a*, and go forwards.
C.   All go backwards with a double bounce, and on *t'a* a heavy tread.
The song repeats, with the following evolutions:

172

x'. Pivot to the original orientation.
A'. *Kwanshare* forwards.
B'. *Kwanshare* gradually into two parallel files.
C'. Double bounce in place.
Santa Clarans add another song repeat, with these complications:
A". Two leaders split the group into two circles, each by guiding his file with the *kwanshare* movement.
B". Proceed backwards in the double circles.
C". Work back into two parallel files with *kwanshare,* and double-bounce in place on arrival.
z (coda). Double-bounce in place, face to face.

In addition to the tempo and beat, the melodic character distinguishes *kwanshare* songs. *Xoxeye* tunes start with a low, monotone pulsation and rise to the *xakegi,* then descend again, but *kwanshare* tunes start on the highest note and descend. Also, *xoxeye* songs are more elusive and irregular than the tuneful *kwanshare.*

SAN JUAN TEXTS FOR XOXEYE

The Tewa texts, says Garcia, are interspersed with the usual syallables, which may be archaic or obsolete Tewa; also they include Keresan words. "The texts proclaim the human, animal, and plant fertility by key words - oxua, raingods; oxua, clouds; kwan, rain; kwantan, thunder; tsiguwenu, lightning; soxua, fog." The men in the singing chorus illustrate the key expressions and the cardinal directions by means of gestures, as *kwantuka* - calling the rain from all directions. During passages of vocables they use a pumping motion similar to the women's *xoxeye* gesture (Figure 25, lc). In the sections referring to rain and the *oxua* arriving from the four directions, they use the *ohotayo* gesture like the rain-calling hand movement of the kwirana (Figure 23, and 25, la).

Fast Dance. A.B. (Vocables)
        C. From the north, from the west
          The oxua came with their corn growing power.
        C'. From the south, from the east
          The oxua came with their corn growing power.
Kwanshare. Line 1. ·The shiwana are speaking (Keresan).
        Line 6. The shiwana are singing.

YERE or Snowbird Dance

Men and women alternate in a file and they gesticulate in *yere* as in *kwanshare*, but in a triple rhythm on beats 1 and 3. They hold feather clusters. The dancers enter in a single file, then they turn to the four directions with complex patterns of *t'a*. They work their way into a circle, around the *nansipupinge*, while the chorus moves on the outside. In the circle the dancers do the *kwanshare* motion.

Yere (meaning unknown) fits into the Harvest Dance (*xoxeye-kwanshare*) type of choreography. Such an association is strengthened by Parsons' mention of "Yede" as the Tesuque Saint's Day Dance (1929:209-210). Today it survives as a sporadic performance at San Ildefonso, not always in the summer, thus on Easter Sunday, March 29, 1964, and at the Benefit Dances on July 19, 1964, each time with different songs. Nambe also used special songs for its variant on July 4, 1964.

While the Blue Corn Dance resembles the regulation Fast Dance of *xoxeye, yere* is related to the *kwanshare* Fast Dance. The same is true of the songs. Blue Corn songs belong to the pyramidal type, like most *xoxeye* songs, while the *kwanshare* and *yere* have a simpler form, with a descending trend, especially *yere*. The costuming of Blue Corn-Butterfly Dance resembles that of *xoxeye* in the women's tablitas, though the shapes are different, the former favoring crescent shapes and the latter designed in the terraced cloud symbol shape. Again, for *xoxeye* the men are nude to the waist, but for Blue Corn and *yere* they wear white shirts recalling *penshare* and *yandewa*. All participants in *yere* have feathers in their hair - no tablitas.

All of the crop dances - in spring and summer - may have large groups, but selected groups, especially trained and costumed. In these respects (selection and costuming) they differ from the true Harvest Dance of the Tewa, *tembishare*. They also differ greatly in the dance form and music.

Figure 77 – Santa Clara Song for Blue Corn Dance

Figure 78 – Santa Clara Xoxeye Fast Dance Song

Choice of Formations on Figure 79.

Figure 79 – Santa Clara Xoxeye Formations

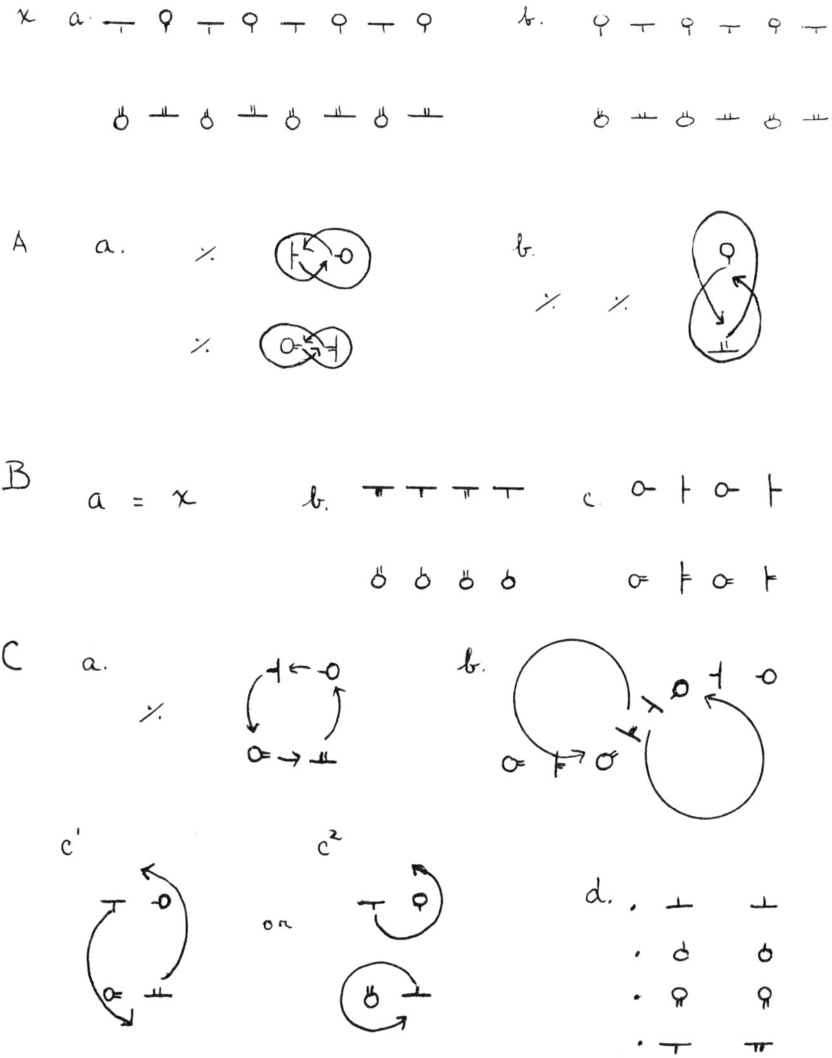

177

Figure 80 – Tesuque Xoxeye Quadruple Formations

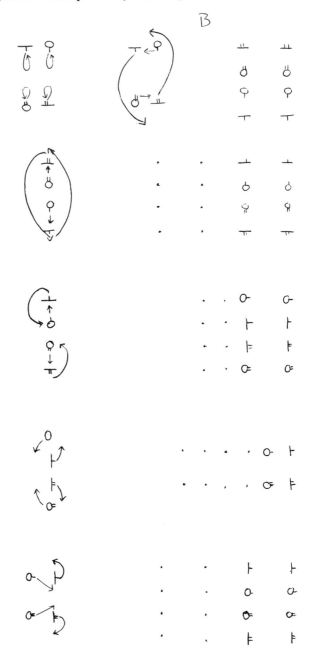

Figure 81 – Santa Clara Kwanshare

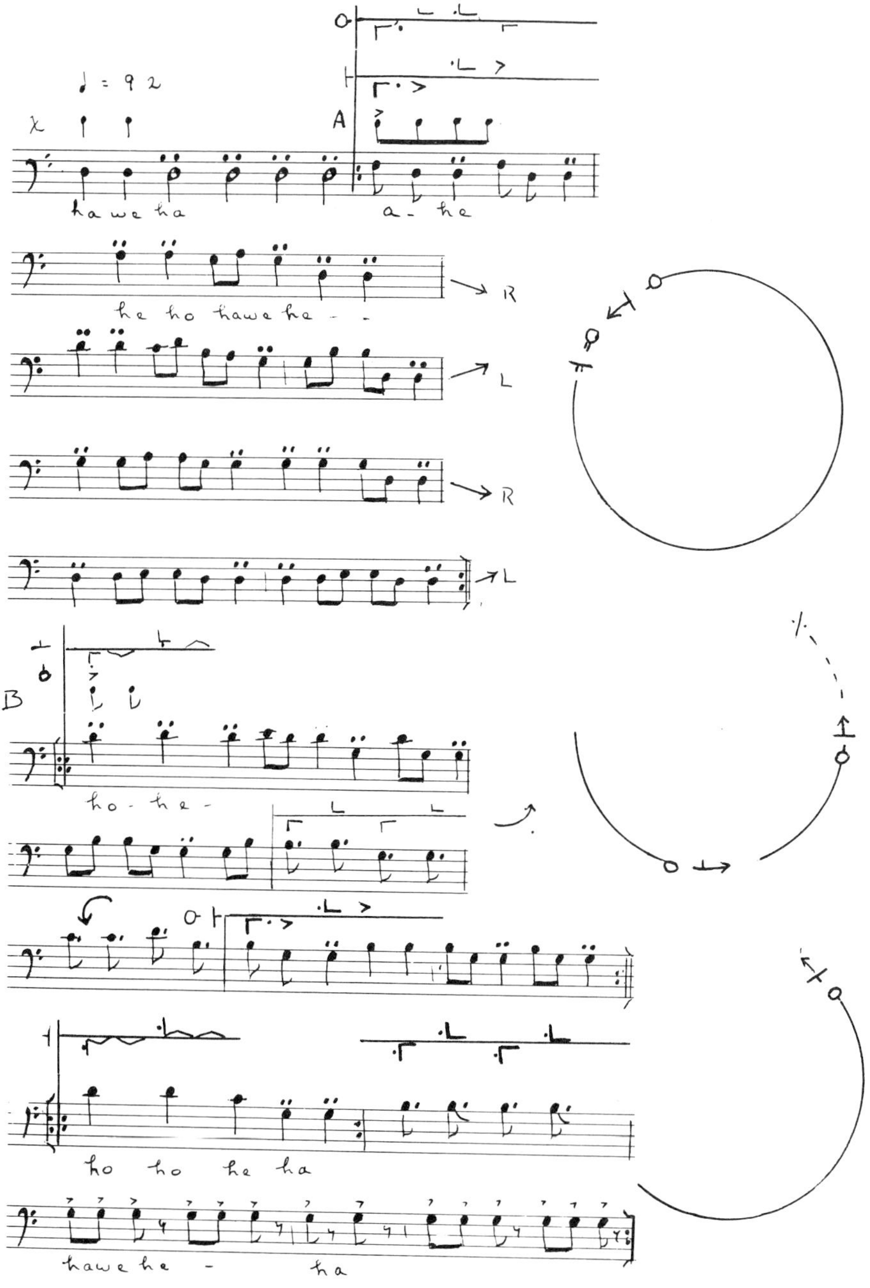

179

Figure 82 – Santa Clara Kwanshare (continued)

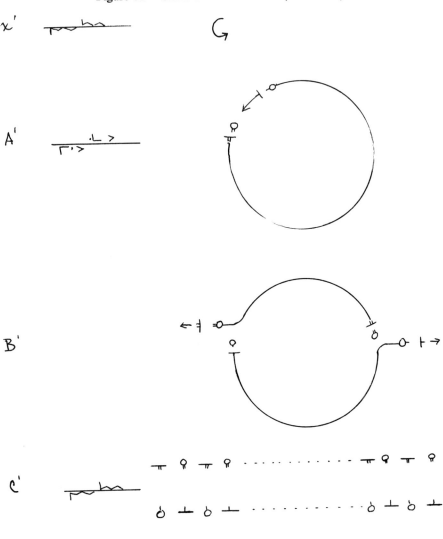

Figure 83 – Santa Clara Kwanshare (continued)

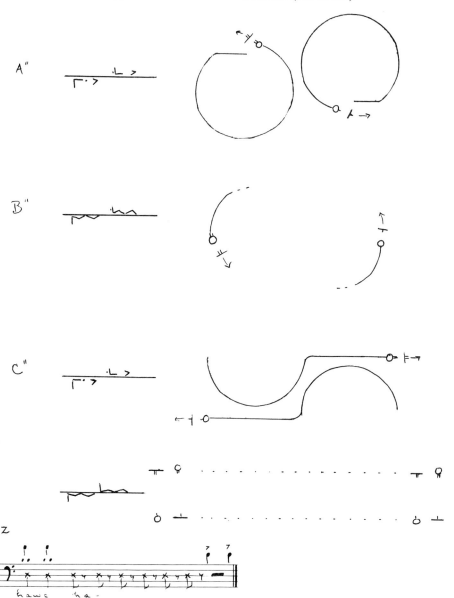

Figure 84 – San Juan Xoxeye (Slow Dance)

Figure 85 – San Juan Xoxeye (Fast Dance)

Figure 86 – San Juan Kwanshare Song

Shi shi wana Katsanoma yawi-

Chowe chowe leo leo

AA BB CC

hapimbe shi wana Kuyu tano ma yawiya —

Form |: A A B B C C :| y y B B C C y y B B C A A B B C C y

184

Figure 87 – San Ildefonso Yere

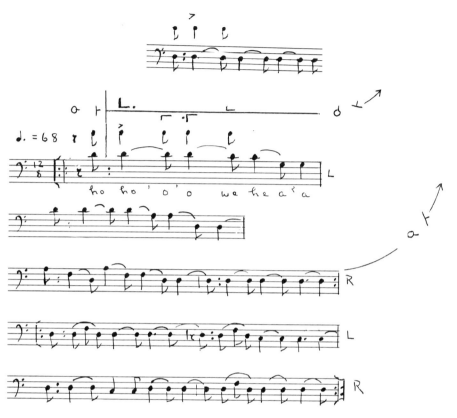

Chapter 15

IN THE FERTILE VALLEY THEY HAVE FLOWERS

TEMBISHARE or Harvest Dance

The Harvest Dance of San Juan and San Ildefonso is a Thanksgiving Ceremony to Mother Earth, *nanechukwiyo*, for fertility and for all agricultural crops. Of all Tewa plaza dances it is most closely integrated with the social and religious organization. It is sponsored by the *kosa* Society with the assistance of the other religious organizations in the pueblo. The laity may join, but usually only 25-30 dancers participate, in addition to the singers' chorus.

It is held every four or five years in late September, for instance on September 20, 1964. It must be on a Saturday or Sunday, because of the wage-earning men; so the final kiva practice takes place on the preceding Friday or Saturday night. There is only one long appearance, starting at about 11 A.M., with four complete performances at the four stations in the south, west, north, and east plazas, and one short song in the practice kiva. The dancers do not wear costumes as for *okushare* or *xoxeye*. But they put on their best Indian clothes. The men wear moccasins, a fancy shirt, good store pants, and a wreath of flowers. The women wear a black manta, wrap-around boots, an *ahigi* (small loose silk shawl tied around the neck and hanging down the back), and Hopi squash blossom hairdo with flowers.

The performers gather in front of the kiva (either kiva). To an entrance song by the separate chorus they dance in a meandering line into the plaza, into position. The traditional order in the file is:

1. Kosa Society, head and assistants
2. Summer Cacique with assistants or faithful laymen of the moiety
3. Winter Cacique with assistants or laymen of the moiety
4. Bear Society Priest and assistant
5. Kwirana Society
6. Game Priest, pingxeng
7. Governor, civil officers, war chief, and assistants
8. Womens' Society, kwiyo
9. Scalp Society Priest (obsolete)
10. Summer Moiety, headed by most faithful lay members.
11. Winter Moiety, headed by faithful male and female members.

186

"After the group has reached the first station, everyone remains in a stationary circular position, while they open bags of gifts. They throw gifts into the middle of the circle where spectators (Indian, Spanish and Anglo) make a mad dash for the gifts. I looked around for people from other pueblos and gave my gifts to them personally. Watermelons, musk melons, and squash are cast upon the ground to break, for Mother Earth.

"Anyone who has not prepared gifts may join the dance anytime. When there were many clowns, they used to 'catch' spectating males and place them in line at the end of the circle.

"The dancers in the circle move clockwise sidewards. They are in the same order as for the entrance. The chorus stands to one side, outside the circle. Each religious group is represented in the dance by its own special song. The songs are in sequence according to the appearance of each religious group. When a head of a religious society or a cacique is featured, he enters the center of the circle, and he and his assistants form a line. His relatives or members of his moiety may join in the line in the center, to 'help out.' First they face one way (say north), then they successively turn in the opposite direction to face, say, south. Men and women join this line, not necessarily in alternation." (Antonio Garcia).

As they side-step with the drum beat, the people in the circular formation swing both arms from side to side at waist level, palms extended and downwards. The principals in the center do the *antege* step in place. They gesture with the right hand, with the arm extended towards the front, right, face level. They move the hand L to R to L in a small arc, palm forward. The gestures may symbolize, respectively, an invocation to the earth and to the sky. But the Tewa have no clear concept of such symbolism.

The formation, direction, and gestures are unusual. So are the songs. The melodies are pitched lower than usual, with recurrent passages in the lowest range. They have a heavy, persistent, slow beat, pervading formulae, and special vocables "howe howe; hau hau." The entrance song alone does not use the formulae. It is faster than the ensuing songs and interpolates "hapimbe." The initial, central, and terminal formulae are marked x, y, and z in song 1. They are the same in the other songs. They alternate with variable melodic sections - usually just A, B, A', B', etc. - in many repeats, written below the songs. The clearest pattern of repeats, in the songs the *kosa,* is a fourfold repeat of the entire song. In the other songs the tendency is towards four repeats, however, with irregularities. The melodies have descending trends, with the highest point usually at the beginning of the first theme, thus quite different from line dance songs.

On the other hand, the song texts express the same ideas as the texts for *tunshare,* with some of the same expressions and also some new phrases. Many songs refer to flowers and crops, but some also mention deer, eagle and parrot tail feathers, or dew baskets.   Sometimes they refer to the performers of the specific episode, as the *kosa* or *kwirana.*

187

TEXTS FOR TEMBISHARE

Entrance Song - Vocables, with Keresan words in the second-to-last line -
"East, long time ago."
1. Kosa - x. (Vocables)
      A.   In the outskirts of the Pueblo, at blue sun lake
           Kosa men are singing beautifully.
      y.   (Vocables)
      B.   Beautifully they are singing.
      z.   (Vocables)

2. Summer Cacique - A. (Vocables). Who asked me to gather flowers?
      Dark corn girls asked me to gather yellow flowers.
      B. Who is urging me?
      C. Yellow corn boys, blue corn boys - filili-
      They urged me to gather dark flowers.

3. Winter Cacique - A. Shiwana
      B. Right here in San Juan over the kiva (are clouds).
      C. The oxua have flowers there.
      And then it rains in San Juan.

4. Bears - A. B. (Archaic). In turquoise village.
      A'. I have medicine herbs in turquoise village.
      B'. 1) Dance kilt, I made this right away.
      2) White, emroidered manta, I made this right away.
      I have medicine herbs.

5. Kwirana - A. Lots of kwirana, lots of watermelons, lots of muskmelons
      we planted, we harvested, we offered.
      (Archaic).
      B. (Vocables).

6. Game Priest - A. (Vocables).
      B. Somewhere at deer lake, Deer oxua boys are
      singing beautifully.
      C. Wampum stick flower; in the mist flowers are blooming
      beautifully.

7. Officers - A. Star flower baskets.
      B. In the heavens are baskets.
      C. They are eagle tails.
      (y B C z x A B) C'. They are parrot tails.

8. Women's Society - A. B. (Keresan and vocables).
   A'. Speckled corn maidens;
   they carry dew baskets on their heads.
   They are going to receive fertility
   because they are female.

9. Scalp Society - (Not recorded)

10. Summer Moiety - A. The shiwana are singing (Keresan).
    B. (Vocables)
    A'. Beyond the Pueblo atsikumu lake.
    1) Summer oxua boys have made it beautiful.
    2) Summer oxua girls have made flowers.

11. Winter Moiety - A. B. (Vocables) Shiwana
    C. (Vocables)
    A'. Beyond the Pueblo at flower lake
    B'. Flower raingods, boys, girls are making beautiful
    sounds.
    B". With their male breath they are producing white
    and red flowers.

Figure 88 – San Juan Tembishare: Entrance

190

Figure 89 – San Juan Tembishare: Dance for Kosa

191

Figure 90 – San Juan Tembishare: Dance for Summer Cacique

Figure 91 – San Juan Tembishare: Dance for Winter Cacique

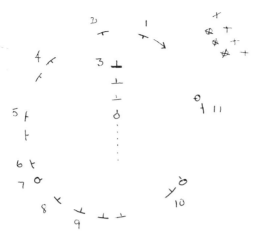

3.

shi — wa na shi —, wa na hi ya

shi shi wa na shi — wa na shi — wa na

ne we ne we o ke tema ko- re

o xu a o-o xu a xu a dim povi sa elang

o Ke i Kwa nang

x A y A z x B y B y a' z x B y B y a' y x A y A z x

Figure 92 – San Juan Tembishare: Bears

Figure 93 – San Juan Tembishare: Kwirana

194

Figure 94 – San Juan Tembishare: Game Priest

x A y A y B (A') z x B y B' y B' z x B y B y B' y B z x
A y A y B z x

Figure 95 – San Juan Tembishare: Scalp Society

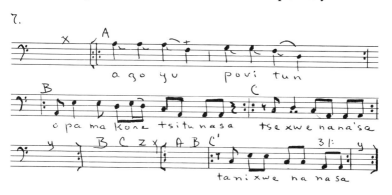

x |: A A B B C C y :| B C z x |: A B C' C' C' y :| B C z x

Figure 96 – San Juan Tembishare: Kwiyo

196

Figure 98 – San Juan Tembishare: Winter Moiety

197

Santa Clara Bull Dance at Puye (above), and Tesuque Buffalo Dance in 1921 (below)

Chapter 16

ABOVE THE DORMANT EARTH

BEAUTIFULLY GAME IS EMERGING

After the harvest comes the traditional hunting season - for Anglo hunters as well as Indians. The fall and winter appear appropriate times for animal dances. Traditionally the Pueblos held hunting rituals and dances while the earth slept, and they still hold many game animal dances at that time - Nambe's Elk Dance on October 4, animal mime during some Christmas and and Twelfth night celebrations, and the San Ildefonso Saint's Day January 23. However, more and more the Buffalo Dances are extending into the warm seasons. In 1957 the spring was filled with Buffalo Dances. And summer shows feature many animal dances. *Penshare* remains in its traditional timing - but *penshare* is distinct from the so-called Buffalo Dances.

KONSHARE or Buffalo Dance, Game Animal Dance

Buffalo impersonators may approach the pueblo at dawn as in the *penshare* prelude, but with a Buffalo Mother as decoy and with a cast of hunters in Plains costumes, or with herders in blankets (Spinden 1915:111, Roediger 1941:190). In the plaza dances the cast and the choreography show many variations. The salient types include:

Type 1. A basic cast of two Buffalo men, one or two Buffalo women, and a Hunter.

Type 2. Pairs of Buffalo men and women in multiple, up to six couples.

Type 3. Two Buffalo and one or two women, with two side lines of Deer or small Buffalo with one horn.

Type 4. Two to four Buffalo couples with a cortege of mountain Game Animals, Deer by twos, two Antelope, two Mountain Sheep, and, until recently, two Elk; the Buffalo distinguished by hoary heads and the Game Animals by antlers and other items of costuming.

Type 5. A line of young Buffalo with several young Mothers, called "Fertility Buffalo Dance" at Puye Cliffs shows.

The Buffalo always tread upright with a heavy gait, the Women with a lighter step. The Hunter (Game Priest) also dances upright, and, like the Buffalo men, he manipulates a rattle and a set of small bow-and-arrow. The Game Animals lean on foresticks. The Deer are dressed as in *penshare* and they stride as in the *penshare* Dawn entrance and the *ange'i,* or they bounce in place. The young Antelope run about at random. The Mountain Sheep gambol or they join the line of Deer.

The Buffalo group shows its meteorological symbolism in details which evidently have remained unchanged (Roediger 1941: 184; Dutton 1955:14). The men have serpentine lightning designs on their hide kilts, and the women wear bustles with sun symbols.

All types of *konshare* follow a traditional procedure, with three songs, performed by a separate chorus of singers and drummers. The first song, which is sometimes an Oklahoma or Jicarilla war dance tune, serves for the entrance into the plaza and for the final recessional to the next plaza or into the kiva. The second, "slow" song accompanies a slow dance which varies in choreography. The third "fast" song has equally variable choreography in two parts. The dance songs are traditional in each pueblo and are rarely newly composed. Nambe uses the same songs as the Santa Clara summer moiety. All have vocables.

EXAMPLES

Type 1. One woman is customary only in Tesuque (resembling Keresan custom). Santa Clarans dance the type with two Mothers at Puye. Two couples with an attendant danced in the San Ildefonso north plaza on Easter Sunday, 1957. They trod in a simple, C C circle during the slow dance, with quarter-turn pivots. During the fast dance they ambled forward and back, then they trod in the *konshare* step which combines *antege* and *sunu*. The couples circled each other. Whitman saw this basic "Hopi" type on March 14, 1937 in the south plaza (1947:137). Parsons saw it in January, 1926 in Santa Clara and San Juan (1929:196).

Type 2. On Easter Sunday (April 21), 1957, six Buffalo couples, without a Hunter, but with guards, represented the summer moiety in Santa Clara. After the entrance the singers grouped in the east plaza, facing east, while the dancers lined up in double file, facing the chorus. They readjusted this in the other plazas, by the conservative summer moiety plan.

The winter moiety featured two couples at Puye, July 25, 1964. They generally used the same formations and steps as the summer dancers in 1957, with two differences. As customary at Puye programs, they used only two songs, thus combined their entrance with the slow dance. During the fast dance they added an extra part, with oblique patterns. Their procedure (choreographed with music) was:

1. Slow Dance: Tread *(dikonyi)* in a C C circle, forward, then sideward, then forward, all facing the same way at all times.

2. Fast Dance:

200

A. To drum tremolo, amble forward, pivot and return, at right angles to the axis of the files; genuflex at every turn.

B. To duple beat - a. (same tune as A.) In place, do the *konshare* pawing step in place, pivoting from side to side in unison.

b. (new tune) Run obliquely right forward for a measure, sidle into place for a measure. On repeat, run and return left.

A. Reverse orientation with a parallel half-circuit, to tremolo.

B. As before, but facing the other way.

1. Exit with song and choreography of entrance.

Type 3. San Juan has two versions of the *ko'e*, Little Buffalo Dance. While there is always a central group of two Buffalo and one Mother, the side lines can be White or Black Buffalo, with appropriate kilts, all with one horn on the right side, four feathers next to the horn, small gourd and bow in R and L hand. They used to alternate with two appearances each in one day, representing, respectively, the winter and summer moieties. They appeared on New Year's and San Juan's Day. But they have been dwindling in popularity. In 1959 there were only four Little Buffalo, in 1961 and 1963 only two, as prelude to the San Juan's Day *Kwitara*. The choreography represents the full cast:

1. Slow Dance:

With *dikonyi*, tread in two files into plaza (south plaza) arranged as shown.

2. Fast Dance:

A. To tremolo, Big Buffalo lead files in opposite circuits; woman stays in place.

B. To duple beat (same tune), do *konshare* step in place.

A. B. Repeat in reversal.

This type is still a great favorite in San Ildefonso. Frank Turley reported a variant with side lines of Deer, and two Antelope and "Shepherds" following the Buffalo, on January 23, 1960 (communication). Usually, however, the side dancers are the one-horned Buffalo. This seems traditional. Photographs go back to 1893 (Spinden 1915: 102, 113-114). Parsons gives a good description of a variant in Tesuque, for the Saint's Day, November 12, 1926:

"At noon the dancers emerge from the Winter people's kiva - the choir down first as usual, the men to stand in two lines, the drummers in front. The dancers begin to dance as soon as they leave the ladder, taking positions in two lines vis-a-vis, eighteen men and women alternating in each line, thirty-six in all. After the short dance in front of the kiva they proceed in dance step to the singing of the choir along the road around the south side of the town. In this progress, as in later circuits, they are led by 'their father,' who during the dancing in place stands off a little distance from the dancers. . .

Above and Below: San Ildefonso Buffalo Dance

202

"Passing into the court, the two lines form at right angles to the spruce-set door of the house of the Winter Town chief. The door opens and out comes the Hunt chief, who is 'their father,' then the Fire Society chief from a rite of cleansing, then the two Buffalo Old Men with the Buffalo Woman between the men. Led by 'their father,' the Buffalo group dances a serpentine down the middle, the attendant lines executing a special dance movement, the women standing in place, the men stepping out first to one side of the line and then to the other and uttering sharp, shrill hoots or yelps. As soon as the Buffalo group reaches the end of the line, the movement changes, all the dancers facing now east, now west, and taking a lively stamping step, the men as usual stamping more vigorously than the women, who hold their right arms at right angles to the body, the left arm folded against it. The men make the half-turns to east and west with a quick forward nod of the body. Between these two dance movements - the serpentine figure and the hollow square or turning figure - the standard bearers lead their respective lines around in a circling quadrille-like movement. These three movements are repeated three times." (1929:201 and 1939, II:836-840).

The dancers repeat the three-part dance in front of the church, in front of a spruce-tree in the court, in front of the Winter Man's house. Then the Buffalo group retires to his house, the two attendant lines retire to the kiva. They appear again before dinner, twice after dinner.

Type 4. While this description sounds eleborate, the mixed Game Animal Dance can have even more complex choreography. Nambe presents a simple version, with two Buffalo couples, and small Deer, one pair at Puye 1964, two pair on October 4, 1963 at Nambe. The plan for the fast dance was:

A. To tremolo, Buffalo amble forward and return, while Deer stride to the other end of the Buffalo double file.

B. To beat, Buffalo do *konshare* step in place, while Deer double-bounce in place, leaning on their foresticks.

A. B. Repeat in reverse.

At Puye the Nambe dancers and the Santa Clara summer progressives present more elaborate versions, to the music in the following example.

On Sunday, March 3, 1957 dancers of the summer moiety performed a Game Animal Dance to traditional songs, without any curtailment, and with an expanded cast. The dancers were: 4 Buffalo men, 4 Buffalo women in the lead; then 24 Deer in double file, from adults to five-year-old boys; 2 Mountain Sheep, 2 young Antelopes. In addition, they had a large chorus, gesticulating during the singing. The movements between the groups were at times very contrapuntal:

1.   Entrance (into first plaza) from practice kiva, chorus leading, then standing to let the dancers pass; singers and dancers walking in direct paths, the Game Animals meandering.
2.   Slow Dance, with chorus in place, west of dancers.
A. C.   *Dikonyi* by Buffalo group, toward chorus, forward, then sideward, then forward, in double file, facing other line during side steps. Animals circle with *dipenyi.* Face about on y.
B. C.   All reverse and change places by *interchange* pattern shown on diagram, the Buffalo with parallel semi-circuit, the Deer and Mountain Sheep with opposite circling. Face about on zy.
B. C.   Back to original orientation, sideward, then forward.
3.   Fast Dance.
A.   Tremolo,Buffalo forward and back, Deer circle.
B.   Beat, Buffalo with *konshare* step, at right angles to orientation, in place; during b pivot in installments, swing right arm forward on each phrase beginning; then *t'a;* repeat ab.
A'.   Change orientation and places with Game Animals by *interchange.*
B'.   Like B., facing other way.
A".   Reverse by *interchange.*
B".   Like B.
1.   To entrance song, all meander to next plaza, chorus leading and letting dancers pass to their stations for the slow and fast dances.
The dances recur in each plaza as described, with adjustments to the orientation and available space.

Type 5. This variant, limited to the Puye programs, differs from the other Buffalo dances in several ways. The boy Bulls lean on foresticks. After the entrance, in a line, the boys and girls dance as follows, in a reversal of the usual procedure for a Fast Dance:
A.   To a duple beat, all paw the ground, facing plaza center.
B.   To a tremolo, the girls balance in place, while the boys meander forward and return, at right angles to the line, moaning "mu-uh." In 1963 they charged members of the audience, especially aggressive photographers.They did not repeat this comic play in 1964.

KERESAN COMPARISON

If Santa Clara's Type 4 is intricate, it is nothing compared to the complexity and variety of Keresan Game Animal Dances. The Tewa produce counterpoint by synchronizing different themes of the groups. The Keresans do this too. In addition they invent new combinations and evolutions (Kurath 1958b:446). For each appearance they devise new designs and

204

they repeat the complete set in mirror design (Kurath in Lange 1959:539-545). San Felipe may have ten distinct choreographies on February 2. Finally, the Keresans, at any rate Cochiti, rotate Game Animal and Eagle Dance in a regular three-year cycle on January 6, while the Tewa schedule for midwinter is optional.

Figure 99 – Ground Plans: Types of Konshare

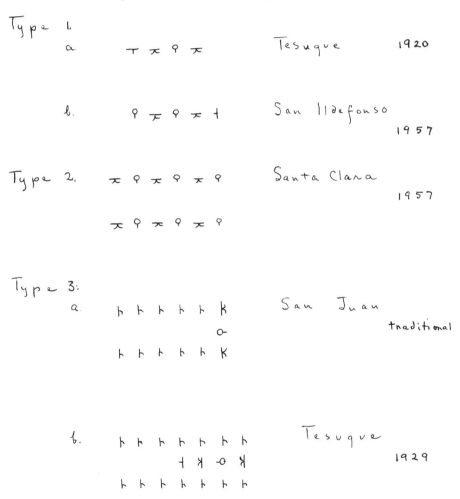

Figure 100 – Ground Plans: Types of Konshare (continued)

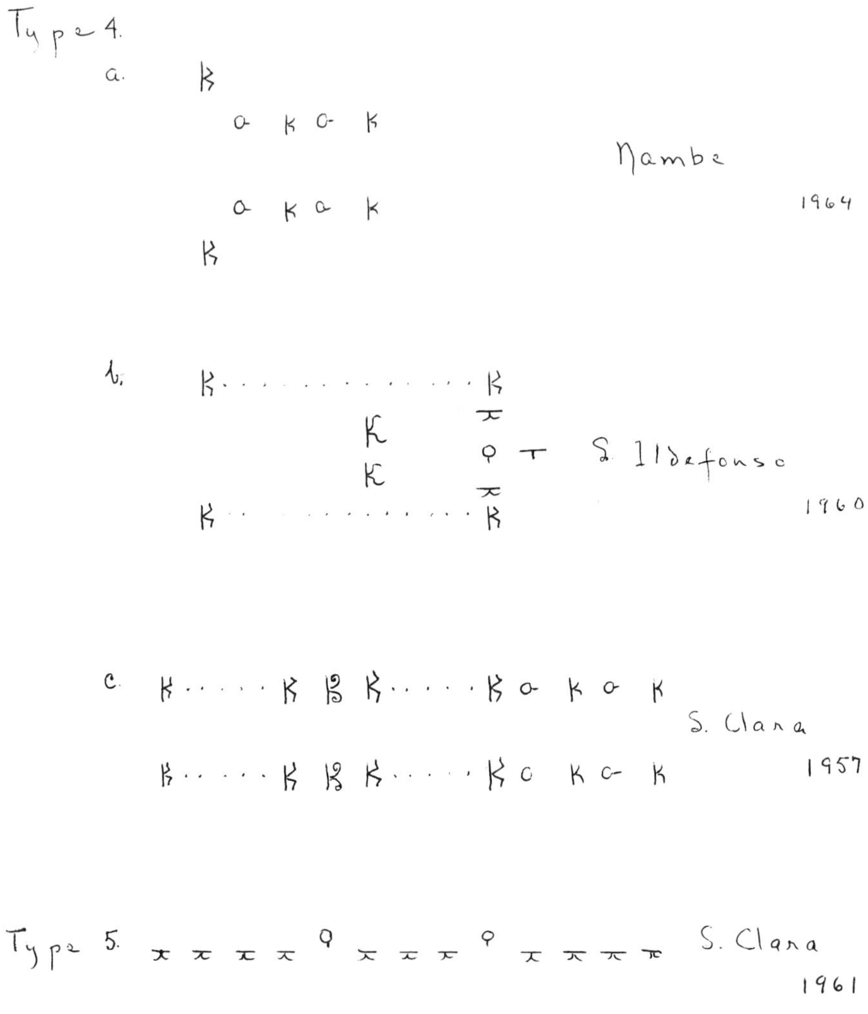

Type 4.

a.   ꝁ

    a ꝁ a- ꝁ

                              Nambe

    a ꝁ a ꝁ   1964

  ꝁ

b.   ꝁ · · · · · · · · · · · · ꝁ

                  ꝁ   ᙮

                  ꝁ   ᳡ ⊤ S. Ildefonso

    ꝁ · · · · · · · · · · · · ꝁ   1960

c. ꝁ · · · · · ꝁ ꝁ ꝁ · · · · ꝁ a ꝁ a ꝁ

                                  S. Clara

  ꝁ · · · · · ꝁ ꝁ ꝁ · · · · ꝁ c ꝁ c- ꝁ   1957

Type 5. ⊼ ⊼ ⊼ ⊼ ᳡ ⊼ ⊼ ⊼ ᳡ ⊼ ⊼ ⊼ ⊼ S. Clara

                                         1961

206

Figure 101 – Konshare Type 2: Santa Clara Winter People

Figure 102 – Konshare Type 2: Santa Clara Winter People (continued)

2. Fast Dance

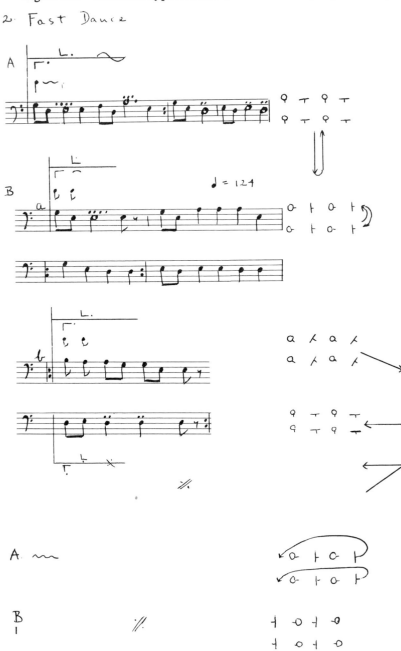

208

Figure 103 – Konshare Type 3: San Juan Ko'e (Slow Dance)

Figure 104 – Konshare Type 3: San Juan Ko'e (Fast Dance)

Figure 105 – Konshare Type 4: Nambe Game Animal Dance

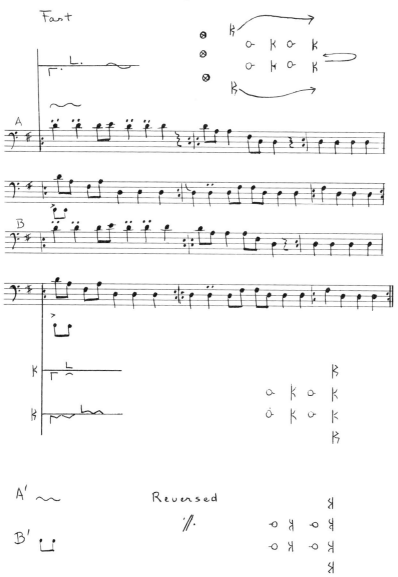

Santa Clara Game Animal Dance, slow dance (above), and interchange

Figure 106 – Konshare Type 4: Santa Clara Game Animals, Summer People (Entrance)

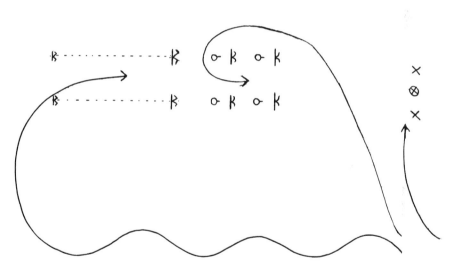

Figure 107 – Konshare Type 4: Santa Clara Game Animals (Slow Dance)

Figure 108 – Konshare Type 4: Santa Clara Game Animals (Fast Dance)

Figure 109 – Konshare Type 4: Santa Clara Game Animals (Plaza Circuit)

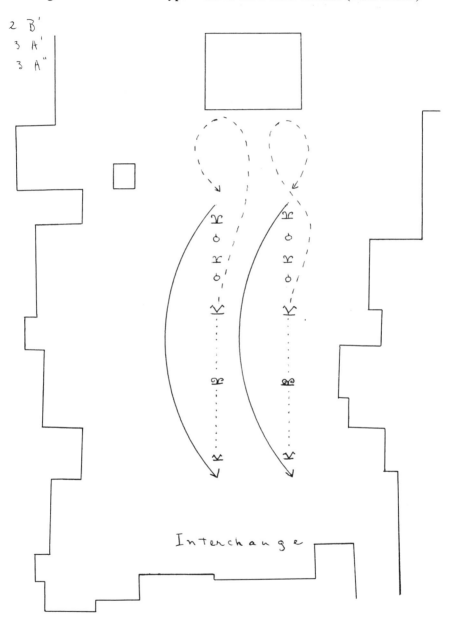

Figure 110 – Konshare Type 4: Santa Clara Game Animals (Plaza Circuit)

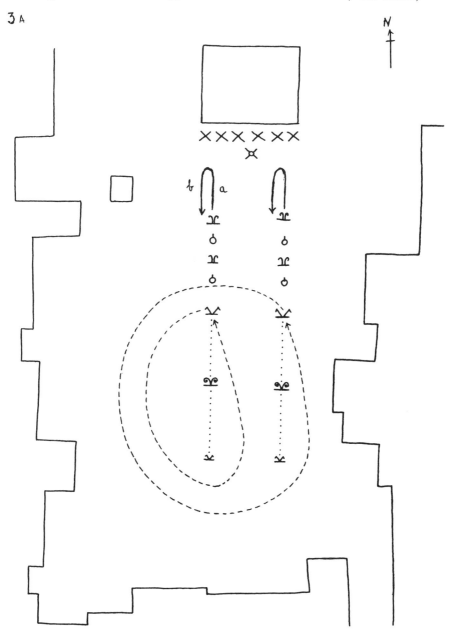

San Ildefonso Eagle Dance, part 3, the hop

218

Chapter 17

THEY COME WITH THUNDER AND LIGHTNING

The Keresan ritualists associate Eagle Dances with Game Animal Dances, thus representing creatures of the sky and earth. The Tewa ceremonialists do not similarly associate these two dances, which use different movements. They are more apt to connect *konshare* with *kwitara*. However, all Pueblos notice the structural similarity between the three ceremonies.

TSESHARE or Eagle Dance

Tseshare is not a hunting dance, nor necessarily a winter dance. Rather, it is traditionally an early spring dance, and at present it may appear at any time. The eagle connotes sky powers. "Wings are symbolic of sunbeams." (Dutton 1963:57, n. 197). "The eagle is supposed to have direct intercourse with the sky powers, and is much venerated. It is not uncommon, even now, to see specimens of the Golden or American Eagle kept in captivity in the pueblos, where they are treated with every mark of respect. The Eagle Dance is a dramatization of the relationship believed to exist between the eagle and man and deific powers. The young men are costumed as eagles, one a male and the other female, and in the course of the dance they imitate almost every movement of these great birds." (Dutton 1955: 14).

Tseshare used to have curative powers. It still has potency for rain, thunder, and lightning, analagous to the "Thunderbird" of the Great Plains. There is, however, no evidence of a connection with the "Plumed Serpent" concept of the Pueblos. While it is losing ritual prestige, it is in the ascendency as a show dance, because of its beauty.

Tseshare has the same structure as *konshare;* in its complete form an entrance, slow dance, fast dance in two parts, and exit. The song type is also the same, with descending trend and sequence. However, each Tewa pueblo uses a special set of songs, and each version shows a different combination of basic movement themes. The circling entrance is generally the same everywhere, but the pueblos vary other themes. For the five pueblos, the themes correspond as follows in the labels on the choreographies:

Flex and Extend (flap wings)	Santa Clara	2A
	San Juan	2Ab
	San Ildefonso	3Ab

219

	Nambé	2A
	Tesuque	2A
Sway from Side to Side	Santa Clara	3A
	San Juan	2A
	San Ildefonso	2A
	Nambé	1
	Tesuque	2A
Hop to Side on One Foot	Santa Clara	2B
	San Juan	2B
	San Ildefonso	3B
	Tesuque	2B
Double Circle	San Juan	2C
	Nambé	2B

The choreographies show other differences, the greater length of the Santa Clara version, the use of three men in the Nambé recurrence of circlings, and the quadruple alignment in Tesuque.

Santa Clara - Two Men
1. Sedate entrance in C C circle, with toe-heel step. z walk forwards.
2. A. Fold and open wings, in place side by side, to tremolo.
   B. Hop to right on L foot, tilting L; reverse, to duple beat.
   z. Flex by degrees to crouch, then extend to erect posture.
   This is supposed to represent priming for flight. Repeat.
3. A. Sway to right and extend, to left and extend, with forward step of knee-bend and straight, to a triple beat. (Looking for prey.)
   B. Walk ahead in meander, one man behind the other.
   A-. z. Like A.
2. As before.
1. Exit like entrance, reversed.

San Juan - Two Men
1. Entrance in C C circle, with toe-heel step.
2. A. Walk in circle, swaying from side to side, flexing and extending. Flex to crouch by degrees, and extend. Tremolo.
   B. Men side by side, hop to R, then to L. Repeat. Double Beat.
   C. Hop in double circle (2 men in opposite directions), swaying to L and R, then with level wings in a double bounce. Repeat.
   Hop on R, pivoting L; double bounce and hop in C circle. Reverse.
   A. Like A. B. Like B.
1. Exit, reversing entrance.

220

San Ildefonso - Two Men
1. Enter as in other pueblos.
2. Double bounce in C C circle.
3. A. a. Walk in circle with sway.
    b. Flex and extend by degrees.
    B. Hop to R on L foot; reverse. Flex and extend. Repeat.
1. Exit.

Nambé - Three Men
1. Enter in file, C C, swaying R and L, with step-bend, step-bend.
2. A. Flex and extend, while walking bouncy, forward. Tremolo.
    B. With bouncy walk, circle R, tilting R, in unison. Duple beat.
    Reverse three times.
1. Exit with entrance song and step.

Tesuque - Four Men
1. A. Enter in pairs in a straight line, with a slow step-bounce.
    B. Cross by twos, meandering and swaying R to L.
2. A. Facing by pairs, flex and extend. Tremolo.
    B. All facing same direction, in a square, hop R and L in rhythm -
    3 hops R, 3 L, 7 R, 3 L, 3 R, 7 L, 7 R - always landing on both
    feet and holding a count at end of each phrase.
(Choreographed from silent film by Portia Mansfield).

The differences have local reasons, also, in part, reasons of derivation.
The Santa Clara version - not the only one in the pueblo - reached the
pueblo from the Hopi 35 years ago, thanks to the Hopi-Tewa (see Chabot
1944a). It is a specialty of the winter people, though a summer moiety
singer made the tape recording I used. The San Juan version is of Laguna
origin. It is recognizable partly by the realistic mask with beak - a Laguna
earmark (Dutton 1955:15). In general, details of costuming distinguish the
local versions, an aspect which I did not investigate. (See Roediger 1941:
195).

EARLIER TEWA VERSIONS

The themes are obviously traditional, and obviously variable in order,
when one considers earlier descriptions. On Christmas Day in 1927,
Parsons witnessed an Eagle Dance in Santa Clara. Two men emerged with
five singers from the house of the winter chief. They approached each
other, swayed, hopped, and circled. They danced four times, in each plaza
(1929:206-207). In 1930 Buttree published a Tesuque version, with a

musical score. She described a successive, circular entrance, then a "menacing" wing flapping, circling, hopping, and swaying exit (1930:60). In 1931 the Evans sisters described a San Ildefonso version, with a different song from the enclosed. First the two Eagles circled C C with a chant to tremolo; then, to a slow song, they circled with a toe-heel in opposite directions; then to a bi-partite, fast song, they swayed from side to side and squatted low, hopped to the side, rotating their wings; finally they circled out (50). The only recognizable previous version is a San Ildefonso recording of the same song I have choreographed (Ethnic Folkways FE 4420, Band 5).

VERSIONS TO THE EAST

The spectacular mime has captivated many tribal members in the Plains and Woodlands, not to speak of White boy scouts. The Eagle Dance has become indispensable in all shows, from Oklahoma to at least Toronto and Manitoulin Island. The only Algonquians who have performed the song and dance accurately are two Meskwaki brothers, Charles and Frank Pushetonequa. Charles learned it as a student in the Santa Fe Indian School. Algonquians in Michigan and Ontario have diluted the dance, using any old song, hopping ad lib, and inventing their own scenarios. They portray an eagle swooping on its prey, or being shot and dying. They copy the costume.

Figure 111 – Santa Clara Eagle Dance (Tseshare)

Figure 112 – Santa Clara Eagle Dance (continued)

heye - weyeyeye heye he ya' a ya'a he ya

hene ya'a — hene ya hi ya

heye -

224

Figure 113 – Santa Clara Eagle Dance (continued)

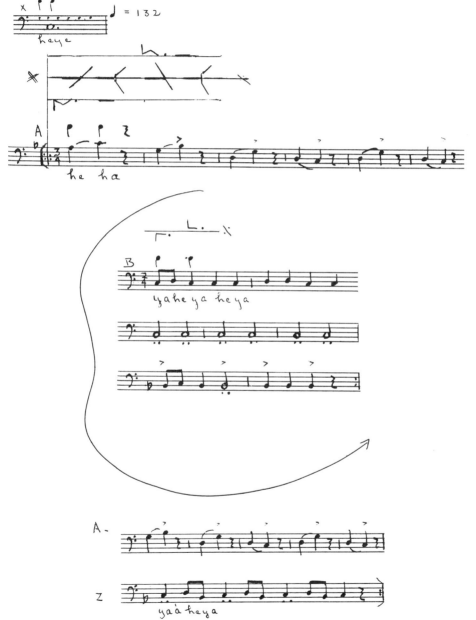

Figure 114 – San Juan Eagle Dance

Figure 115 – San Juan Eagle Dance (continued)

Figure 116 – San Juan Eagle Dance (continued)

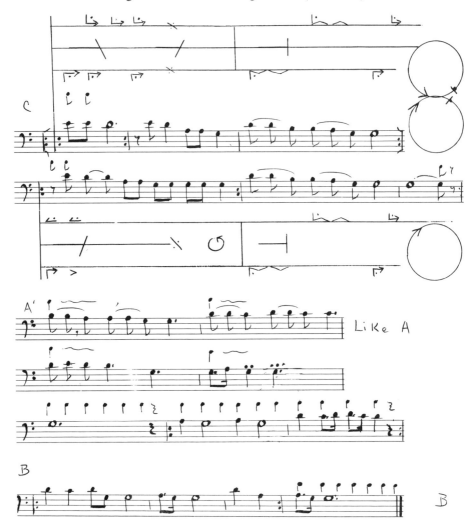

228

Figure 117 – San Ildefonso Eagle Dance (Entrance Song)

Santa Clara Eagle Dance at Puye, part 1, the entrance

Figure 118 – San Ildefonso Eagle Dance (continued)

Figure 119 – Nambe Eagle Dance

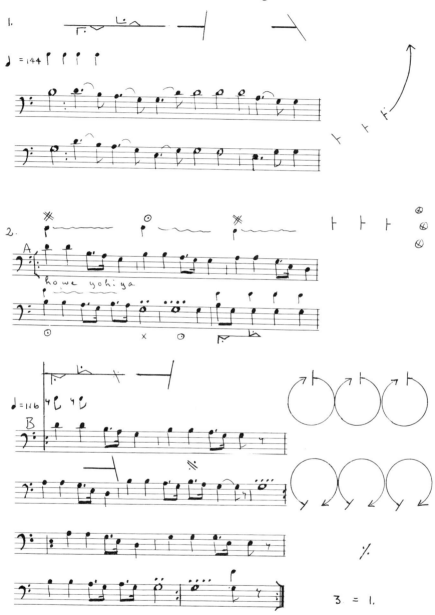

Figure 120 — Tesuque Eagle Dance Choreography

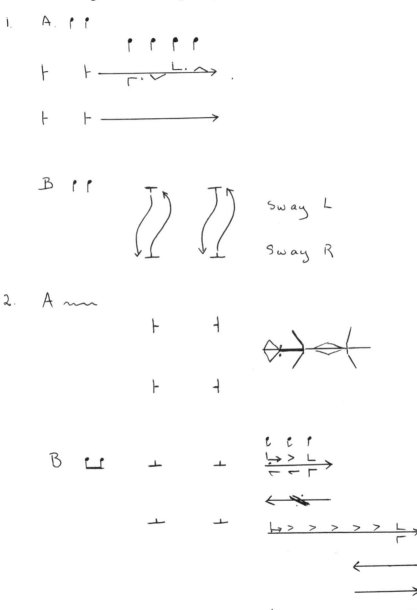

Chapter 18

PLEASURE DANCES FOR ANY SEASON

A number of dances can appear at any time of year, for the entertainment of spectators or the pleasure of participants or both. Dances like *kwitara, tséshare, ba'a,* and *pangshare* belong to the secular category, though *kwitara* has a tinge of sanctity. They all have vague allusions to war and peace. They are for groups of mixed couples. In the first three the men wear Oklahoma costumes.

KWITARA or Comanche Dance; formerly *Fraseshare* or French Dance.
Structurally *kwitara* belongs to the same type as *konshare* and *tseshare* Eagle Dance, with the same kind of songs by a separate chorus. Choreographically it resembles *konshare.* It has been replacing *konshare* and *xoxeye* in the Saint's Day dancing at San Juan and Tesuque, and it has long had a place in the Saint's Days of Santa Clara and San Ildefonso. In 1963 it alternated with *konshare* at the Nambe October 4 fiesta. It is an inevitable feature of shows, alongside other dances of its type.

On many occasions it is associated with very secular features. During Saint's Days all pueblos permit concession stands. San Juan has a carnival outside the dance plazas, and the inhabitants celebrate with drinking parties after *kwitara.* However, Tesuque admits no such features. *Kwitara* is a dignified performance, for the well-being of the people - a generalized supplication for the pueblo's welfare.

The spirited and colorful dance is supposed to emulate the fierce Comanche, as the alternate name implies. Some natives think that it started as a victory dance after a raid by the Comanche two centuries ago. At times this connotation becomes evident, as in the 1943 celebration during World War II, on the Saint's Day. At shrines there were banners for men sent home from Air Corps bases, and dancers wore V symbols for victory (Chabot 1944b). Comanche associations appear in song words, as "wiketaya" (meaning unknown), in the men's steps, and in their costumes. There is much whooping and yelling.

The general plan is very similar in all pueblos on all occasions, as illustrated from San Juan:
1.   Entrance from kiva (either kiva). The dancers are in two files, two men, two women, as in *xoxeye.* The chorus follows them. There may be 4 couples or as many as 20 (40 dancers).
2.   Slow Dance, to song with slow, even beat. The double file meanders

in a C C circuit into place, with a stately tread like *dikonyi.*

3.   Fast Dance, with bi-partite structure.

A. To tremolo, all amble back and forth at right angles to dance line (NS, if line is EW). They genuflex at each change of direction.

y. Transition with duple beat, men priming for next part with hops in place.

B. With the same melody as for A, men hop back and forth between the pairs of women, with pendulum action, NS. They flex and extend their bodies, yelling; at phrase ends they face about and dip and raise small banners. The women gently balance from foot to foot, in place, with small pivots from side to side.

A'. The two male leaders guide the lines in opposite (heraldic) semi-circuits, to face the other way.

B'. In the new placement, the men hop back and forth as before, with a simple Oklahoma war dance step.

1.   With the first song, the performers file into the next station, or into the kiva.

There are local differences, especially in the songs. Each pueblo, in fact in San Juan each singer, has special songs, some old, some new, all in a style resembling Oklahoma dance songs (see Kurath 1961:6). Each pueblo follows its own circuit customs. San Juan *kwitara* uses the north and south plazas (Figure 7). Tesuque dancers use two stations at right angles in the one plaza (Figure 12). In the Puye performances Santa Clara's summer people use from two to five stations. On July 23, 1961 they were so animated that they added a fifth performance to the four-fold plaza circuit. Santa Clarans file to the reversed position with a parallel semi-circuit. In the slow dance they have more *t'a* than other pueblos. Nambe men swing their banners sharply up and down during the turns in the fast dance, while other pueblo men swing them in an "8" design. In all pueblos except Tesuque, small boys and girls join the ranks.

The costume variations are individual rather than local. The women fit a Tewa-type costume to their Tewa steps, with wrapped boots and mantas. But they prepare silken mantas and shiny capes in many colors. On their sleek hairdo they fasten a feather cluster over the left ear. The men wear kilts, vertical strips of bells, bustles in many colors, and a choice of roaches or war bonnets. They do not use long leggings as in Santa Clara in the 20's (Parsons 1929:208) nor do they carry guns as in the San Juan Frase Share (ibid.:209). They avoid the miscellany of an Oklahoma war dance, in costumes and steps.

TSESHARE or Dog Dance

In this show dance the music, choreography, and costuming are nicely

234

Above and Below: Comanche Dance at San Ildefonso (ca. 1930)

235

Comanche Dance at Nambe

Santa Clara Comanche Dance performed at Puye (1961)

236

simplified. Yet they retain the essence of the "bi-partite" structure and the Plains-derived style. The general plan is:

1. Entrance of two or four couples of young men and women in single file, alternating; the women holding their partner on the leash of a hand-woven Tewa belt. To a fused entrance-and-slow song, they meander into their position in the plaza (Puye as observed).

2. A. To tremolo, the youths, on the leash, tread back and forth in small arcs, limited because of the small radius of the belt.

A. B. To a beat, they hop in place or in arcs.

A'. Same or variant, as A.

B'. Same or variant, as B.

Now as to the variants: Two Santa Clara youths arc in opposite directions during A and B, then they converge and diverge during A' and B'. Children, by fours, group in a square, girls on the outside. During A the boys scramble for coins that young women toss on the ground. During A B they hop from foot to foot, with body flexion and extension.

Two San Juan youths, in artistic black kilts and collars, with small roaches and tiny banners, pivot apart and together during A, raising and lowering the R hand with the banner in measure 2, 4, 6, 8. The girls hold the belts loosely. Only the youths progress slightly. On B they use the same pattern, but with low leaps and larger arcs. Repeat. All exit as they entered.

The "Dog Dance" is also called the Tanoan Peace Dance. Also, it has the same choreography as the Nambé Snake Dance, except that there are no girls or belts in the Snake Dance. We decline to unravel the enigma of nomenclature. (Evans 1931 describes the Dog Dance of San Ildefonso, with a song similar to San Juan's.)

BA'A or Belt Dance

The Belt Dance also doubles as a Tanoan Peace Dance. It was a scene from an ancient peace drama where two leaders decided an issue by combat for two men, and where episodes of war were enacted. The drama concluded with the braiding of a peace belt (Hewett 1930: 131-132). Some Tewa say that it symbolizes family ties. In any event, the present dance has no drama of war, just a two-part scene of belt weaving.

Three youths and three girls, or three couples of children use the Tewa hand woven belts. Each girl holds one end of a belt, and her partner holds the other end. In that respect *ba'a* resembles *tséshare.* In other respects *ba'a* differs. It has an entrance and a dance song, and the songs are descendingly sequential, but they are not bipartite, with drum tremolo and beat. In Santa Clara and San Ildefonso the songs and dances differ somewhat, in addition to a lower pitch of the Santa Clara songs. The procedures are as follows:

237

Santa Clara

1. Entrance - The three couples *antege* in a single, alternating file, in a C C circle. (Children just walk). Boys hold one end of belts, then at end of the song, each girl pivots and thereby winds the belt around her waist, then unwinds.

2. Dance - Partners hold two ends of belt. While the girls *antege* in place, the boys weave a braid as in a maypole dance, but with the pattern of an English "hey" for three couples. On the song repeat they unwind the braid. Traditionally the youths should hop with *yandewa* step.

1. Exit like entrance.

San Ildefonso

1. Entrance - The three couples describe a wide arc in pairs. The girls walk with small steps. The boys toe-heel and change to a trot during a rhythmic change, as shown. At song's end the girls pivot for the belt-winding around their waists, as in Santa Clara.

2. During the first song repeat, the girls stand in a row, while the boys, each holding a belt, hop away from the girls and back to them. On the second repeat, the partners hold the belts and the boys weave them as in Santa Clara. They leap during a brief rhythmic change. On the third repeat they unwind the braid.

1. Exit as they entered.

Evidently the increasing popularity of this excellent show piece is limited to Santa Clara and San Ildefonso. Children perform it on Puye Cliffs, not always with great precision. On January 6, 1964 they danced it in Santa Clara Pueblo. Children of the San Ildefonso north plaza performed it on March 15, 1964; youths danced it for the "Benefit" public programs on July 19, 1964. It has spread to White Indian teenagers as far east as Michigan. It is well suited to such shows because it lacks sanctity and excells as a nice picture. Boys always wear Oklahoma war dance costumes. Tewa girls wear mantas, but White girls prefer Plains costumes.

PANGSHARE or Captive's Dance

Pangshare is also a couple dance; but it is a social dance. It rarely appears in shows (at Nambe Falls, July 4, 1963). It is not fancy, nor is it costumed. It is for fun. After a wedding or other festive, ecclesiastical event, sometimes the evening after a show, the Tewa and their guests may dance *pangshare.* They wear ordinary clothes.

It is a very hybrid series of dances, with five parts of obviously different derivations, each part blended with the local Tewa style:

1. "Grand March," with two files proceeding in opposite directions; forward *antege* step. (Fusion of Tewa circuit and Anglo "Grand March" before a square dance). Any number of couples can participate.

238

2. Double file of men and women in separate lines; *antege* to one side parallel, face-to-face, then to other side. Resembles Rain Race Dance which, however, is for men. Also resembles the Isleta Hunci (Densmore 1957:73-76).

3. Couples in two separate files, face-to-face. Men approach women during A, place R hand on partner's shoulder and pivot C C during A'. Reverse (hand on R shoulder, pivot C) during A. Return to place during A'. Repeat whole dance as often as desired. (See last Chapter on derivation.)

4. A "Waltz." In ballroom position, couples circle the room C C. The step-close (pause) and triple-meter song blend Tewa and European patterns (Fig. 135).

5. A Round Dance. This resembles the *tembishare* pattern in a C circling, face to center with a side step, but it has no connection with *tembishare*. It is a Tewa adaptation to the Fortynine and Victory Rounds of Oklahoma. Arm-in-arm, dancers progress L with a limping step to an iambic beat. The illustrative songs by Juan Chavarria are from Oklahoma and from the Wisconsin Winnebago, due to visits. With these and other songs and also original compositions, Tewa couples can end a *pangshare*. Or they can spend an evening on Puye after a show with just Round Dances.

The Tewa puzzle over the questions of etymology and of origins. Does the term, "captive's dance," refer to a former war captive who introduced the dance or a section of the suite; or does it signify the women, who are held captive in the pivot of the third section? On this question I pronounce no opinion.

But formal analysis suggests an accumulation of the five parts from as many origins, perhaps Ute, certainly White and modern Oklahoman. The dances show varying degrees of Pueblo-ization. Part 1 uses *antege* and t'a. Parts 2 and 3 also use variants of *antege,* along with foreign features, such as contact between partners. This feature, which derives from European social dancing, is more prominent in the "Waltz" or "Vals." The blend of native and European step and rhythm is very clear in this fourth part. The last part has remained close to the prototype, the modern Pan-Indian Round Dance of Oklahoma tribes. It is separable from the rest of the *pangshare* suite and can be danced on various social occasions by itself. Also, the songs may appear without dancing when a group of boys get together and "feels like bursting into song " (Garcia). On such occasions the men and boys may compose new songs in the Oklahoma style or in a semi-Pueblo style (see the report by Roberts). The mixture extends to the introduction of English texts.

PAN-INDIAN DANCES IN TEWA TERRITORY

The Round Dance belongs to another conglomerate which developed in Oklahoma within the last century, an aggregate of dances which includes the Grass, alias War or Kiowa Dance, Stomp or Snake Dance, and others. The Tewa have introduced the War Dances in shows, with songs resembling the Round Dance type, but with different choreography. The Tewa find them suitable for uncompromisingly tourist occasions, as in Manitou Springs (Colorado) shows, and they encourage their execution by youngsters desirous of exhibiting fancy steps. The Tewa have accepted the Round Dance as a social affair, but they do not include it in shows, as do more easterly tribes. They have ignored the antiphonal Stomp Dances.

It is unlikely that the Pueblos will integrate any of the Pan-Indian repertoire into their ceremonialism. In the first place, the dances were secular before they reached the Tewa, though they probably derive from ritual Scalp Dances of the Plains and certainly from rituals of Woodland Indians. In the second place, Pan-Indianism developed in Oklahoma because of the proximity of many unrelated tribes and because of a psychological need. To the Oklahomans the dances are symbols of their Indianness, and also are important factors in inter-tribal gatherings. For the Tewa such problems do not exist. They have a rich repertoire of their own and do not need dance symbols of tribal pride, as do tribes with long-dwindling ceremonialism (Kurath 1957a, 1959b). They do not need the imports for shows or sociability. They perform them for fun, with zest and skill.

Figure 121 – San Juan Kwitara

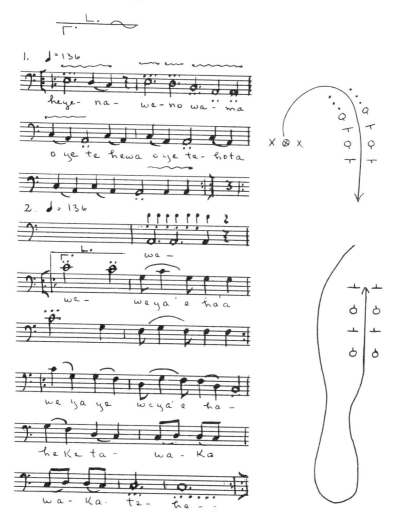

Figure 122 – San Juan Kwitara (continued)

242

Figure 123 – San Juan Kwitara (continued)

Figure 124 – San Juan Kwitara (continued)

Figure 125 – Santa Clara Kwitara Songs

Figure 126 – San Juan Dog Dance

Figure 127 – Santa Clara Dog Dance

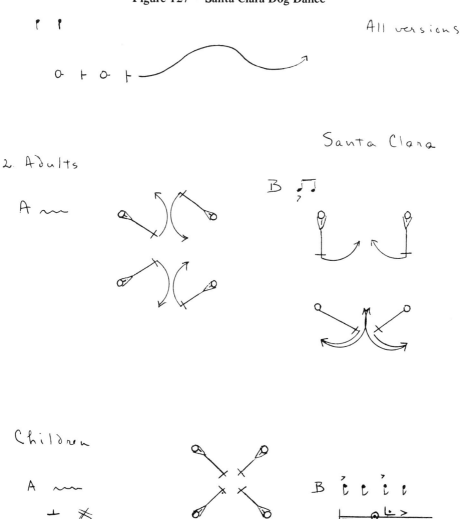

All versions

a ⊢ a ⊢

Santa Clara

2. Adults

A ∿

B ♪♪

Children

A ∿

B ♩ ♩ ♩ ♩

Figure 128 – Santa Clara Ba'a Belt Dance

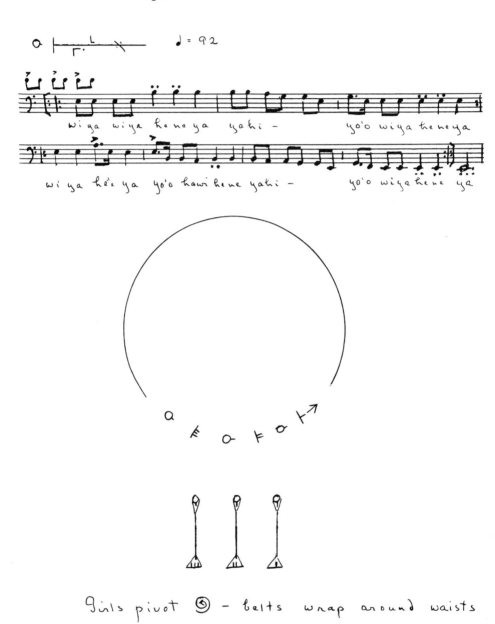

wi ya wi ya ke ne ya yahi – yo'o wi ya ke ne ya

wi ya ke'e ya yo'o hawi he ne yahi – yo'o wi ya ke ne ya

Girls pivot ⟳ – belts wrap around waists

Figure 129 – Santa Clara Ba'a Belt Dance (continued)

Figure 130 – San Ildefonso Ba'a Belt Dance

2.²   Weaving

2.³   Unwinding

Figure 131 – Santa Clara Pangshare (1)

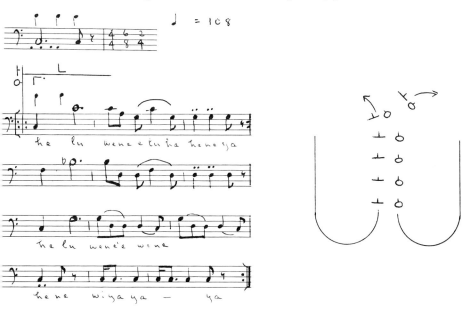

he lu wene e ku ha hana ya

he lu wene'e wene

he ne wi ya ya — ya

Repeat

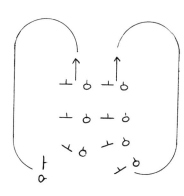

Figure 132 – Santa Clara Pangshare (2)

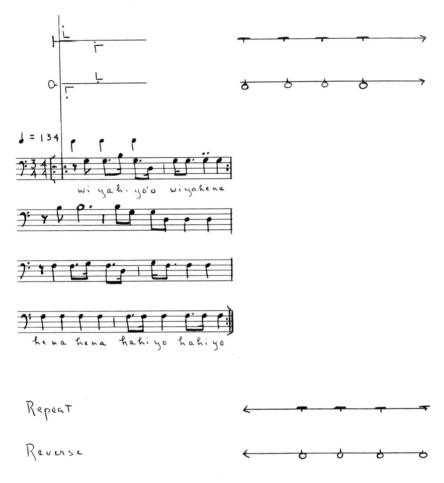

Figure 133 – Santa Clara Pangshare (3)

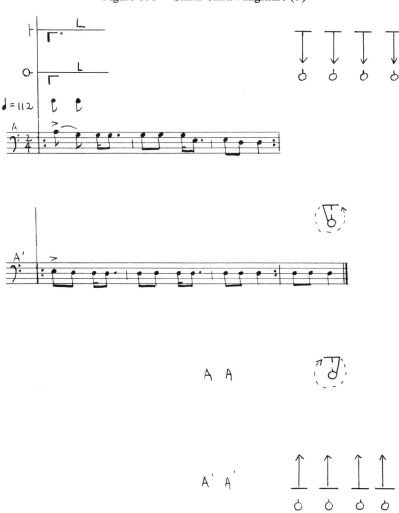

Figure 134 – Santa Clara Pangshare (4)

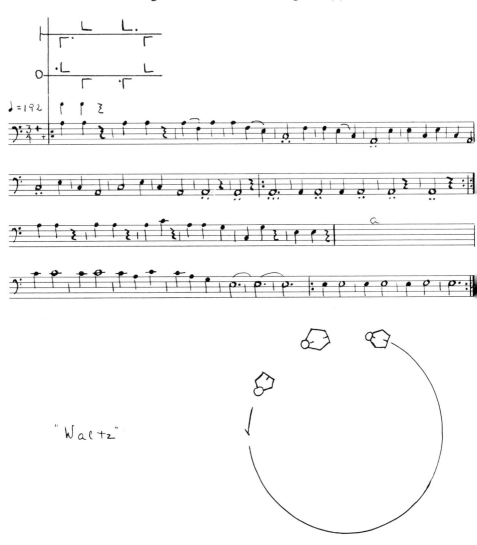

"Waltz"

Figure 135 – Santa Clara Pangshare

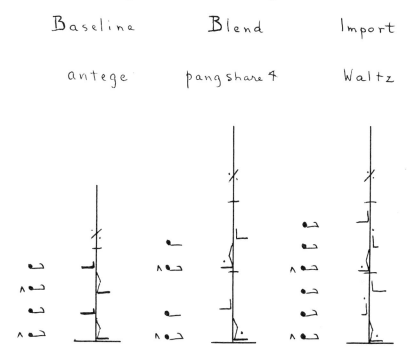

Baseline

antege

Blend

pangshare 4

Import

Waltz

Figure 136 – Pangshare (5) Round Dance

♩ =74

A

ya'e yawe yo'o ha we

B

ya'a ya'e ya'e wiha hena yo

C

ya'e - - yo'o yohowiha

Z

wiyaya wiyayaya

Oklahoma Round

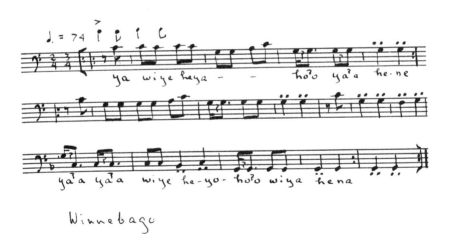

♩. = 74

ya wiye heya - - ho'o ya'a he-ne

ya'a ya'a wiye he-yo-ho'o wiya hena

Winnebago

Chapter 19

MATACHINES: A MIDWINTER DRAMA FROM IBERIA

The dance of the *Matachines* has acquired a respected place in the Pueblo ceremonial repertoire, despite a Hispanic origin and a Mexican transmission. In San Juan it is a traditional Christmas celebration, December 24 and 25. In San Ildefonso it usually also celebrates Christmas Day. In Santa Clara the performances are less fixed, within the months of January or February. In 1963 it was a feature in the Puye Cliffs Ceremonials. The dance drama is a winter play in other pueblos: Taos, Cochiti, Jemez. In Spanish-American villages it may be a summer attraction, as on June 13 at San Antonito. In Alcalde it can appear at Christmas and also for the festival of Santiago, July 25.

The *Matachines* (or *Matachina*) are ten men in San Juan. The number varies in other villages. The *Matachines* always dance in two parallel files and interweave in complex figures. Their costume is a combination of Plains trousers and moccasins, vari-colored tunics and capes, mitres with two feathers, one above each ear, and long, gay ribbon streamers. The soloist and leader is called *Monanca* (Sp. Monarca). He may wear other kinds of trousers and a Plains beaded vest. He always wears a crown, with streamers, but with a more conical shape than the Matachines' and with a small crucifix at the top. He and the *Matachines* manipulate a feathered trident in the left hand in horizontal motions, and they vertically shake a small gourd rattle in the kerchief-covered right hand. They move the tridents more like kerchiefs than like rigid objects. The ribbons also enhance the fluidity of the movements, especially the *Monanca's*.

A small girl follows in the wake of *Monanca*, or dances among the *Matachines* as a soloist. She is called *Malinche*, echoing Malintsin, Cortez' mistress, as *Monanca* echoes Montezuma. Ordinarily she wears a white communion dress, but in 1964 in San Juan she wore a fluffy, light blue skirt and a white sweater. She had wrapped Tewa boots. She wore a delicate coronet and a feather spray on her black flowing hair, though a wreath is customary. As she trips daintily behind *Monanca*, or pivots when he turns, she sets off his elastic vigor. When not dancing, she and *Monanca* occupy two chairs at the rear of the dance lines, vis-a-vis a fiddler and guitarist who sit by the front of the lines.

The true actors of a play are two clowns, *tsaviyo* or *abuelos*. Since their behavior and costumes are quite different from those of the ceremonial, midwinter *tsaviyo* of San Juan, we will call them *abuelos*. They wear anything from kachina-like, home-made masks to rubber dime store masks, and anything from tatters to cowboy outfits or women's skirts. In 1964 they appeared in olive-green fatigues, with cone-shaped, ear flapped masks. Both always wield a long whip, with which they tease a small bull, *el toro*, a boy in the hide and hair of a bull. He leans on two foreleg sticks. At times the *abuelos* and *el toro* wander on the outskirts of the lines; sometimes they copy the dancers; at times they join in the dancers' formations. As a dramatic climax the bull charges the dancers and the *abuelos*. The *abuelos* tease him with their whips, symbolically kill, castrate, and quarter him. Someone shoots a gun into the air, just for the noise. Then the *abuelos* revive the bull. The *Matachines* ignore the play.

That ends the dance, with the line dancers kneeling. Then the whole procedure starts all over again, at another station.

In the course of the afternoon on Christmas Day the company gives eight performances, at eight stations, in front of the church and the priest's house, in the south and the north plazas, by the *Monanca's*, *Malinche's*, the Summer Cacique's, and the Winter Cacique's homes. Against the white snow and the adobe walls the brilliant colors blaze in the sunlight, and the capes and ribbons waft in the wintry wind. The *Matachines* are creatures of fantasy, disguised by black eye-fringes and kerchief half-masks.

CHOREOGRAPHY

The formations and steps are more intricate than in typical Tewa dances. They are fitted to the rhythm, tempo, and phrasing of simple harmonized tunes in polka or jig time. Though performed in good Tewa style, the patterns derive from European longways, and can be identified by European terms. The formations are two lines in place; cross-over; down-the center by soloists; various forms of meander (vibora); advance and recede; and cast-off (separation and circling by the lines). The steps are combinations of polka or two-step, pas de basque, and leg swing with a forward kick. Others are Tewa pats, runs, hops, and skips. Pivots conclude many phrases.

Each character or group of characters uses special step types:

la. Polka (step-step-step-hop), combined with pivots, is the step of the *Matachines* and *Monanca* at the entrance and at the winding figure towards the end.

lb. A two-step (polka minus the hop) is the step of one of the *abuelos* when he accompanies *Malinche* during her winding maneuvers.

2. This has two consecutive parts:

a. Three sets of patting steps, then a swinging kick, which are preliminary to the recurrent step of soloist and group, when *Monanca* dances up and down between the lines, when he "kneels" and then "stands" the ten men. The "enchainement" fills 12 measures.

258

Above and Below: San Juan Harvest Dance (1970)

259

Monanca (left) and line dancer, San Juan (1964)

b. A combination of pas de basques, pats, and hopping pivots, filling 10 musical measures, for the *Monanca* and *Matachines*. *Monanca* dances with more vigor and more flourishes, with turning of the body and leaning to right and left. He hops while the line dancers bounce. He coordinates the steps with the body twists and the swaying of the trident in such an exquisitely fluent manner as to justify the invention of a dance-script device. I have connected the personal glyphs and also the gesture kinemes, so as to represent the swaying. Below the glyphs I show the step rhythms, which are not always identical with musical rhythms.

3.   Tiny steps, forward, backward, or turning, belong to *Malinche*.

4.   A hop from foot to foot is *el toro's* progression when he meets the the *Matachines* successively in patterns of corners and down-the-center.

5.   A combination of polka, pat, and swinging kick, three sets backwards starting L, then three starting R; three forward, then two polkas and a swing-kick, for the *Monanca* and line-dancer during a cast-off, 8 measures for each movement phrase.

In addition, during interludes, *Monanca* and *Malinche* make passes at at each other like the sign of the cross, with the trident.

COMPOSITION OF THE DANCE DRAMA

	Tune	Step	Formation	Performers	Special Action
I.	1	1a	Two lines	Monanca, Malinche, Matachines	Entrance, salute
II.	2	2	Down center Cross-over	Monanca Matachines	Matachines in place
			Down center	Monanca	Matachines kneel as Monanca pivots past
	1			Monanca, Malinche	Make passes, she takes trident
III.	3	3	Meander	Malinche	Matachines kneel,
		1b		Abuelo	shake rattles
	1			Monanca, Malinche	Passes
	3	3,1b	Meander	Malinche, abuelo	
	1			Monanca, Malinche	Passes, he takes trident
IV.	2	2	Down center	Monanca, Malinche	Matachines rise
V.	4	4	Corners, down center	Toro, Matachines	Toro charges Monanca
VI.	5	5	Castoff	Monanca, Malinche, Matachines	Toro charges abuelos
	6	6	Advance, recede	Matachines	
VII.	2	2	Down center	Monanca, Malinche	Matachines kneel
VIII.	7	1a	Meander	Monanca, Malinche	Toro killed, revived

261

DEVIATIONS

There are many variations in the performance in one day, within San Juan, not to speak of inter-village variations. In 1964, during the late afternoon of December 24, the San Juan *Matachines* reversed the castoff. That is, the two lines filed down the center, crossed in the back, and returned to the front, instead of filing down on the outside. Choreographic variations are, however, minimal compared to the behavior of the clowns. The *abuelos* can do anything. They make fun of the dancers by exaggerating or by lagging behind in their tempo. They join the formations at will. In 1964 during Part III, both *abuelos* accompanied *Malinche* during her meandering, one *abuelo* in front, one in back. Then only one *abuelo* accompanied her during the reversal, as a guide. Later on she meandered alone or with just the *Monanca.* On another repeat of the drama, one *abuelo* advanced between the two lines of kneeling *Matachines,* just after Part VII. With mock reverence, he deposited his whip before the musicians, bowed, retreated, then returned to bow and retrieve his whip, and finally joined the seated *Monanca* and *Malinche.* On one occasion, *el toro* gored an *abuelo,* who fell down. The other *abuelo* massaged and raised the wounded one. They can invent all kinds of by-play for the contest. In between dancing and acting, the *abuelos* act as guards, re-arrange streamers and other disarrayed costume items. In 1964 another guard and costume-fixer wandered around in a plaid shirt and a feathered camera, emulating the blank expression of a tourist photographer. Many other fine points must be seen to be believed.

MUSIC AND DANCE

In San Juan, as in most pueblos, the accompanists are a team of fiddler and guitarist. They play in the style of Hispanic folk fiddlers and guitarists. The fiddler plays European duple time and jig time tunes, with a drone on an open string, A or D. The guitarist uses conventional harmonies, mostly in tonic and dominant chords, as illustrated with the first tune. They repeat each tune many times, as often as necessary to complete a figure.

The steps fit the tempo and phrasing of the music. For instance, the ten-measure dance series fits to the ten-measure tune 2, while the eight-measure dance series fits to tune 6. Sometimes the dance phrase overlaps the musical measures, as the three plus three pivots of the *Monanca* against the measures of song 2. In this section II, the pauses after some of the steps recall *t'a,* with their rhythm of 1 2 pause.

As in many Tewa dances, the dancers ply gourd rattles. The duple pulsation of their native instruments mingles with the strident strings.

When the *Matachines* kneel, they can devote their whole attention to the manipulation of their rattles, and they shake them in combinations of eighth and quarter note beats. When they and the *Monarca* combine the vertical rattle impulse with the horizontal swing of the trident, and with the intricate steps, they are accomplishing a feat of coordination.

In the lower part of several illustrations the scores of the Santa Clara music represent a remarkable adjustment of the European tunes to the native drum and voice idiom. More about the blend later on.

REPORTS BY OTHER OBSERVERS

Previous authors have rarely tackled the musical scores and the choreography. In fact, to my knowledge, only the Evans sisters wrote down the San Ildefonso *Matachines* steps, to Herzog's transcriptions of fiddle tunes (1931:80). The steps and tunes resemble those of San Juan, but they are not identical. The Taos tunes, published by Taos Recordings, are also similar. Likewise similar are the tunes in the Spanish-American villages near the Tewa (Robb 1961).

Most of the reports are verbal descriptions. They show similarities between pueblos and over the years, but they also indicate differences. I shall quote two descriptions twenty-three years apart. Both reports generalize on the behavior, but they emphasize the San Juan versions:

"The dancers form in two long lines and at times the dance is reminiscent of a Virginia Reel or a modern square dance. Generally the Governor selects the dancers, who are ten in number. He also appoints the dance leader or Monarco (the Monarch), and the clowns or Abuelos (grandfather) as they are called. The other characters include a young girl, Malinche, dressed as if for Communion, and a young boy wearing a full bull hide and horns. The ten dancers and the Monarco. . .carry a trident in one hand and a tin can rattle covered by a fancy handkerchief in the other. . .

"The first dance is always performed right outside the church. The musicians take their places on chairs provided and the dancers form two lines facing them. Opposite the musicians is usually a chair for the Monarco, who leads the dance followed by the little Malinche. The bull through most of the action just stands to one side of the musicians. The musicians start their tune and the dancers begin in a slow stately dance led by the Monarco. The Monarco dances up and down between the lines of dancers and as he passes each pair they pivot [not in 1964] and kneel until the Monarco gets to the end of the line and takes his seat. Then the little Malinche takes the Monarco's rattle and dances in and out between the dancers with occasional pauses where she bows in the middle facing the musicians. She returns the

263

rattle to the Monarco, and dances back down the center as the Matachines rise and resume dancing in place. Then follows a series of cross-overs and follow-the-leader movements all done with the utmost precision. Finally the bull comes charging down between the dancers to be met halfway by the Malinche who waves a handkerchief at him. This is repeated several times, after which the bull, maddened by the passes of the Malinche, charges at the Abuelos. He pretends to gore them and they use their whips to torment him. Finally one of the Abuelos shoots the bull (at Alcalde with a toy gun) and he falls dead. The Abuelos then pretend to butcher the bull and distribute the meat to the people. Finally the bull gets up and leaves and the dance ends with the Matachines all kneeling." (Feder 1962).

"Early in the afternoon the ten dancers form in two rows, the two Mexican players of violin and guitar seated at one end, a San Juan drummer standing alongside, and next to him the little boy "bull," whose back is covered with a complete cowhide, including horns and tail. The boy carries two sticks to bend over on, like animal impersonators in the game-animal dances. Monanka (Monarco) stands between the dance rows, with the Malinche, the little girl dancer, behind him. She is about ten, with short brown hair and light skin, heavily powdered. Yellow cotton dress, with wide sash, a handkerchief pinned in front, wreath of white artificial flowers, white woolen gloves, wrapped moccasins. Sometimes Malinche dances arms akimbo, but mostly with arms crossed in front, taking small Indian-like steps, dancing very soberly, surely, and imperturbably.

"In the first figure each Matachin revolves where he stands, to right or to left, taking European gliding steps and moving his three-prong stick, 'matachina ma,' or hand, languidly, fanwise, in front of himself. Stick in left hand, kerchief-covered rattle in right hand. The headdress of the Matachin looks like a bishop's cap, with small gilt or silver crosses pinned in front, and on each side an eagle feather. The eagle-wing or tail feathers are topped with downy feathers except in two cases where tiny American flags are substituted - cross, eagle feather, flag, symbols to us of the threefold culture of the Pueblos! The face is hidden by a fringe of jet to the nose and by a silk kerchief raised cowboy fashion from the neck to the mouth. Beaded cloth trousers, beaded moccasins, beaded armbands, and belts of bells.

"In the second figure, Matachina kneel on both knees (one knee, Cochiti), each vis-a-vis couples in turn. Monanka sits in a chair at one end. He gives his stick and his kerchief-covered rattle to Malinche, who proceeds to dance alone, weaving in and out of the kneeling figures. She returns the stick and rattle to Monanka, making passes which may be the sign of the cross. In the third and final figures there is a variety of quadrille-like changes of position by the Matachina, Monanka weaving in and out with Malinche dancing close to his heels. (Alcalde)

"Meanwhile the two Abuelos, the Grandfathers, have been valeting the dancers, straightening out displaced streamers, or picking up pebbles from where the dancers are to kneel. The Grandfathers wear ordinary store clothes and shoes, and each a large mask of hide, with nose and ear flaps, the back and top showing a fringed seam. On the side of one mask are printed a horse and five-pointed star. "Merry Christmas" and other words are scrawled on each mask. Each Grandfather carries a thong whip, and calls out in falsetto.

"At the close of the third figure the 'Bull' makes a dash at one of the Grandfathers, who falls as if gored. A gun is shot off by somebody behind the musicians, and the bull drops dead. Then the other Grandfather goes through the motions of quartering the bull with his whip. Throughout the performance the War captain has checked the crowd of lookers-on, and two or three old men have stood on the outskirts of the dance group. Now one of the old men speaks to the musicians, bidding them accompany the dancers for dinner to the house which is labelled in large letters "Governor of San Juan." (Parsons 1939, II:852 ff.).

Parsons tells about sequels - a church service at 3:00 P.M., then a procession with saint's images, with choir singing in Latin, a meeting by the procession and the Matachina between the graveyard and the court, and the joining of the two groups. The procession halts several times for lively dancing by the Matachina company, before the little kiva, and again by the churchyard. [This is reminiscent of Yaqui custom.] Then the saints are returned to the church.

All writers emphasize Mexican, un-Indian aspects, alongside some native features.

AN IMPORT FROM EUROPE

Tewa open-mindedness extended to the utilization of imports from White aggressors. Not only did they accept the *Matachines* drama from the Spanish missionaries. They gave it a place in their ceremonial calendar, and they even justified its acceptance by an origin legend.

"These ceremonies are believed to have been introduced by a mythological figure from the south; this was an Indian god who wore European clothes... The god is often identified with Montezuma, and the Indian names Payatemu (Keresan) and Poseyemu (Tewa) may represent phonetic distortions of the Aztec form of Montezuma." (Dozier 1958:445). [Poseyemu means "dewfall." See slow *tunshare* 1.]

According to historical facts, Franciscan missionaries first presented a relative to *Matachines,* Los Moros, at San Gabriel in 1598. They hoped to replace native ritual dramas and were pleased at the ready acceptance.

Actually, the Tewa merely added the drama to their aboriginal repertoire, just as they added the Catholic pantheon to their own (ibid.:445-446). In time they modified the steps and costumes to fit their style. Some pueblos like Santa Clara composed vocal and percussion music on the Spanish model, while others, like San Juan, kept the fiddle and guitar music.

The drama flourishes in Mexican villages as well as in the pueblos. It also flourishes in Mexico, where it was introduced in the sixteenth century, under the Matachines name among the Yaqui, Tarahumara, and Huichol, and under other names among the Aztecs, Otomi, Maya, and other native peoples (Beals 1945:167-168; Kurath 1949, 1957b; Spicer 1954:85, 1962: 510).

Observers and scholars have argued over the origin of the drama (De Huff 1932, Kanellos 1956, Robb 1961, Lea 1963-4, Kurath 1957b, and others). Some tend to consider it Arabic, because of the name. In fact, *Matachin* derives from Arabic mudawajjihin (Pl. mudawajjihen), meaning "they face each other" or "they wear faces." Either meaning would be applicable. Also, double-file dances and stringed instruments are at home in Arabia and diffused to Spain, along with other aspects of Moslem culture. The current theory tends to interpret the Matachin and other dances of the "Morisca" family as European vegetation rites which became identified as the battle between the Moors and Christians during and after Moorish occupancy of Iberia. Many variants of the drama survive in Spain and other regions of Europe, as dramas or sword plays, at midwinter or Corpus Christi (Foster 1960:163, 221-225).

The Renaissance Matachin of France was a court entertainment by buffoons who made passes at each other with wooden swords, like the passes between the San Juan *Monanca* and *Malinche*. The tune, published by Arbeau (1588:157), resembles English Morris tunes, Basque Sword Dance tunes (Barandiaran 1963, esp. pp. 60 and 80), as well as Mexican variants (Kurath 1949:102, Robb 1961:97-100). There are tunes in duple metre, with typical rhythms and cadences like the end of the San Juan tune 1. There are many jig tunes, and melodies with a "dotted rhythm" like the San Juan tune 3. They are played by fiddle and guitar or harp, or at times by a one-man combination of flute and tabor, both in Europe and in Hispanic America.

The instruments must have seemed strange to the sixteenth century Tewa. And the tunes must have appealed only because of novelty, with their foursquare structure and the melodic rises at conclusions. Yet the Tewa must have recognized common features, such as rhythmic units 2, 3, 4, 10, and 11 (see Figure 35). Also the Pueblo musicians had native songs with rising-falling melodies and diatonic scales.

The scales of the San Juan hispanic tunes and the Santa Clara drum-

and-voice adaptations show tendencies towards blends. The San Juan tunes include five-tone scales, and the Santa Clara songs include a six-tone scale (song 4), as well as sparser scales. In the case of both series, the sparse and narrow scales are at the beginning and end of the drama and the full scales in the middle. However, the Santa Clara tunes have a generally descending trend, similar to the *konshare* melodic type.

In San Juan the only indigenous musical feature is the rattle rhythm. But in Santa Clara the native quality is reinforced by Tewa ceremonial texts in song 4. They speak of the kachina village, of the pueblo of Santa Clara (xapo); of poseyemu sendo newa poali (Poseyemu, the Great One, here he came); of fog and wheat growing power.

Though I have not seen the Santa Clara version, I would suppose that the steps have more Tewa quality than in San Juan. But even in San Juan the dancers have effected a blend between the European polka and pas de basque, and the native foot-pats, knee-bouncing, and treads. Especially the little *Malinche* is Indian in her delicate tripping. The pivot is common to both dance styles, while the straight-legged kick (the sixteenth century "grue") is un-Tewa. Among mimetic actions, the Bull's striding on fore-sticks has no Iberian prototype, but it has a striking prototype in the gait of the Tewa Game Animals. The actions of the *abuelos* are also Tewa in character, notwithstanding the costuming.

The *abuelos* are not a Tewa interpolation in the drama. For the European - and also Old Mexican - *Moricas* include masked clowns in the cast. Iberian prototypes include other symbolic and behavioral features familiar to the Tewa, such as ritual death and revival, animal impersonations, crowns, bells, feathers. The transvestite woman of Europe and Mexico would have seemed familiar to the Tewa; however, the Tewa *Malinche* is a girl, not a boy. Combat does not feature in native Tewa dances, as it does in Europe and in ancient and modern Mexico. Possibly the trident replaces the sword. Above all, the symbolism of welcoming a new season and new vegetation had much to do with the Tewa acceptance of the Christian-pagan ceremony, with its familiar and exotic features.

On the surface, the formations seem European, with familar figures. Actually, they are elaborations on basic designs known to the Tewa. They are not quadrilles or square dances. They are longways, with a basic pattern of a double-file, and progressions with meet-and-retire, cross-over, meander, successive face-abouts, cast-off, and down-the-center. The *Matachines* formations are more intricate than the longways even in *xoxeye* and *konshare,* and they sometimes operate differently, but they contain enough familiar features for acceptance.

One of the exotic applications of a native motif is the meander. The *Malinche,* and later on the *Monanca,* wind among the *Matachines* in a manner that is not Tewa but is common in Europe. This brings to mind one Pueblo instance of such a figure, the winding of the San Felipe "Malinche," Buffalo Mother among the Game Animals on February 2. Is this an instance of transference from *Matachines* to *konshare*? And might this Keresan device suggest that some of the *konshare* patterns were inspired by the Iberian longways figures? Very likely they were.

The two "abuelos" with Tony Garcia at San Juan (1964)

Figure 137 – Matachines Music and Choreographies

Figure 138 – Matachines Music and Choreographies

Figure 139 – Matachines Music and Choreographies

 2.

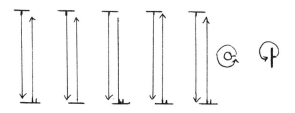

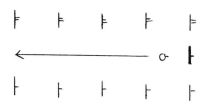

2.

Santa
Clara

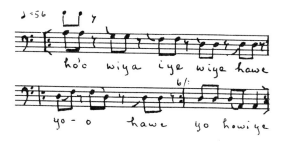

♩=56

ho'o wiya iye wiya hawe

yo - o hawe yo howiye

Figure 140 – Matachines Music and Choreographies

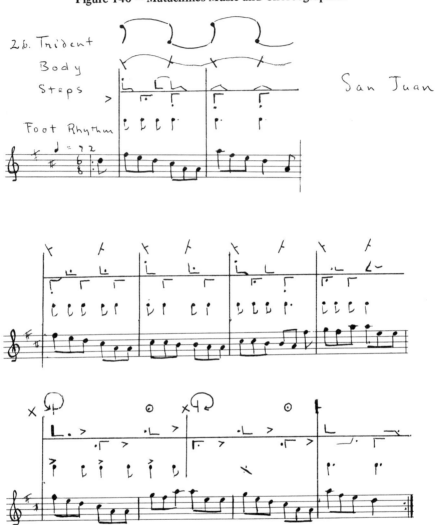

Matachines Kneel

Figure 141 – Matachines Music and Choreographies

273

Figure 142 – Matachines Music and Choreographies

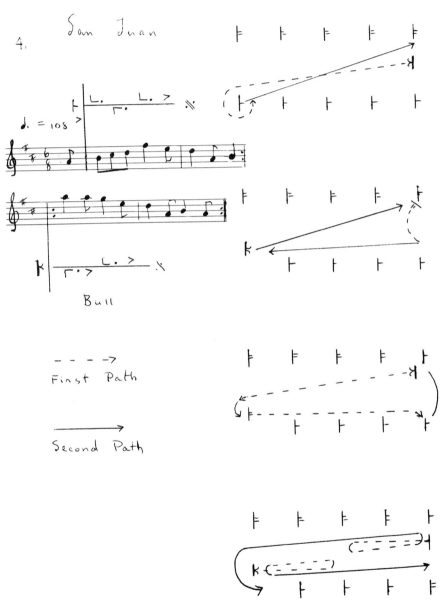

Figure 143 – Matachines Music and Choreographies

5.

Step of 6.

San Juan

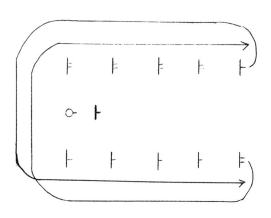

4.

Katsina owimba Xapo owinge wi he

Santa Clara

Figure 144 – Matachines Music and Choreographies

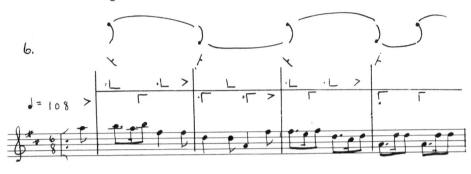

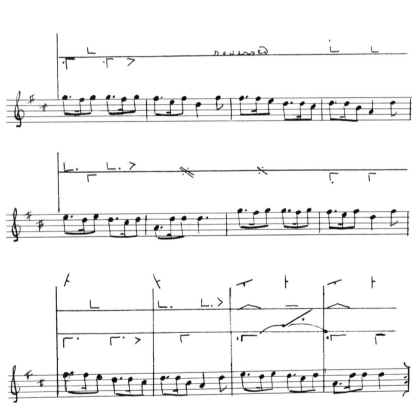

Figure 145 – Matachines Music and Choreographies

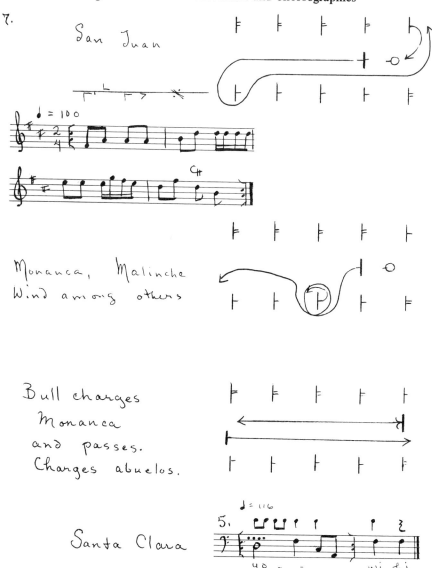

7.

San Juan

♩ = 100

Monanca, Malinche
Wind among others

Bull charges
Monanca
and passes.
Charges abuelos.

Santa Clara

♩ = 116

5.

yo - - with hi

277

Figure 146 — Scales: San Juan and Santa Clara Matachines

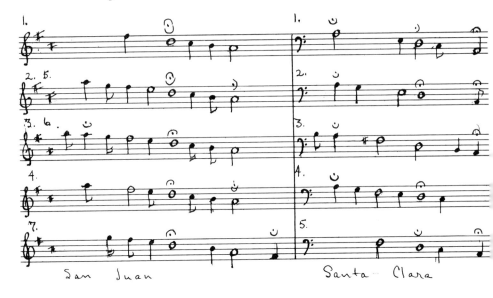

San Juan   Santa Clara

Chapter 20

RITUAL RADIATION AND RECEPTION

The previous chapters have shown varied dance and music forms. They have also shown that the forms are not chaotic. Though a few dances are unique, the most important ceremonies fall into two large groups, with different developments of basic patterns. This chapter will approach, rather tentatively, the complex question of origin, and will try to distinguish native Tewa patterns from imported patterns.

In a few recent importations, history supports theories of exotic origin. Usually native traditions are the only clues besides comparisons of forms. Intertribal similarities may have several causes: chance; sharing of an extensive, ancient substratum; contact and sharing of the same environment; and diffusion (Service 1964).

In music and dance, the element of chance is reduced to simple items like walking. The similarity of a step or formation between the Pueblos and Serbians might be due to chance; but within North America the likenesses arouse suspicions of connections. A circle dance with the same direction and step indicates intertribal borrowing, especially if song types are similar.

The other three causes range from speculation to certainty. Speculations on primordial relationships could lead to Siberia, Australia, or Patagonia, but they will here stay within reasonable geographical boundaries. Definition of relationships within the immediate Tewa surroundings reaches into many common cultural aspects. The tracing of diffusion by conquest or trade can seek aid in historical facts.

THREE WIDESPREAD FEATURES

Three aspects of Tewa ceremonialism find echoes in many rituals of aboriginal America. They are directional symbolism, gestures, and sacred clowns. Directional symbolism permeates the ritualism of all Pueblos; it extends through Middle America and through the Plains and part of the Woodlands. Gesture codes were well-developed throughout arid-America down to Yucatan, in the Plains, and in British Columbia. Sacred clowns appear everywhere, but not everywhere in guises similar to the Pueblo.

Directional symbolism emphasizes the four cardinal directions as in the Tewa circuits. It includes the vertical dimensions in gestures. All studies of Pueblo Indian religion stress the six directions and sometimes the center, in the cosmologies as well as in ritual actions (Parsons 1939:100, 284; Lange

1961:135, 231). They show that the cardinal directions are associated with the same seasons, and that they vary in their associations with gods, animals, corn maidens, plants, and colors. From the Rio Grande to the Hopi mesas dances recur at four stations and gestures invoke the raingods (Parsons 1939; I :372). At Zuni the center receives special emphasis (Dutton 1962a:169). Neighboring tribes exploit directional symbolism, as the Navajo with their four sacred mountains and the center (Hester 1962:850) and the Apache with their *gahe* makers representing mountain spirits of the four directions.

Similar beliefs and customs extend through the mountains of adjacent Middle America. The aboriginal Tarahumara shamans bring offerings to the four winds in the Rutuburi dance (Lumholtz I:330). The mestizo Concheros dancers to the south precede their plaza appearances with libations to four-directional deities, which seem like descendants from the prehistoric Aztec raingods, the Tlalocs. The Maya still invoke the four rain-bringing Chaacs. Before the Conquest the Aztecs and Maya associated deities with animals and colors as well as with directions, in different combinations from the Tewa. The Maya dedicated each New Year ceremony to one of the four year bearers or Bacabs, two benevolent ones for the south and east, two malevolent ones for the north and west. The Aztecs observed counterclockwise circuits in offerings and processionals. They even expanded the altar circuits to interurban proportions in the hurried circuit of Huitzilopochtli, Ypaina Huitzilopochtli. Sometimes Aztec priests offered sunwise libations, to the east at dawn, the south at noon, the west at sunset, and the north at midnight; while flute-blowing priests addressed the east, west, south, and north in a cruciform pattern analogous to the Tewa alternate stations in the plazas (Kurath and Marti 1964: 10, 87).

Directional worship and fourfold repeats used to govern the rituals of the Great Plains and western Woodlands, and they persist among some Siouans and Algonquians (see Wissler et al 1912-1916). Such numerical ritual was especially significant in the Sun Dances and in Calumet Dances (Densmore 1918:85 ff.; Fenton and Kurath 1953: 274-275). To this day the Ponca hold a Sun Dance with four dancers as the four winds or four eaglets, lasting four days and nights (Howard and Kurath 1959). Great Lakes Algonquians address their Pipe Dance to demigods of six directions. They must repeat all other dance songs four times. But this symbolism does not extend to the Iroquois, who build all rituals on the principle of dualism.

Gesture codes were strongly developed in Middle America and in the Plains. The Aztec and Maya gestures may have resembled the rain calling and fructifying gestures of the Tewa *kosa*. They were limited to sacred functions; they were stylized and probably rhythmical. Codices show priestly gestures, while descriptions also tell of group gesticulations (Kurath and Marti 1964: 116-127). The Plains sign language survived till recently, while the Middle American code has long been extinct. The Plains code included many resemblances with Pueblo gestures; but it was utilitarian and non-rhythmical (Thomkins 1926). On the other hand, the Kwakiutl code is a dance phenomenon with specialized conventions (Erna Gunther n.d.ms). In their damp homeland, Great Lakes tribes appropriately mime swans' wings, and fish fins. They dispell, not lure, rainclouds.

The Tewa clowns have many relatives elsewhere, as to their appearance, functions, and behavior. Parsons and other authors have elaborate descriptions of their appearances in Pueblo kivas and plazas. The most complete summary parallels the behavior of Pueblo and Mayo-Yaqui figures (Parsons and Beals 1934). While the Tewa *kosa* and *kwirana* most closely resemble the Keresan comic ritualists, the *tsaviyo* recall the Yaqui *chapayekas* meaning "long, slender noses." They have similar masks of hide, with earflaps and noses. They also are related to the Papago Easter "devils," the *djidjur* and *novico,* the Navajo *to'neinili,* one of the *ye'i,* and the Apache *hlibahi* who accompanies the *gahe.* They do not resemble the many buffoons in Mexican dance dramas, but they seem to have affinities with the Plains-Ojibwa masked *windigokan* and the Dakota *heyoka* (Kurath 1949:100, 1956a:109-110).

Not all of the ghostly maskers are alike in appearance and function, but they have certain powers in common. They all have purificatory, curative, rain-bringing, and phallic potency. They are awesome as well as comical, and are often associated with spirits of the ancestors. They engage in parodies as well as in serious ritual procedures. They act in anti-natural manner, often grotesque and obscene. In the Pueblos they have become fused with agricultural symbolism, in the Plains with war powers. Most of the clowns form sacred societies by vow and are highly organized despite their individual behavior. In this respect they resemble the Iroquois False Faces, who wear unique types of masks, and who have their own songs and dances independent of other groups.

All of these clowns and others appear related. They seem to have their roots in very ancient beliefs and ceremonies, possibly emanating from a common, primordial source. The directional actions also seem to survive from a vast, ancient substratum. Direction concepts and gesture codes reached their most elaborate developments in pre-Cortesian Middle America and they may have diffused to the Pueblos and Plains from this source (Tomkins 1926:93). No one will ever know. But we do know that the Pueblo sacred clowns fully enact the patterns of the directions by means of symbolic gestures, and thus combine the three great ceremonial features.

INTER-PUEBLO MANIFESTATIONS

The Eastern and Western Pueblos share specific group dances as well as the three widespread features. At the same time, each area and each village has developed special variants. All of the Pueblos, and only the Pueblos, highly prize their agrarian line dances, which are modelled on the secret kachina ceremonies. The Hopi and Zuni use the same formation with face-abouts and the same step as do the Tewa. Parsons considers the San Juan Turtle Dance a variant of the "Good Kachina" Dance of Zuni (1939, II:985). The Hopi kachina songs, which are always newly composed, resemble the songs for *okushare* and *antegeshare* in the pyramidal structure, full vocal tone, and powerful pulsations, but they are more complex and emphatic. Kachina songs by Hopi-Tewa are more like the Tewa *ange'i*, (observation from tape recordings by George List). The line dances of "Deer Kachina" appear related to the distinctive *penshare* at least in choreography. The songs are not available. Parsons compares the San Juan Deer Dances with those of Zuni and Jemez (1939, II:916). White speaks of the Santa Ana Deer Kachina (1942:92).

The Keresan forms are closest to those of the Tewa, especially in Cochiti, which lies nearest to Tesuque. The Keresans share the more elaborate dances, which include women and double files, as Basket and Corn Dances. The singers have borrowed songs from each other, as the Keresan Turtle Dance song. They receive them partly through careful listening as spectators, partly through actual participation. For the best singers and dancers are welcome to help out at each other's fiestas. Tewa have borrowed Keresan texts, without understanding them, but doubtless realizing the identity of thoughts in the verses (Kurath 1960c). The Keresan music has a special character, which awaits further definition and comparison with the Tewa. In all cases the choreographies and songs show greater complexity, as does the whole ceremonialism (Robb 1964; Dozier 1961; Lange 1958; Kurath 1958b).

Inter-Pueblo borrowing of social and ceremonial features has been a lively process. The borrower remains aware of the source for a long time. Thus, Santa Clarans still recognize the Zuni Basket Dance as distinct from their own, and the San Juan dancers distinguish the Tewa and Hopi Butter-fly Dances. They have received these dances by intervisiting and also by permanent migrations of individuals, of a Hopi to San Juan, of returned Hopi-Tewa to Santa Clara. They have also borrowed dances that the various Pueblos derived from other tribes and developed in their own ways, as the Buffalo Dances.

While the Pueblos ultimately received maize from Middle America and many concepts and ceremonial forms along with the commodity, they have developed their special dances for rain and crops. The songs have no equivalents anywhere else. It would be idle guessing to ask whether the kachina-type line dances were inventions by the Hopi, Zuni, Keresans, or Tanoans. They are Pueblo.

ENRICHMENT FROM OTHER TRIBES

Within the last few centuries the Pueblos have borrowed and remolded many "enemy dances." The enrichment has by no means been a one-way process. On the contrary, the Pueblo legacy to Navajo and Apache ceremonialism, especially to masked dancing, has extended over many years (Parsons 1939, II:1039-1063). Exchange with the Navajo was most intensive before 1700 A.D. and lagged in the second half of the eighteenth century (Hester 1962:87-91). This affected the Hopi more than the Tewa. But Navajo are still frequent visitors at Tewa fiestas, and sometimes they become permanent inhabitants. Tewa men have learned Navajo songs along with the peculiar vocal style. Tewa women parody the *yeibichi*, somewhat to the indignation of visiting Navajos. But the Tewa have not adopted serious Navajo ceremonies.

The influence of the Apache is more extensive than in the Western Pueblos, because of the greater proximity to the Tewa, and the frequent contacts with the Jicarilla to the immediate north. When the Jicarilla lived east of Taos the contacts usually took the form of raids, but now the relations are more amicable. Many Tewa attend the Round Dances at Stone Lake on September 15. An ancient and evident influence is manifest in the Dawn songs of *penshare*. These songs have Apache words and also the triad scales of Apache music (McAllester 1961). Furthermore, the clowns in the plaza dance are called "Apaches." Some contacts filtered through Taos or Picuris. Parsons thinks that the Tewa borrowed the idea of relay races from the Jicarilla via Taos (1939, II:1057). Garcia and Roberts are interested in this problem, and they plan to discover song analogies. The Tewa have thoroughly incorporated their borrowings in their ceremonies. At present they are learning contemporary Mescalero Apache lore. The students at the Albuquerque Indian School perform an excellent version of the *gahe* masked dance, thus re-borrowing their loan of yore. They use this only in shows.

The present location of the Jicarilla used to be the residence of the Ute, now in southern Colorado. In the eighteenth century the Ute frequently visited Taos and San Juan for trade or raid, and they inspired a now obsolete "Ute Dance." It seems likely that the "captive" that gave the name to the Tewa *pangshare* was Ute. The first song for the march in circles resembles the Northern Ute Lame Dance songs, especially Densmore's No. 40

(1932:109).Women danced this double circle with a limping step apparently similar to *antege*, thus congenial to the Tewa. The third *pangshare* dance, with two approaching rows of men and women, recalls the Ute Double Dance and song (ibid.:118-119). Such derivation must be conjectural, especially since Densmore's study was further north. But the geographical origin of the dance finds support in two facts. When northerly Abiquiu was a Tewa village, the inhabitants were very fond of *pangshare*, "el baile de los cautivos" (Harrington 1916:*3*, 38). Also, the dance does not feature in the Western Pueblos. Songs for the Hopi "Panshale," demonstrated by George List, turned out to be Round Dance songs of the '49 type. As a further tie with the Ute one can mention the use of the morache or notched stick in the Ute Bear Dance. The Tewa, however, use the morache in *antegeshare* and *tunshare*, not in *pangshare*.

The contacts with tribes of the southern Plains were usually not amicable. The Comanche repeatedly raided the Pueblos, Taos and Pecos about 1750, Galisteo in 1774 (Parsons 1939, II:1030-1033). The Pawnee possibly preceded the Comanche (ibid.:1037). Before the seventeenth century the Pueblo men set forth into eastern New Mexico for buffalo hunts. The murals at Kuaua and pictographs at Galisteo indicate prehistoric forays and early veneration of the imposing beast's powers for procreation, its association with lightning and rain (Dutton 1963:74, 218). Pueblo singers claim Kiowa and Comanche provenience for the Buffalo, *kwitara*, and Eagle Dances. But the Buffalo dances would seem to have developed from an earlier, native Pueblo ceremonialism, to have combined with mime of other horned beasts, specifically *penshare*, and to have mutated under Plains influence. The dance and its solar costumes may have drawn inspiration from the combined concept of the Comanche (and other Plains tribes), who venerated and mimed the buffalo during their great annual Sun Dances (Linton 1935:420-428). The buffalo heads and the hide costume of the Hunter show Plains origin, but the dance is unlike the Plains BuffaloDances. Formerly the Siouan dancers milled about; now the Oklahoman groups clomp in a circle, in Algonquian fashion (Kurath 1956b). As to the Deer in *konshare*, they behave unlike any other Deer mimes, from the Yaqui to the Wisconsin Ojibwa. They are the only Deer striding with the aid of foresticks. The contrapuntal formations are Pueblo, not Plains or Woodland.

The performers in *kwitara* use Pueblo double file progressions. They do not tread with the *antege* step, in masks, as do the Kumanche of Zuñi (Raymond 1960-61). Rather, in the fast dance the men's steps derive from Plains modern War Dance steps. Their costumes also imitate Oklahoma males, while the women's costumes and actions remain more Tewa in style. The Plains men, however, improvise step combinations individually, without formations; and they use more varied steps than the *kwitara* dancers. The Tewa say specifically that they emulate the ferocity of the Comanche, and they sometimes insert Comanche words into the songs. They have not integrated the dance into their ceremonialism and their style as completely as the Buffalo dances. *Kwitara* would appear a more recent import, without ecological meaning.

The Eagle Dance differs even more from the typical line dances of the Tewa. Yet it retains ritual power, and formerly served as a true curative and procreative rite. Eagle ceremonialism has a wide and deep distribution. It may connect the Tewa with the Aztecs (Parsons 1933, 1939, II:1018-1020). But the Tewa do not pit light-bringing Eagles against sinister Jaguars. They equate the two youths with male-female duality, as did the Pawnee in their Hako, and they circle in a similar manner (Fenton and Kurath 1953:275-276). The Tewa Eagles toe-heel, and they flex like Plains dancers, but in general they do not copy Oklahomans. Rather, the Oklahomans have copied them and have included an Eagle Dance in their shows. So have the Algonquians, even to Toronto, in their own vigorous style. Thus the mime, which derives at least in part from the Plains, has bounced back to its originators and beyond.

These three dance types display different kinds and amounts of exotic qualities. Yet their musical structure is identical. Does the structure clearly resemble that of the Kiowa and Comanche? The Buffalo entrance songs may be recent Kiowa or other Plains war dance songs. The structure of the fast dance has the same binary form, with tremolo and then duple beat, as the Pipe Dance, alias Calumet Dance or Contest Dance of Oklahoma. Pipe Dance is historically related to the Eagle Dance (Fenton and Kurath 1953). Many tribes now feature the Calumet Dance and others with the same kind of structure - the Bean Dance, the Shawanoga or Corn Dance of the Great Lakes, many Iroquois dances. For each part they have a suitable movement. Pipe, Bean, and Corn Dances are now part of the Pan-Indian repertoire, which developed in Oklahoma. But did the songs and their dances derive from present Oklahoma? Aboriginal Comanche songs have disappeared. According to a Kiowa, John Bosin, the original Kiowa ritual songs do not have this structure. But songs of the Pawnee and the adjacent Omaha did at the turn of the century. The Dakota also have the structure in their Sun Dance songs, at any rate, in a sample recorded by Willard Rhodes at Wamblee, South Dakota. The Sun Dance song resembles the Tewa type most closely; for it uses the same tune in parts A and B, while the Pan-Indian songs use a new tune for B. Perhaps the song type emanated from the Central Plains and reached the Tewa and other Pueblos via the Kiowa and Comanche. Or perhaps it reached them in several ways, directly from the Pawnee, then in the eighteenth century, and again in the twentieth century, indirectly.

The Tewa employ the same structure in other dances, all in exotic style except one. The Rainbow Dance is Pueblo in style and ideology, but the Dog Dance and Belt Dance have more affinity with the Oklahoma repertoires. The Tewa claim them as Tanoan. Very likely they are Tanoan creations on the established "Kiowa-Comanche" pattern, for show purposes.

The Shield Dance, with the binary structure, is certainly Pan-Indian. And the other show dances - Kiowa War Dance, Hoop Dance - leave no doubt as to their derivation, in their style and in their ostracism from the ritual roster. They are solo exhibitions, theoretically for men, in practice also for little boys and girls. Though the Tewa do not specialize in these dances as much as the Taos people, they dance them with zest, to genuine Oklahoma songs. They received them by peaceable means, by intervisiting, and fairly recently. Parsons claims a recent introduction among the Tewa in 1929 (224). Brown (1961) has evidence for an earlier date in Taos; in fact, he reports a claim that Taos dancers invented the Hoop Dance.

Taos certainly aided the transmission of the show dances and also of the social round dances, the Victory Dance and Fortynine of Oklahoma. Taos dancers display these on July 4, but the Tewa rarely use them in shows (only at Nambe on July 4). They and visitors join in the circle after shows or after domestic festivals like weddings, sometimes as conclusion to a *pangshare*. As Don Roberts will discuss the origin and the Tewa versions, I will here only confirm the Plains provenience, probably among the Cheyenne, with flowering in Oklahoma and a vast diffusion within the last decades, now even to the Iroquois (Kurath 1957a, 1963b).

The Longhouse Iroquois of Ontario and New York State are much less receptive to such imports than are the Tewa, partly because of distance, partly because of concern for the preservation of their own ceremonial dances. Several centuries ago they accepted and reworked distant forms, as the Eagle-Calumet complex. Thus they received some of the same influences as the Tewa, from the core of the Central Plains. But they apparently neither gave nor received direct influences within historic times. Their communal ritual dramas and their particular songs and dances differ from those of the Tewa, most conspicuously their circular, improvisatory corn dances, with antiphonal singing. Yet they share many patterns with the Pueblos, especially the pulsation and resonant vocal technique, also the scales of songs which both received from the central core. More intriguing are the similarities that cannot be traced to the Plains core, as the calendric festivals for vegetable and animal spirits, the moiety duality, albeit in different guises, and several motion patterns. For instance, the Iroquois frequently stomp forward, then sideward, then forward, as do the Tewa in the slow Buffalo and the first *yandewa* sections. The postures and earthbound styles are similar. Strikingly similar are the jiggling arm movements of women dancers (Kurath 1964). The similarities may be residues from a very old source, the maize complex, which the independent agriculturalists have each developed in a special way.

The examples show that the Tewa are receptive to new ideas and that they owe some of their artistic variety to ingenious recreation from exotic inspirations.

VARIATIONS ON EUROPEAN THEMES

If the Tewa recreations of Plains themes are ingenious, their novelties on European themes are strange and fantastic. Actually, they have rarely accepted inspiration from European dance and music. They welcomed the *Matachines* Dance from Spain, by way of Mexico, but they have amalgamated the imported figures with their own styles and ideas. Each pueblo has evolved a different compound of Iberian and native elements - not only the Tewa but the Keresans and the Jemez inhabitants. The Hispanic origin remains discernible.

The mutation invites further observation and recognition of the admixture in the Pueblo and Spanish-American localities, their derivations from a sixteenth century prototype, and their relation to the modern counterparts in the other Americas, Europe, and even Africa.

The only other Tewa borrowing from Europe is more modest and more clearcut. It is the waltz in *pangshare,* which so neatly blends the Tewa and and Hispano-Viennese step. More recent popular dance forms of the Anglo have not inspired the Tewa. Santo Domingo once included a jitterbug variant in the Corn Dance, but the Tewa dancers have never deviated from their traditional *xoxeye* patterns. They have not introduced Anglo features into their show dances, except for mechanical devices such as the expendable loudspeakers. They are mechanically adept and are ever exposed to popular and art music and dance of the "Western" civilization, but they have not attempted a fusion. They have not even mixed themes from Gregorian chants into their ceremonial songs, though they are quite capable of such a mixture. They more readily accept saints and cars to their plaza ceremonies than hymns and twists.

POSTLUDE

The dances and music reflect the Tewa past and they express the present. They retain much of their original meaning in economy and beliefs, because of the constant environment. They remain still more integrated with the socio-religious structure. They have lost none of their artistic beauty and precision, and have undergone some enrichment. Unfortunately, the prestige of the kiva and of ritual activities is fading. On the other hand, the last few years have brought a resurgence of enthusiasm for plaza dances, revivals of obsolescent dances, and inclusions of new imports or creations.

Partly the florescence has taken the form of public, semi-secular shows. This brings up the question of the future. Will the dances gradually arrive at the status of theatrical, secular performances? Would the status as fine art serve to improve or to deteriorate the performance quality? Secularization seems on the way, but, if anything, the quality has improved within the last eight years, in the direction of professional standards.

Whatever the directions of development, there is no future in the imitation of show dances from Oklahoma. Conversely, there is no gain in transferring dances to White groups, who may achieve some understanding but who would be desecrating the sacred heritage. In the future, a great art can flourish only by continued reverence for the meanings, and by florescence from within the Tewa communities. The Tewa may welcome encouragement from White connoisseurs. But they must create their own dance and music forms of the future. They can. They are capable of absorbing new ideas and of creating new forms in dance, as they have done in painting and in handicrafts.

Appendix I

TEWA AUDIO-VISUAL SOURCES

RECORDINGS

San Juan: Antonio Garcia, tape recordings of most dances with singers of
the sawipinge.

Manuel Archuleta, disks "Songs of the Red Men," A9994,
A9996, A9997 (published Tom Tom Record Co. n.d.).

Santa Clara:Donald N. Brown, tape recordings, partly published in "Music
of the Pueblos, Apache, and Navajo" (The Taylor Museum,
Colorado Springs, 1962).

Gertrude Kurath, tape recordings.

Juan Chavarria, tape recording.

PHOTOGRAPHY

All Five Pueblos:

Hugh Miller, 8 mm. sound films (Fairchild), all except Nambe.

Donald Roberts, 8 mm. sound film, Nambe.

Gertrude Kurath, 16 mm. silent films (Bolex).

Portia Mansfield, 16 mm. silent films.

Donald Brown, Bertha Dutton, Gertrude Kurath, Hugh Miller,
Jeanne Miller, Donald Roberts, 35mm. slides, monochromes.

Museum of New Mexico Photographic Collection, monochromes.

Appendix II

PUYE CLIFFS SAMPLE PROGRAM (1964)

Saturday, July 25		Sunday, July 26
	10:00 A.M.	Rain Dance (Singer)
Belt Dance	10:30 A.M.	Nambe Pueblo Comanche Dance
Nambe Buffalo	11:00 A.M.	Basket Dance
Belt Dance	11:30 A.M.	Bull Dance
Rain Dance	12:00 A.M.	Buffalo Dance
Rainbow Dance	1:00 P.M.	War Dance (Dog Dance)
Corn Grinding	1:30 P.M.	Blue Corn Dance
Buffalo and Deer Dance	2:00 P.M.	Nambe Pueblo Spring Dance
Nambe Snake Dance	2:30 P.M.	San Juan Eagle Dance
Butterfly Dance	3:00 P.M.	Comanche Dance
Harvest Dance	3:30 P.M.	Morning and Evening Dance

Dances are by Santa Clarans unless otherwise specified.

Appendix III

THE CONSTRUCTION OF DANCE INSTRUMENTS

MAKING A GOURD RATTLE

Tools - knife, awl, small and large pebbles, rawhide strips, paint or mud from a sacred slough (naposhun), a dried, flat gourd, or a small, pear-shaped gourd (Communication, Cleto Tafoya).

1) Scrape discoloration from gourd with knife.
2) Clean out fiber from inside by shaking large pebbles, because of the improved sound without fiber. This is a job for children.
3) Bore holes with file-point or awl, a larger hole at the handle end, a small one at the other end.
4) Insert small pebbles from an anthill as sound makers.
5) Carve a short cottonwood stick and insert through gourd, through both holes.
6) Fasten handle with rawhide strips through a slit in the upper end of stick.
7) Bore hole in handle and attach rawhide loop.
8) For ceremony, apply mud, for tourists paint in bright colors.

MAKING A MORACHE OR SCRAPING STICK

Tools - stick about 2 ft. long, 2" x ½" thick of medium soft wood, smaller stick about 8" x 4" x 3", knife, paint.

1) Cut notches along edge of long stick, 1" wide, ½" deep, ½" apart, except for handle space. Round edges smooth.
2) Round small stick for scraping.
3) Paint designs on sticks, if desired. Nowadays may varnish.
4) For playing, place on inverted, bowl-shaped basket, at slight angle, and rub short stick up and down on large stick.

CONSTRUCTION OF DRUM AND STICK

Tools - hollow cottonwood log, hide, thong, mallet, chisel and gouge, knife, paint.

1) Select hollow log with uncracked shell, size vary according to desires - say, 12 in. diameter, 22 in. height.

2) With mallet, chisel, and gouge, carefully extend the hollow, until shell is about 1-2 ins. thick.
3) Round off top and bottom edges with knife.
4) Plug knotholes, if any.
5) Stretch rawhide both ends, to extend about 5 ins. beyond edge, down sides. Tack to sides. Hide must be wet and well soaked.
6) Lace thong through perforations in edge of hide - 10 to 12 holes round. Lace slantwise and perpendicular alternately. To extend thong, tie on more lengths. Tighten.
7) Cut spaces between lacings curved or pointed.
8) Attach two thong handles by top lacing.
9) Paint with one of customary designs.

Tewa singers can make drums, but they usually procure them from Keresan, especially Cochiti craftsmen. San Ildefonso craftsmen can provide small ones. When in use, drum is held as shown on photographs.

DRUM STICK

Stick of hickory or ironwood - 18 ins. long, ½ in. thick, knob at end. Pad knobby end with down or cotton, cover with small piece of hide, tie. Pad should be 1 ½ ins. thick.

TEWA PUEBLO ROUND DANCES

By Don L. Roberts

The Round Dance is one of the most popular and widely spread Indian dances. This dance is known by a variety of names, and the Pueblos sometimes refer to it as the Taos Dance.

In the Round Dance, the participants form a circle around the singers. The dancers often hold hands or lock arms and move with a short bouncing side step. A clockwise circuit is usually followed, but at times, as at the Nambe Falls Ceremonial on July 4, 1964, the direction is changed at random.

Although Round Dances are very popular with many Indian tribes, they now play a diminishing role in Tewa culture. Round Dances were formerly done in connection with weddings and fiestas, as well as for enjoyment. They were also performed after the completion of sacred ceremonial dances so that all could join in and have a good time. Now Round Dances are found mainly at dance festivals such as the Puye Ceremonial and the Nambe Falls Ceremonial.

Formerly, Round Dances often served the function of providing a meeting place for members of the opposite sexes. This role has now been assumed by "American" dances featuring jazz, rock and roll, and western bands. Even the fiestas for the patron Saint of a Pueblo now often end with a dance hall type dance. The younger members of the Pueblo especially prefer this style of dance over the Round Dance.

ORIGIN OF TEWA ROUND DANCES

Although the evolution of the Round Dance is rather obscure, it appears that the Northern Plains Indians were the originators of the form. It is likely that the Round Dance traveled to the Pueblos by one of two routes. Gamble has stated that the Round Dance was introduced to the Oklahoma tribes by the Dakota Sioux in the early 1900's (Gamble 1952: 101). Since Taos Pueblo maintained rather close ties with the Oklahoma Indians, it would have been easy for Taos to have acquired the Round Dance from their Oklahoma friends.

A less likely possibility is that the Round Dance was transmitted from the Northern Plains to Taos by the Western Plains Tribes. The Gros Ventres, a Northern Plains tribe, are known to have introduced the Round Dance to the Arapahos around 1890 (Nettl 1955:327). The Arapahos, or their neighbors, the Cheyennes, could have passed the Round Dance on to Taos.

Despite this foreign origin, Taos considers the Round Dance to be within its traditional ceremonial system, even though many of the songs have been recently composed and some are borrowed from the Oklahoma tribes (Brown 1961:38). This illustrates the readiness with which new songs can be assimilated by a culture, and thus explains why the same Round Dance song may be found in widely separated areas. From Taos, the Round Dance diffused to the other Pueblos.

DESCRIPTION AND MUSICAL ANALYSIS

Six Round Dance songs with English texts form the base of this study. Although they were all recorded at San Juan Pueblo, these songs are typical of those sung in the other Tewa villages. The songs, which contain English texts along with vocables or nonsense syllables, were chosen for their novelty.

"Sixteen Times" (Fig. 147) is one of the most popular Round Dance songs, and is found throughout the United States. Willard Rhodes has published two versions of this tune. One, sung by a Navaho woman, resembles the Tewa rendition, but has an extended text with an added melodic line (Rhodes 1963:11). The other, an unidentified example, presents basically the same melody as the Tewa song, but the text has been completely changed (Rhodes 1952:131). The Ojibway's sing another similar but simplified version of "Sixteen Times" (Kurath: personal communication).

"Sixteen Times," as sung at San Juan, uses a pentatonic scale (Fig. 147). An unusual feature is the "blue third" which results from the interchange of a minor and major third. Although the musical form is simple, AABCC, the structure is of interest. Section B also appears as the last part of C, and the last part of A is found, in a slightly different form, in B and C.

"Are You From Oklahoma" (Fig. 148) has an interesting drum beat. It starts in a triple pattern and then changes to a duple. Thus, the drum rhythm of two is in direct contrast with the vocal rhythm of three. This rhythmic struggle is characteristic of many Round Dance songs. The musical form is AABB'CCAA. A and B are quite similar and B' differs from B only by the addition of one beat necessitated by a change of text. The San Juan singers think this song is from the Plains.

The origin of "Do You Remember the Mockingbird?" (Fig. 149) is not clear. Several San Juan musicians feel it was composed at San Juan, and a stylistic analysis tends to support this opinion. The presence of a rather complex musical form, ABABCB'A'B"AB, and a hexatonic scale, which contains more tones than the four songs known to have come from the

Plains, suggests Pueblo origin. Also, the reappearance of section A with English words may be a Pueblo feature since the only other song this is found in ("My Sweetheart Come To Me") was definitely composed at San Juan. The conflict between the drum and voice (triple versus duple) is present throughout the song.

"My Sweetheart Got Mad At Me" (Fig. 150) is another Round Dance song that has gained wide-spread popularity. A comparison with a recording of this song made some twenty-five years ago shows that only minute changes have occurred during that period. The singers at San Juan claim that the song was composed there. Although this is doubtful, there is no evidence to refute their view. A unique feature of this song is the use of three different cadence tones, since the normal pattern is for all phrases to end on the tonic. The first phrase concludes on the fifth, the next on the fourth, and the last on the tonic, making a descending series of cadences. Also unusual is the fact that the fifth is sung more than any other pitch in the song, and even the fourth is heard almost as often as the tonic.

"My Sweetheart Come to Me" was composed by Benjamin Archuleta of San Juan (Fig. 151). While the other songs are sung in the higher tessitura characteristic of Taos and Plains voices, this one, sung a fourth to a sixth lower, falls within the normal San Juan singing range. The musical form, which is the most complex of all these songs, is Intro AABBBB' AABBBB'C AABBB'C. Segmentation is present, since section B is repeated three times before finally falling into the cadence pattern. The melody in A and B terraces downward until it cadences on the tonic. Section C then rises twice before descending to the tonic. Again, as in "Sixteen Times," the "blues third" is present, as first the major third and then the minor third appear in the cadence pattern.

"One-Eyed Ford" is another popular number on the "Round Dance Hit Parade" (Fig. 152). It is likely that this song dates from the early part of the century. Some feel it was composed at Taos, but the exact date and place of composition remain unknown. The melody, where the English words appear, has a definite leaning towards the style of popular hit tunes. It would be rather easy to place harmony under the tune and make a catchy waltz out of it. The scale is simple (pentatonic), and the tonic, second, third, and fifth notes of the scale are the main tones. This is the only song in which both the second and third tones are important.

CONCLUSION

In Plains Round Dances, there is a general musical form, AABB', that most songs adhere to. This consists of an introduction, the repeat of the introduction, the chorus with the first ending, and the chorus repeated with a second ending (Powers 1961:98).

294

There is no single form for Tewa Round Dances. The six transcribed songs each have a different form, and none fit the AABB' pattern of the Plains songs. This suggests that the Tewas change the form of borrowed Round Dance songs to fit the more complex structure of their own musical heritage. Even where the imported melodies and words remain the same, the musical form is changed.

The musical forms of the transcribed songs are:

> AABCC
> AABB'CCAA
> AABAABCCAAB
> ABABCB'A'B''AB
> I AABBBB' AABBBB'C AABBB' AABBB'C
> AABAABCC AABAABCC AAB

From these diverse form structures, it is possible to suggest only one distinct over-all Tewa feature—concluding a song with a repeat of the opening section (either A or both A and B). However, since this occurs in only four of the six songs, a firm statement on this point can not be made. Further study is needed to clarify the matter.

The cadences of all of the songs have, with slight deviations, the same rhythmic pattern (♪ ♪. ♪ ♪ ♪ ♪. ♩ ♩ (♪)). Plains Round Dances also use this type of cadence rhythm. It is commonly called the "Scotch snap."

The tempo of most Tewa Dance songs is ♩=87-90. This pace is slightly faster than the ♩=60 to ♩=74 found in the majority of Plains Round Dances studied. The reason for the more rapid Tewa pace is not known unless it reflects an influence from Taos, where most of the tempos seem to be above =100. Although many Tewa Round Dance songs tend to rise a half or whole step in pitch towards the end, there is little change in the tempo.

Four songs have a pentatonic scale, and two are hexatonic (Fig. 153). It is interesting to note that of the two songs, using the hextaonic scale, one is known to have been composed at San Juan and the other is thought to have been. Since the other four probably are of Plains origin, one can suggest that the Round Dance songs composed by the Tewas have a more complex scale pattern than the imported songs.

The root of the songs is usually the most important tone followed, in order of consequence, by the fifth, fourth, octave, and sixth. The ambitus varied from an octave to a tenth. Three songs had a spread of an octave, one of a ninth, and two of a tenth. The relative importance and frequency of the intervals sung is shown by the following list, which gives the total number of times each interval appeared in all of the songs combined.

Perfect octave · · · · · · · .20
Major sixth · · · · · · · · · .20
Perfect fifth · · · · · · · · ·30
Augmented fourth 4
Pefect fourth 105
Major third 62
Minor third 184
Major second 319
Minor second 3
Perfect unison 172

The time and reason for adding English words to Round Dance songs can not be definitely ascertained. It is, however, likely that the Tewas began using them about fifty or sixty years ago. Two reasons for this are prevalent among the Pueblos, and both are likely to have some truth in them. Some feel that when English became the basic language of communi-between Tewas and non-Tewas, English words were added so all present would understand the texts. Others think that the students at the first government Indian schools were eager to use their newly learned know-ledge of the English language, and did so by incorporating English words into Round Dance songs.

In conclusion, the following basic differences between Tewas and Plains Round Dances can be defined. The Tewa songs have faster tempos although they do tend to be slower than those performed at Taos. The Tewas use more complex scales for the songs they compose than for those they borrow. Songs sung, and particularly those composed by the Tewas, tend to fall in a much lower vocal tessitura. Finally, the Tewas have no set musical form for Round Dance songs, although it may be a unique Tewa feature to conclude a song with the phrase or phrases with which it began.

Figure 147 – "Sixteen Times"

he yo he yo

Oh yes I love you hon- ey dear, I don't care if you're mar - ried

six- teen times I'll get you yet.

he yai hai yai he yai hai ho

297

Figure 148 – "Are You from Oklahoma?"

Figure 149 – "Do You Remember the Mockingbird?"

Figure 150 – "My Sweetheart Got Mad at Me"

Figure 151 – "My Sweetheart Come to Me"

Figure 152 – "One-Eyed Ford"

Figure 153 – Scales of Round Dance Songs

BIBLIOGRAPHY

Aberle, S. D.
1948   *The Pueblo Indians of New Mexico: Their Land, Economy, and Civil Organization.* Amer. Anthrop. Assoc. Memoir 70.

Anonymous
1928   The Animal Dance at San Ildefonso. *El Palacio* 24 (7-8): 118-122.

Arbeau, Thoinot
1588   *Orchésographie.* Paris.

Arnold, Charlotte
1928   The Dance at Nambe. *El Palacio* 24 (2): 26-28.

Bandelier, Adolf F.
1926   *The Delight Makers.* New York: Dodd, Mead, and Co.

Barandiaran, Gaizka de
1963   *Danzas de Euskal Erri.* San Sebastian: Coll. Aunamendi.

Beals, Ralgh L.
1945   *The Contemporary Culture of the Cahita Indians.* Bureau of American Ethnology Bulletin 142.

Brown, Donald N.
1961   The Development of Taos Dance. *Ethnomusicology* 5 (1): 33-41.
1962   *Masks, Mantas, and Moccasins: Dance Costumes of the Pueblo Indians.* Colorado Springs: Taylor Museum.

Buttree-Seton, Julia M.
1930   *The Rhythm of the Red Man.* New York: Barnes.

Chabot, Maria
1936   Defense of the Dance. *New Mexico Magazine* 14 (10): 16-17, 46-47.
1944 a   Feast Day at Santa Clara Pueblo. *El Palacio* 51 (10): 200-201.
1944 b   Saint's Day Celebration at San Juan. *El Palacio,* ibid.: 192-193.

Chapman, Kate Muller
1925   Sun Basket Dance at Santa Clara. *El Palacio* 18 (3): 42-46.

Clark, Anna Nolan
1941   The Circle of the Seasons. *New Mexico Magazine* 19 (1): 18-19, 43.

Collier, John
1948   *Indians of the Americas: The Long Hope.* New York: Norton.
1949   *Patterns and Ceremonials of the Indians of the Southwest.* New York: Dutton.
1962   *On the Gleaming Way.* Denver: Alan Swallow.

Colby, Banjamin N.
1963   Folk Science Studies. *El Palacio* 70 (4): 5-14.

Coze, Paul
1952   Of Clowns and Mudheads. *Arizona Highways* 28 (8): 18-29.

De Huff, Elizabeth Willis
    1932   December Indian Dances. *New Mexico Magazine* 10 (11): 14-15, 45-47.
    1936   Dances for Increase. *New Mexico Magazine* 14 (7): 16-17, 44-45.
    1937   Rituals of Rhythm. *New Mexico Magazine* 15 (7): 14-15, 37-38.

Densmore, Frances
    1918   *Teton Sioux Music.* Bur. Amer. Ethnol. Bull. 61.
    1922   *Northern Ute Music.* Bur. Amer. Ethnol. Bull. 78.
    1924   *Pawnee Music.* Bur. Amer. Ethnol. Bull. 93.
    1932   *Yuman and Yaqui Music.* Bur. Amer. Ethnol. Bull, 110.
    1936   *Cheyenne and Arapaho Music.* Southwestern Museum Papers 10. Los Angeles.
    1938   *Music of Santo Domingo Pueblo.* Southwest Mus. Pap. 12.
    1957   *Music of Acoma, Isleta, Cochiti and Zuni Pueblos.* Bur. Amer. Ethnol. Bull. 165.

Dozier, Edward P.
    1954   The Hopi-Tewa of Arizona. *Univ. of California Publications in American Arch. and Ethnol.* 44: 229-376.
    1957   Rio Grande Pueblo Ceremonial Patterns. *New Mexico Quarterly* 27 (1): 27-34.
    1957   Spanish-Catholic Influences on Rio Grande Pueblo Religion. *Amer. Anthrop.* n. s. 60 (3): 441-448.
    1961   Rio Grande Pueblos. In *Perspectives in American Culture Change* (ed. E. H. Spicer): 94-186. Univ. of Chicago Press.

Dutton, Bertha P.
    1955   *New Mexico Indians and Their Arizona Neighbors.* Santa Fe: New Mexico Association on Indian Affairs.
    1962   *Indian Villages Past and Present, Santa Fe Area.* Santa Fe: Museum of New Mexico Press.
    1963 a   *The Indians of New Mexico.* Museum of New Mexico Press.
    1963 b   *Sun Father's Way.* Albuquerque: Univ. of New Mexico Press; Santa Fe: School of American Research, Museum of New Mexico Press.

Driver, Harold E.
    1961   *Indians of North America.* Univ. of Chicago Press.

Evans, Bessie and May G.
    1931   *American Indian Dance Steps.* New York: Barnes.

Feder Norman
    1962   Matachines: A Photo Essay. *American Indian Tradition* 8 (2): 79-82.
    1964   Origin of the Oklahoma Forty-Nine Dance. *Ethnomusicology* 8 (3): 290-294.

Fenton, William N. and G. P. Kurath
    1953   *The Iroquois Eagle Dance, an Offshoot of the Calumet Dance.* Bur. Amer. Ethnol. Bull. 156.

Foster, George
    1960   *Culture and Conquest.* Viking Fund Publ. in Anthrop. 27.

Gamble, John I.
    1952   Changing Patterns in Kiowa Indian Dances. *Acculturation in the Americas, Proc. and Selected Papers of 29th International Congress of Americanists* (ed. Sol Tax). University of Chicago Press.

304

1960   Fortynine: A Modern Social Dance. *American Indian Hobbyist* 6:86-88.

Garcia, Antonio, Juanito and Gregorita Trujillo
1966   Tanoan Gestures of Invocation. *Ethnomusicology* 10 (2): 206-7.

Goggin, John Mann
1937-8 Calendar of Eastern Pueblo Festivals. *New Mexico Anthropologist* 2(1): 21-23 and 2 (5): 89-94.
1938   Notes on Some 1938-1939 Pueblo Dances. *Ibid.* 3 (2): 30-32.
1939   Additional Pueblo Ceremonies. *Ibid.* 3 (3-4): 62-63.

Gunther, Erna
n.d.   *A Preliminary Analysis of Kwakiutl Dancing.*

Harrington, John P.
1916   *Ethnogeography of the Tewa Indians.* Bur. Amer. Ethnol. 29th Annual Report.
1942   *The Indians of the Southwest.* Santa Fe: Leaflet of the School of American Research, Museum of New Mexico.

Henderson, Alice Corbin
1923   Dance-rituals of the Pueblo Indians. *Theatre Arts Monthly* 7(4):109-115.

Henderson, Junius and Harrington, John P.
1914   *Ethnozoology of the Tewa Indians.* Bur. Amer. Ethnol. Bull. 56.

Herzog, George
1936   A Comparison of Pueblo and Pima Musical Styles. *Journal of American Folklore* 49 (193): 305-306.

Hester, James J.
1962   *Navajo Migrations and Acculturation.* Museum of New Mexico Papers in Anthropology 6.

Hewett, Edgar Lee
1930   *Ancient Life in the American Southwest.* Indianapolis: Bobbs-Merrill. and Bertha P. Dutton
1945   *The Pueblo Indian World.* Appendices by J.P. Harrington. Albuquerque.

Hill, Gertrude
1954   *Bibliography: Pueblo Indian Dances and Ceremonies.* Santa Fe: Library, Museum of New Mexico.

Howard, James H. and Gertrude Kurath
1959   Ponca Dances Are Mimes and Music. *Ethnomusiocology* 3 (1): 1-14.

James Ahlee
1925   Crow Dance at San Ildefonso. *El Palacio* 8 (10-11): 229-230.

Kanellos, Vascos
1956   Rituals in the Old Tradition. *New Mexico Magazine* 34(12): 24-25, 59.

Kurath, Gertrude P.
1949   Mexican Moriscas. *Journ. Amer. Folklore* 62(244): 87-106.
1956   Masked Clowns. *Tomorrow* 4(3): 106-112.

1957 a   Pan-Indianism in Great Lakes Tribal Festivals. *Journ. Amer. Folklore* 70 (276): 179-182.

1957 b   Origin of the Pueblo Indian Matachines. *El Palacio* 64 (9-10): 259-263.

1958 a   Plaza Circuits of Pueblo Indian Dancers. *El Palacio* 65 (1-2): 16-26.

1958 b   Game Animal Dances of the Rio Grande Pueblo Indians. *Southwestern Journ. Anthrop.* 14 (4): 438-444.

1958-9   North American Indian Summer Festivals. *Folklorist* 5 (2): 220-221.

1959 a   Winter Calendar of the Rio Grande Pueblo Indians. *Folklorist* 5(3); 247-249.

1959 b   Menomini Indian Dance Songs in a Changing Culture. *Midwest Folkore* 9 (1): 31-38.

1960 a   Panorama of Dance Ethnology. *Current Anthropology* 1(3): 233-254.

1960 b   Cochiti Choreographies and Songs. In Charles Lange, *Cochiti:* 539-556.

1960 c   Calling the Rain Gods. *Journ. Amer. Folklore* 73(290): 312-316.

1962   Rituals for Sustenance. *Folklorist* 7(1): 8-11; 7(2): 41-47; 7(3): 70-78.

1963 a   Tewa Plaza Dances: A Photo Essay. *American Indian Tradition* 8(2): 16-21.

1963 b   Modern Pan-Indian Dances and Songs. *Folk Musician and Singer* 8(1): 4-8.

1963 c   Stylistic Blends in Afro-American Dance Cults of Catholic Origin. *Papers Michigan Academy of Science, Arts and Letters* 48: 577-584.

1966   *Tewa Choreographic Music.* Studies in Ethnomusicology 2: 4-19.

- - - - and Sanuel Marti

1964   *Dances of Anahuac.* Viking Fund Publ. in Anthrop. 38.

La Farge, Oliver

1930   Plastic Prayers: Dances of the Southwestern Indians. *Theatre Arts Monthly* 14: 218-224.

1960   *The American Indian.* New York: Golden Press.

Lange, Charles H.

1957   Tablita or Corn, Dance of the Rio Grande Pueblos. *The Texas Journal of Science* 9 (10: 39-74.

1958   The Keresan Component of Southwestern Pueblo Culture. *Southwestern Journ. of Anthrop.* 14(1): 34-50.

1961   *Cochiti: A New Mexico Pueblo, Past and Present.* Austin: Univ. of Texas Press.

Laski, Vera

1957   The Raingod Ceremony of the Tewa, a Religious Drama. *The Masterkey* 31: 76-84.

1958   *Seeking Life.* American Folklore Society Memoir 50.

Lea, Aurora Lucero-White

1953   The Basket Dance. *New Mexico Magazine* 31(6): 18, 55.

1954   Prayer to the Sun. *New Mexico Magazine* 32(3): 22, 37.

1963-64   More about the Matachines. *New Mexico Folklore Record* 11: 7-10.

Linton, Ralph

1935   The Comanche Sun Dance. *Amer. Anthrop.* n. s. 37: 420-428.

List, George

1962   Song in Hopi Culture, Past and Present. *Journ. of the International Folk Music Council* 14: 30-35.

306

Lumholtz, Carl
1903   *Unknown Mexico,* 2 vol. London.

Mason, Bernard
1938   *Drums, Tom-toms, and Rattles.* New York: Barnes.

McAllester, David P.
1961   *Indian Music in the Southwest.* Colorado Springs: Taylor Museum.

Merriam, Alan P.
1964   The Arts and Anthropology. *Horizons in Anthropology* (ed. Sol Tax). Chicago; Aldine Publishing Co. Pp. 224-236.
1965   *The Anthropology of Music.* Evanston, Ill.: Northwestern Univ. Press.

Mills Mollie
1931   Bringing Back the Sun. *New Mexico Magazine* 9(12): 24-25, 42.

Nettl, Bruno
1956   *Music in Primitive Culture.* Cambridge: Harvard Univ. Press.

Ortiz, Alfonso
1963   *A Processual Analysis of a Social Movement in the Rio Grande Pueblos.* MS. M. A. Thesis, Univ. of Chicago.

Parsons, Elsie Clews
1922   The Ceremonial Calendar of the Tewa of Arizona. *Amer. Anthrop.* n. s. 24(1): 209-229.
1924   Tewa Kin, Clan, and Moiety. *Amer. Anthrop.* n.s. 26(1): 33-339.
1926   *Tewa Tales.* Mem. American Folklore Society 19.
1929   *The Social Organization of the Tewa of New Mexico.* Mem. Amer. Anthrop. Association 36.
1933   Some Aztec and Pueblo Parallels. *Amer. Anthrop.* n.s. 35(4): 611-631.
1939   *Pueblo Indian Religion,* 2 vol. Univ. of Chicago Press.

- - - and Ralph Beals
1934   The Sacred Clowns of the Pueblo and Mayo-Yaqui Indians. *Amer. Anthrop.* n. s. 36(4): 491-514.

Powers, William
1961   American Indian Music: the Social Dance. *American Indian Tradition* 7(3): 97-104.

Raymond, Jerral
1960-61 The Kumanche Dance of the Zuni Indians. *Folklorist* 6(3): 400-402.

Rhodes, Willard
1962   Acculturation in North American Indian Music. *Acculturation in the Americas, Proc. and Selected Pap. of the 29th International Congress of Americanists* (ed. Sol Tax): 127-132. Chicago.
1963   North American Indian Music in Transition. *Journ. of the Intern. Folk Music Council* 15: 9-14.

Robb, J. Donald
1961   The Matachines Dance – a Ritual Folk Dance. *Western Folklore* 20(2): 87-101.
1964   Rhythmic Patterns of the Santo Domingo Corn Dance. *Ethnomusicology* 8(2): 154-160.

307

Robbins, W.W., J.P. Harrington, B. Freire-Marreco
1916   *Ethnobotany of the Tewa Indians.* Bur. Amer. Ethnol. Bull. 55.

Roberts, Don L.
1964   A Brief Guide to Rio Grande Pueblo Dances. *Quarterly of the South-western Association of Indian Affairs* 1(2): 12-15.

Roediger, Virginia M.
1941   *Ceremonial Costumes of the Pueblo Indians.* Berkeley and Los Angeles: University of California Press.

Saldaña, Nancy H.
1966   La Malinche: Her Representation in Dances of Mexico and the United States. *Ethnomusicology* 10(3): 298-309.

Santa Fe Railway Indian Village
1948   Souvenir Brochure. Chicago Railroad Fair.

Service, Elman R.
1964   Archaeological Theory and Ethnological Fact. *Process and Pattern in Culture:* 364-375. Chicago: Aldine Publishing Co.

Sinclair, John L.
1951   *The Story of the Pueblo of Kuaua.* Pap. School of American Research No. 45 (from *El Palacio* 58, 7).

Smith, Watson et sl.
1952   *Kiva Mural Decorations at Awatovi and Kawik-a.* Pap. Peabody Museum of Amer. Arch. and Ethnol. v. 37.

Spicer, Edward H.
1940   *Pascua: A Yaqui Village in Arizona.* Univ. of Chicago Press.
1954   *Potam: A Yaqui Village in Sonora.* Amer. Anthrop. Assoc. v. 56, no. 4, Pt. 2, Mem. 77.
1962   *Cycles of Conquest.* Tucson: Univ. of Arizona Press.

Spinden, Herbert J.
1915   Indian Dances of the Southwest. *American Museum Journal* 15(3): 103-115.
1933   *Songs of the Tewa.* New York

Stevenson, Dorothy
1963   Song of the Deer. *New Mexico Magazine* 41 (11-12): 30-33.

Steward, Dorothy N.
1950   *American Indian Ceremonial Dances in the Southwest.* Santa Fe.

Steward, Julian
1931   The Ceremonial Buffoon of the American Indian. *Pap. Mich. Academy of Science, Arts and Letters* 14: 187-207.

Stubbs, Stanley
1950   *Bird's-eye-view of the Pueblos.* Norman: Univ. of Oklahoma Press.

Tomkins, William
1929   *Universal Indian Sign Language of the Plains Indians of North America* (reprint edition 1941). San Diego.

308

Underhill, Ruth
  1948   *Ceremonial Patterns of the Greater Southwest.* Monographs Amer. Ethnol. Soc. 13.

Van Stone, Mary R.
  1935   The Matachina Dance. *El Palacio* 40(1-2): 10-12.

White, Leslie A.
  1935   *The Pueblo of Santo Domingo, New Mexico.* Amer. Anthrop. Assoc. Memoir 43.
  1942 a   *The Pueblo of Santa Ana, New Mexico.* Amer. Anthrop. Assoc. Memoir 60.
  1942 b   The Impersonation of Saints Among the Pueblos. *Pap. Mich. Academy of Science, Arts and Letters* 27: 559-564.

Whitman, William
  1940   The San Ildefonso of New Mexico. In *Acculturation in Seven American Indian Tribes* (ed. R. Linton). New York.
  1947   *The Pueblo Indians of San Ildefonso.* Columbia Univ. Contributions to Anthropology 34.

Wissler, Clark, et al
  1912-16   *Anthrop. Pap. Amer. Museum of Natural History 11.*

Woods, Betty
  1948   Matachines Dance at Jemez. *New Mexico Magazine* 26(12): 6.

PUBLISHED DISC RECORDINGS CONSULTED FOR THE STUDY

Archuleta, Manuel
  n.d.   Dance of the Corn Maidens. *Songs of the Redmen* A-9996 (III). Chant of the Buffalo Dance. *Ibid.* A-9997 (IV).

Brown, Don and David McAllester
  1962   *Music of the Pueblos, Apache and Navaho.* Colorado Springs: Taylor Museum.

Frezquez, Adolfo and Tranquilino Lucero
  n.d.   *Taos Matachines Music.* Taos Recording and Publication.

Rhodes, Williard
  n.d.   *American Indians of the Southwest.* Ethnic Folkways Recordings F E 4420.

Other Transcriptions from Field Tape Recordings by the author, Antonio Garcia, and Donald Brown.

ML
3557
K96

Kurath, Gertrude Prokosch.
    Music and dance of the Tewa
pueblos, by Gertrude Prokosch Kurath,
with the aid of Antonio Garcia.
Santa Fe, Museum of New Mexico Press,
1970.
    viii, 309 p. illus. 23 cm. (Museum
of New Mexico. Research records, no.
8)
    Bibliography: p. 303-309.

    1. Indians of North America--New
Mexico--Music. 2. Indians of North
America--Dances. 3. Tewa Indians--
Music. I. Garcia, Antonio.
II. Title.   III. Series: Santa Fe,
                    (Cont. on next card)